World Wisdom
The Library of Perennial Philosophy

The Library of Perennial Philosophy is dedicated to the exposition of the timeless Truth underlying the diverse religions. This Truth, often referred to as the *Sophia Perennis*—or Perennial Wisdom—finds its expression in the revealed Scriptures as well as the writings of the great sages and the artistic creations of the traditional worlds.

The Essential Shinran: A Buddhist Path of True Entrusting appears as one of our selections in the Perennial Philosophy series.

Spiritual Masters: East & West Series

This series presents the writings of great spiritual masters of the past and present from both East and West. Carefully selected essential writings of these sages are combined with biographical information, glossaries of technical terms, historical maps, and pictorial and photographic art in order to communicate a sense of their respective spiritual climates.

The Essential Shinran

A Buddhist Path of True Entrusting

Compiled and Edited by
Alfred Bloom

Foreword by
Ruben L.F. Habito

World Wisdom

The Essential Shinran: A Buddhist Path of True Entrusting
© 2007 World Wisdom, Inc.

Most recent printing indicated by last digit below:

10 9 8 7 6 5 4 3 2

Library of Congress Cataloging-in-Publication Data

Shinran, 1173-1263.
  [Selections. English]
  The essential Shinran: A Buddhist Path of True Entrusting / compiled
and edited by Alfred Bloom; foreword by Ruben L. F. Habito.
    p. cm. – (Spiritual master – East & West)
  ˉ Includes bibliographical references and index.
ISBN-13: 978-1-933316-21-5 (pbk. : alk. paper)
ISBN-10: 1-933316-21-7 (pbk. : alk. paper)
  1. Shin (Sect) – Doctrines – Early works to 1800.   I. Bloom, Alfred.
II. Habito, Ruben L. F., 1947-   . III. Title.
BQ8749.S552 2007
294.3'926–dc22

                                                        2006029986

Printed on acid-free paper in The United States of America.

For information address World Wisdom, Inc.
P.O. Box 2682, Bloomington, Indiana 47402-2682

www.worldwisdom.com

CONTENTS

FOREWORD

Shinran's Religious Message for Our Time

The Pure Land Buddhist tradition has been a major player in the shaping of Japanese history, culture, and society since medieval times, and is in fact acknowledged as "one of the largest Buddhist movements in the world."[1]

Communities of Pure Land Buddhist devotees came to be formed outside of Japan in the nineteenth century with the migration of contract workers to Hawaii, to continental United States and Canada, and also to different regions of Latin America. The Eastern (Higashi) and the Western (Nishi) Hongwanji Temple complexes, headquarters of the two major Pure Land Buddhist traditions located in Kyoto, continued through the years to send clergy from Japan overseas to minister to the religious needs of these communities of adherents. In the United States, followers of Pure Land Buddhism have taken on the name "Buddhist Churches of America," counting many first, second, and successive generations of Americans of Japanese ancestry as members, but also with a number of Western-born (non-Japanese) adherents.

An eminent scholar and leading figure in the academic study of Pure Land Buddhism in the West, Dr. Alfred Bloom, has written several important volumes on this subject, focusing on the life and thought of Shinran. His *Shinran's Gospel of Pure Grace*, first published in 1965, is a groundbreaking study that presented this thirteenth century Japanese Pure Land Buddhist sage and revolutionary thinker to English language readers. This is a scholarly and yet very readable volume that places Shinran in the historical and social context of his time, highlighting the significance of his religious message.

Dr. Bloom's study of and personal reflection on the life and thought of Shinran led him, by his own account, to become a Pure Land devotee in 1974. Born of Jewish parentage, his mother had become a converted Baptist, and he grew up in what he describes as a "fundamentalist" kind of atmosphere.[2] His early religious upbringing spurred him on to embark on a spiritual odyssey that led him to this new turn, which continues to inform his

---

[1] Dennis Hirota, ed., *Toward a Contemporary Understanding of Pure Land Buddhism: Creating a Shin Buddhist Theology in a Religiously Plural World* (Albany: State University of New York Press, 2000), p. viii.

[2] Alfred Bloom, "A Spiritual Odyssey: My Encounter with Pure Land Buddhism," *Buddhist-Christian Studies* 10 (1990), pp. 173-175.

academic as well as personal life to this day. He writes: "Shinran's teaching reflects a deeply personal, non-authoritarian, critical approach to religious faith that found resonance in my thinking."[3]

He has now given the world this new volume that gives readers a highly accessible and reliable guide, based on original sources, to Shinran's key ideas seen in the context of his life and religious career.

With the publication in 1997 of *The Collected Works of Shinran* by the Hongwanji International Center based in Kyoto, the total corpus of Shinran's writings has become available in English translation.[4] An indispensable resource for scholars, this two-volume collection includes the systematic treatises written in Chinese with copious citations from Buddhist scriptures and meant for a small circle of educated Buddhist clerics of his time, as well as Shinran's personal letters to devotees advising them on various spiritual and practical issues.

This present volume, *The Essential Shinran: A Buddhist Path of True Entrusting*, provides scholars and general readers alike with a handy guide to the central ideas of this thirteenth century religious genius, culled from his original works in a way that can be readily cross-referenced with the writings found in the *Collected Works*.

Alfred Bloom organizes the material effectively in a way that sheds light on the structure of Shinran's religious message, addressing key questions that a prospective reader would raise. "Who was Shinran?" "How did he understand the human condition?" "What was his view of ultimate reality?" "What did he teach about religious practice as a way to realizing ultimate reality?"

The second section responds to the question, "What do we know of Shinran?" and presents ancient sources that give us a glimpse of major events of his life and religious journey. There are many biographical accounts of Shinran that have been published in different epochs, and Bloom has selected the most relevant passages from Shinran's own accounts in his treatises and letters, from the letters of his wife Eshin-ni, from stories handed down in early oral tradition (*Kudenshō*), and from the earliest biography (called *Godenshō*) of Shinran written by Kakunyo, third Abbot of Hongwanji (1270-1351).

The third section, which comprises the bulk of the collection, presents the key facets of Shinran's interpretation of Pure Land teaching, elucidating

---

[3] Ibid., p. 174.

[4] Published by the Hongwanji International Center. Kyoto: Jodo Shinshu Hongwanji-ha, 1997.

his views on the human condition, the nature of ultimate reality, and the way to realizing and personalizing ultimate reality as a way to overcoming the problematic of the human condition.

The organization of the material resonates with a structural format for understanding religious life offered by the late Frederick J. Streng.[5] With a working definition of religion as "a way of ultimate transformation," Streng's format elucidates on different possible ways of being religious as manifested in the world's traditions, considering each one in the light of its 1) view of the problematic of the human condition, 2) understanding of the nature of ultimate reality, 3) prescriptions toward a personal appropriation of ultimate reality, and 4) social expressions of that appropriation of ultimate reality.

Shinran's view of the *human condition* is aptly expressed in these passages from *Gutoku's Hymns of Lament and Reflection*:

This self is false and insincere;
I completely lack a pure mind.
Each of us, in outward bearing,
Makes a show of being wise, good, dedicated;
But so great are our greed, anger, perversity, and deceit,
That we are filled with all forms of malice and cunning. . . .
Lacking even small love and small compassion,
I cannot hope to benefit sentient beings. . . .
With minds full of malice and cunning, like snakes and scorpions,
We cannot accomplish good acts through self-power. . .
[*Collected Works*, I, pp. 421-422].

This bleak view of the human condition, depicting us humans as unable to save ourselves from this cycle of birth and death by our own powers, is turned around and seen in an entirely new light with the *understanding of the nature of ultimate reality*, centering on Amida, the Buddha of unhindered Light, and his Primal Vow to liberate all sentient beings from their suffering.

Unhindered light is great compassion;
This light is the wisdom of all the Buddhas.
In contemplating that world [of the Pure Land],
It is boundless, and vast, and infinite, like space
[*Hymns of the Two Gateways of Entrance and Emergence, Collected Works*, I, p. 623].

---

[5] Frederick J. Streng, *Understanding Religious Life*, third edition (Belmont, CA: Wadsworth, 1985).

In short, ultimate reality, identified with the Buddha Amida and his Primal Vow, is understood in a dynamic way as compassion-in-action, seeking to save all beings from their different situations of pain and suffering. Human beings need only to entrust themselves totally and wholeheartedly to this compassion, with a single-minded recitation of the Name of Amida in an act of a totally entrusting mind (*shinjin*). This is the *prescribed way to the personal appropriation of ultimate reality*. In Shinran's view, this act is not one that we humans can undertake of our own power, but is itself due to the marvelous workings of the compassion of Amida. An individual who has entrusted himself/herself to Amida in a single-minded way, that is, a person of *shinjin*, receives the inner assurance of rebirth in the Pure Land, and thus arrives at true peace of mind (*anjin*). For such persons who have received this assurance of rebirth, the continued recitation of the Name is no longer seen as an act of supplication asking to be saved and be reborn in the Pure Land, but as an act of sheer gratitude to Amida for this assurance.

This appropriation of ultimate reality is given *social expression* as such persons of *shinjin* form communities of shared devotion and practice, and as they let the compassion of Amida work in themselves toward the well-being of all.

Among those who have found interest and have devoted time to the study of Pure Land Buddhism are Christian scholars and theologians who have noted remarkable congruencies between its message and key religious themes in Christianity. There have been a good number of insightful studies looking into these resonances with Christian theological themes.[6]

Shinran's religious message is one that continues to deserve serious hearing in our twenty-first century global society, marked as it is by woundedness on many levels of our being. Those of us who have been touched and inspired by Shinran's religious message, whether formally affiliated with the community of adherents of the Pure Land Buddhist tradition in different parts of the world or not, may be able to offer significant contributions toward healing this woundedness.

We can begin, taking cue from Shinran, with an acknowledgment of our abject human failure to take care not only of our own individual well-being, but of our well-being as a global family as well. Our individual and communal

---

[6] See for example John Cobb, Jr., *Beyond Dialogue: Toward a Mutual Transformation of Christianity and Buddhism* (Philadelphia: Fortress Press, 1982), pp. 97-143; Paul Ingram, "Faith as Knowledge in the Teaching of Shinran Shonin and Martin Luther," *Buddhist-Christian Studies* 8 (1988), pp. 23-36; Sharon Baker, "The Three Minds and Faith, Hope, and Love in Pure Land Buddhism," *Buddhist-Christian Studies* 25 (2005), pp. 49-65.

failures to cultivate wisdom and compassion, due to many compounded factors, centering on the three poisons of greed, ill-will, and delusive ignorance, have taken their toll on the political, socio-economic, ecological, not to mention spiritual, dimensions of our being.

This acknowledgment of our human powerlessness to save our own selves and our Earth from our own destructive tendencies need not be seen as an abdication of our responsibility of taking steps toward healing our individual and communal woundedness. Rather, this can be the starting-point for taking new directions in our individual and collective lives, whereby we are able to entrust ourselves to the workings of a Power that enables us to overcome our selfishness and pride, and be able to reach out to one another in humility, empowered by wisdom and compassion that is at work in all of us.

Ruben L.F. Habito

INTRODUCTION

Shinran (1173-1262 C.E.) is the founder of the Jōdo Shinshū Pure Land tradition in Japan during the Kamakura period (1185-1332 C.E.) of strife and turmoil following the victory of the Minamoto warrior clan over the effete Taira clan. The movement, once set in motion, eventually became the largest Buddhist sect in Japan from where it spread to the West at the end of the nineteenth century.

With the translation of the writings of Shinran, the Shin Buddhist tradition can now be explored in its depth by Western scholars and students of religion and seekers, as well as members of the tradition. To facilitate this process, this publication text has drawn together important passages and insights of Shinran against the background of his life and spiritual legacy.

The translation of his writings marks a milestone in the development of Shin Buddhism accompanying its emergence from isolation in Western society into the modern arena of interfaith religious dialogue. Through this body of translations, Shinran will inevitably become better known and understood for his religious insight and spiritual creativity. We are hopeful that the volume may play a role in that development.

Translations are very significant and important for bridging cultures. They open the doors into the minds and spirits of ancient, as well as contemporary, thinkers that are otherwise inaccessible to us. Translations are also interpretations. They stimulate new thought and insight in readers. The spread of Buddhism beyond India, the land of its origin, to the diverse Asian countries required the translation of countless Indian Buddhist scriptures. These efforts gave rise to the flowering of Buddhist thought and culture, particularly in China, during the T'ang age (616-906 C.E.) and later in the Sung period (969-1126 C.E.). They also stimulated the development of Buddhism in Korea and Japan, as well as later in Tibet. In these cultures there grew up a veritable garden of spiritual insight, literature, and art. The interaction of the translations, teachers who transmitted Buddhism to the new culture, and their followers gave rise to new forms of religious experience and thought.

Traditions can be revitalized through translation. However, translations, though containing the teaching, do not become vital until people read, study, interpret, discuss, and apply their insights to their lives. Scholars develop their interpretations and analyses of the texts, and their commentaries and writings give guidance to followers on how the text may be used and understood. The diversity of viewpoints becomes a creative catalyst for deepening the thought of the community. The Pure Land tradition took deep root in Japan and through many teachers it has developed a stream of religious experience and thought. Among the various noted proponents of the teaching, Shinran elaborated his distinctive interpretation as a result of his experience of spiritual despair engendered by his failure to fulfill the ideals of Tendai Buddhism. His interpretation was popularized by the eighth Abbot of the Shin tradition, Rennyo (1415-1499 C.E.), who transformed the movement into a religious and social force. It has reached us today as the largest Buddhist sect in Japan, though, despite its prominence there, it has not been very well known in the West. Until recently, the sect has been considered primarily as a Japanese or ethnic religion, restricted to the Japanese ethnic community. While historical and social conditions limited its spread, it is a truly universal teaching. Through the translation of Shinran's writings, however, the teaching is becoming better known through university courses in World Religions and Buddhism or among scholars engaged in Buddhist-Christian dialogue.

The Jōdo Shinshū teaching itself was brought to the West from Japan through the immigration of contract laborers engaged to work on the sugar and pineapple plantations in Hawaii beginning in 1885. Some workers migrated to the continental United States and Canada. The Jōdo Shinshū Hongwanji sect, headquartered in Kyoto, Japan, together with other Japanese Buddhist traditions, sent clergy and established temples to serve the spiritual needs of the Japanese émigré community. The Hongwanji constitutes the largest of the Buddhist sects in the West, since its members came from areas of Japan where it was concentrated.

The sect leaders have always been concerned for the nurture of their members, and particularly the second and succeeding generations who have gradually assimilated into Western culture. Since World War II there have been several efforts to translate Shinran's writings. In 1955 there was the *Shinshū Seiten* or *Shinshū Holy Scriptures* sponsored by the Hongwanji Mission of Hawaii. During the 1960s onward *Nisei* or second generation ministerial candidates studying in Japan engaged in translating and annotating important texts in the Ryukoku University Translation Series. In all, some eight volumes were produced with translations of a ritual text, *Shōshinge* (*Hymn of True Faith*) rendered in several Western languages, as well as translation of the *Sūtra of Contemplation*, a major Pure Land scripture. The effort of translation was taken over by the Hongwanji International Center during the 1980s. It has taken some twenty years for the total corpus of Shinran's writings to be translated and made available to the membership and the general public. This monumental work entitled: *The Collected Works of Shinran* introduces his thought on an unprecedented scale.

The Collected Works of Shinran is a competent, creative, and courageous endeavor to offer Shin Buddhism to the world. It is competent, being the work of a scholarly group who collectively forged the most precise and perceptive meaning of the original texts. It is creative in offering a stimulus for the evolving scholarly Buddhist tradition in the West. It is courageous in opening the ancient texts for scrutiny and analysis by modern scholars of various religious backgrounds. It means that Hongwanji has assumed the responsibility to make Shinran's teaching clear and meaningful beyond the Japanese cultural context. It also holds the potential for Shinran's thought to fertilize religious thought in the world through the process of ongoing contemporary religious dialogue. To forward that effort the accompanying second volume contains introductions to the various writings and useful information concerning the texts used by Shinran and his mode of interpretation, as well as a glossary.

It should be understood from the outset that the texts are not "exciting" reading, like a novel or artistic work. It is a book for study and reflection. The accompanying introductions and study materials greatly assist the student to understand the teaching. *The Collected Works of Shinran* itself, however, lacks the kind of organization that can help the reader navigate its content and easily find passages on any topic. In order to help students and scholars find their way through the writings, this volume offers a comprehensive outline of Shinran's most important ideas and issues which are scattered through the *Collected Works*. The compilation of selected passages in the outline will enable the reader to discover Shinran's insights more easily. We have also placed Shinran in context by summarizing his life and religious contributions. Our approach offers a road-map or guidebook for those who wish to savor his thought and reflect on it for their own edification or study Shinran more deeply. A reader can read through the selected passages or find those of particular interest and then locate the specific context in the complete *Collection*.

Shinran's method in his major work *Kyōgyōshinshō* was to add comments to the passages which he quoted from many sources to support his viewpoint. It is commonly understood that the quotes he employed have become his words, but we have primarily selected his own words and ideas, leaving aside the quotations from other texts. The serious scholar can refer to the complete text. Some writings are more commentarial, where Shinran interprets terms and concepts appearing in works by other writers, which he shared with his followers. Among Shin followers the *Wasan* or hymns and poems are more popular because he wrote them in the common Japanese of the time, making the teaching more understandable. In addition he wrote letters to his followers explaining principles, exhorting or encouraging the members as they confronted various problems. Here we see a more personal Shinran. Included among his writings is a very famous and popular text *A Record in Lament of Divergences*, or *Tannishō* which, though he did not write it, contains important quotations from Shinran assembled by his disciple, Yuiembō. In addition we have included some well-known stories from the tradition and sayings that are not in the received texts. From this variety of writings we glean his spiritual insight, which has made him an enduring and attractive figure in Japanese Buddhism as well as the focus of devotion for followers.

The image of Shinran that emerges from these writings reveals a person who experienced a deep religious transformation through his own struggle as a monk, then as a teacher, spiritual leader, and family man. Shaped by his experiences of exile, marriage, and human relations, Shinran bequeathed to us a heritage of religious insight. We should not be put off by the density of the writing, his or the translators. His spirit is embedded and embodied in these texts. It is our challenge and responsibility to release it into our contemporary world.

In conclusion I want to express my deep appreciation to the World Wisdom Press, its editor Mr. Barry McDonald and his associates Mr. Stephen Williams and Mrs. Mary-Kathryne Steele for their constant encouragement and assistance in the production of this volume. I am deeply grateful to Dr. Ruben L.F. Habito for his foreword which graces this work. We want to express our gratitude to the Jōdo Shinshū Hongwanji-ha sect headquarters in Japan for permitting the use of *The Collected Works of Shinran* as the basis for this book and also for the images used on the cover. We would also acknowledge the labors and skill of the translators: Head Translator, Rev. Dennis Hirota and his associates, Professors Hisao Inagaki, Michio Tokunaga, and Ryushin Uryuzu. Our thanks also go to Rev. Yuho Bruno Van Parijs of the White Lotus Center in Anchorage, Alaska, for his effort in placing the complete *Collected Works* on line on the Internet for easy reference. Also we thank the Matsugaoka Library for permission to reprint the early biography of Shinran, *Godenshō* by Kakunyo, the third Abbot (1270-1351 C.E.), translated by Drs. Daisetz T. Suzuki and Gessho Sasaki and included in *The Collected Writings on Shinran*, published by the Jōdo Shinshū Ōtani-ha sect. Our gratitude also goes to Mr. Wayne Yokoyama for his inestimable help in assisting the project and for his translation of the *Kudenshō*, also a text of the third Abbot, which illuminates Shinran's life and teachings. Our appreciation goes to Bishop Chikai Yosemori of the Honpa Hongwanji Mission of Hawaii and the following ministers: Rev. Akimasa Iwasa, Rev. Eric Matsumoto, Rev. Shindo Nishiyama, and Rev. Toshiyuki Umitani for suggestions on important passages in the writings. Also I express my appreciation to my friends Ms. Kenya-Lee (Tao-che) Province and Mr. Richard Tennes for reviewing the outline and the text.

Finally, any errors, limitations, omissions, or deficiencies in this volume are solely the responsibility of the compiler-editor.

Gasshō (palms together), *Namu-amida-butsu*
Alfred Bloom
Kailua, Hawaii

CONVENTIONS

All quotations from Shinran are from *The Collected Works of Shinran*, unless otherwise indicated.

Diacritical marks and italics are given according to the original source. The terms *nenbutsu/nembutsu*, *bonbu/bombu*, Yuienbō/Yuiembō are written throughout with the *m* rather than *n* for the sake of uniformity.

I. SHINRAN'S LIFE (1173-1262 C.E.)
AND LEGACY

A. Shinran's Spiritual Journey

There is little biographical material concerning Shinran's early life beyond
what is given in his wife Eshin-ni's Letters, some genealogical notations,
and the *Godenshō*. Later biographies attempted to fill in the details, such
as indicating that his mother was Kikko, the daughter of Minamoto Yoshi-
chika. His father was Hino Arinori, belonging to a branch of the famous and
powerful Fujiwara clan. According to the tradition, Shinran's parents are said
to have died when he was about four years (father) and eight years of age
(mother) respectively. Based on these traumatic experiences, Shinran reputedly entered the monastery at the age of nine. This has been a widely held
view in the sect and reiterated over the centuries because of its stress on
impermanence, which is a basic point of Buddhist teaching.

Nevertheless, we know that Shinran's father lived much longer. He had
apparently become a lay-monk and is known as Arinori Nyūdō, a person
who retired from the world. Evidence for this comes from the notation
by Zonkaku (1289-1373 C.E.), the son of Kakunyo and an early scholar of
Shin Buddhism, that Shinran and a brother Ken'u had dedicated a Sūtra as
a memorial after the death of their father. Scholars have generally rejected
the traditional accounts and hold that Arinori and four sons (Shinran, Jin'u,
Ken'u and Yu-i) retired to the monastery possibly as a result of the upheavals
and turmoil that attended the political change brought about by the over-
throw of the Taira clan by the Minamoto in what are known as the Genpei
wars (1181-1185 C.E.), culminating in the famous battle of Dan-no-Ura.

The earliest biography of Shinran written by Kakunyo (1270-1351 C.E.),
the third Abbot, called *Godenshō*, does not provide any information on the
early life of Shinran, other than his entry into the monastery at age nine.
Radical scholars in the early part of the twentieth century questioned the
biographical references of sectarian texts since many of them tended to exalt
and divinize Shinran. The problem was that there was no information on him
outside of his writings and the sect biographies and legends that had grown
up. There were no objective sources.

However, this situation was resolved with the discovery of 10 letters of
Eshin-ni, Shinran's wife, in the Hongwanji storehouse in 1921. From that
time on greater authority was given to Shinran's autobiographical references in his writings and the information they yield. Essentially, the letters,

together with the *Godenshō*, permit us to outline Shinran's life, though details may be lacking.

There are generally four stages in his life progress. The first stage is his life on Mount Hiei. His presence there had been questioned until Eshin-ni indicated that he was a *dōsō*, a type of minor priest in the monastery, functioning in services of continuous *nembutsu*. These services were sponsored anywhere from a week to 90 days for the benefit of nobles who were ill or had died. The merit of the recitations were transferred to the client. Here Shinran must have contacted Pure Land thought, and he is said to have studied in Mount Hiei at the Ryōgon Hall in Yokawa where Genshin (942-1017 C.E.), one of the great teachers in Japanese Pure Land teaching and Shinran's lineage, taught. While in the monastery, Shinran studied the Tendai teaching, while practicing the meditations and disciplines which originated in Zen, Pure Land, Shingon, and Tendai traditions. Mount Hiei was the Harvard University of the time. It brought together many facets of Buddhist practice and teaching in which Shinran is said to have excelled. His thought was greatly influenced by Tendai teaching.

According to Eshin-ni serious questions arose for Shinran concerning his future destiny. He somehow felt inadequate and despite the learning he had achieved, he was unsure that he would ever attain enlightenment. In order to resolve his doubts and anxieties, he undertook a practice of meditating at the Rokkakudō in Kyoto. This temple is alleged to have been founded by Prince Shōtoku and enshrined a figure of Kannon Bodhisattva (the Bodhisattva of Compassion). He meditated there for 100 days and on the 95th day he received a message from Shōtoku that led him to Hōnen (Eshin-ni, Letter 3) whereupon he became his disciple. This event, whatever it involved, was a great turning point for Shinran and for Buddhism.

The *Godenshō* records a dream of Shinran that forecasts his marriage. In the dream Kannon vows to take the form of a woman and together they will spread the *nembutsu* teaching. The text of this dream also appears in Shinran's handwriting but is undated. Kakunyo, the author of the *Godenshō*, placed it in connection with the Rokakkudō experience, though it is not clear that that is its proper place.

Shinran's study (1201-1207 C.E.) under Hōnen constitutes the second phase of his life. He was 29 years of age when he entered the hermitage at Yoshimizu, and, as far as we know, never returned to Mount Hiei. By his own confession in the *Tannishō*, he stated that he would not feel regret if he were deceived by Hōnen, as many people at the time were saying, because he was not capable of any other practice and hell is his determined residence (*A Record in Lament of Divergences* [*Tannishō*] 2). In the *Kyōgyōshinshō*, Shinran exclaimed his joy as he recollected his meeting with Hōnen, his being able to copy Hōnen's major work, the *Senchakushū*, and draw a portrait. On one occasion, as the result of criticism of Hōnen's disciples because of laxity in maintaining precepts, Shinran signed a pledge, using the name Shakkū which had been given by Hōnen. Later, according to Shinran, Hōnen changed his name from Shakkū to Zenshin through a dream.

These events constitute Shinran's claim to be an authentic disciple of Hōnen, though he was excluded from the acknowledged successors by the later Pure Land (Jōdo-shū) sects which claimed Hōnen as their heritage.

The earliest writings of Shinran are notes that he made to the *Sūtra of Contemplation* and the *Smaller Pure Land Sūtra*, possibly before 1217 C.E. They reflect the strong influence of Hōnen.

Hōnen's group did not escape criticism and opposition as his teaching became better known. Essentially Hōnen proposed that the *nembutsu* recitation was fully capable of bringing the highest enlightenment to all people, saint and sinner alike. It undercut the traditional Buddhist establishment. In addition, it undermined the folk religious tradition, since Amida was the sole spiritual power in the universe. As a result of some indiscretions and the insensitivity of a few of his followers, complaints arose from other Buddhist temples. Eventually, the conversion of two women in the court to his teaching, through their relation with some of his disciples, led to their execution and the prohibition and abolition of the movement by exiling leading members, including Shinran. Shinran criticized this event in the *Kyōgyōshinshō* because of its injustice and lack of real investigation. However, Hōnen and Shinran parted, never to meet again. This took place in 1207. Shinran went to Echigo in northern Japan and Hōnen went to Tosa in Shikoku.

The period of exile (1207-1212 C.E.) and his later activities in propagation in the Eastern provinces (1211-1235 C.E.) mark the third phase of Shinran's life. These aspects of his life comprise his time away from Kyoto. Little is known of the period of exile except that he married Eshin-ni and began to raise a family. He had six children with her, though traditional biographies list a child by Tamahi, the reputed daughter of Fujiwara Kanezane.

There is a legend that Kujō Kanezane, a supporter of Hōnen, requested him to designate a disciple to marry his daughter Tamahi in order to demonstrate his teaching that Amida's salvation does not require keeping precepts. Hōnen chose Shinran to fulfill this request, who thereupon obediently married Tamahi.

This story emerges in Shin Buddhism, illustrating its view of total reliance on Amida's Vows. Beyond the fact that Kanezane did not have a daughter by that name, it also contrasts with what we know of Hōnen, who maintained monastic discipline and generally called on his disciples to follow the precepts. While it is clear that Shinran married Eshin-ni, there are suggestions of the existence of another mysterious woman and her son, on whose behalf Shinran later in his life requested assistance from his disciples. Whatever the truth may be in these traditions, we can be clear that Eshin-ni was a central person in the life of Shinran and her letters are an important contribution to assessing his life.

There does not seem to be much evidence of Shinran's evangelistic activity in Echigo since only one disciple is known from that area. We may consider that Shinran lived for a period of some five years in exile, contemplating his life and the teaching he received, as well as his future work.

When he was finally pardoned, he remained in Echigo for a few years because of the birth of a child. Finally, he set out for the Kanto region, though it is not clear why he chose that area. However, his dream vision tells of the masses yearning to hear the teaching and perhaps he believed he could propagate the *nembutsu* without great interference in the Eastern provinces.

A significant event took place in 1213 C.E. as Shinran traveled from Echigo to the Eastern provinces of Kanto. It signals a transformation in Shinran's understanding of religious faith. On that occasion he made a vow to recite the three thousand sections of the Pure Land Sūtras for the sake of all beings to bring them to enlightenment. He began the process but suddenly stopped, realizing this was not the true way to bring about their salvation. Rather it was *jishin kyōninshin*, which means that the true way to repay the Buddha's compassion was to share the faith one received with others. This statement comes originally from the Chinese Pure Land teacher Shan-tao (613-681 C.E.), but it gave Shinran a clue to his ministry, which was to approach people directly and share the teachings with them. The original method was indirect and magical without requiring any contact with people. It also reflects his mission, which he received in the vision in the Rokakkudō.

Shinran remained in the Kanto area for about twenty years, and we can see the results from the major disciples with whom he communicated and in various lists of disciples from that period. The Shin Buddhist movement began from this time and Shinran nurtured several leaders who were outstanding in their commitment and devotion to him and his mission. From the various sources 74 disciples are known, of which three were women and the remainder men. The full number of disciples is not entirely clear but by some estimates may range in the hundreds and thousands. It is assumed that the persons mentioned in the listings were leaders of larger bands of followers. The example for this is Chū Tarō of Ōbu who was the leader of 90 people. Scholars have also discussed the social class of Shinran's disciples. They range from farmers and peasants to townspeople, merchants, and lower level samurai. The teaching itself, reflecting a universal character, does not indicate a particular class connection.

During the period of evangelization, Shinran probably began the composition of the *Kyōgyōshinshō*, which is his major text and resource for knowing his teaching in detail. Essentially it is an anthology of Sūtra and commentary passages selected from a variety of primarily Pure Land teachers as well as other Buddhist texts. Interspersed with the quotations, Shinran made his own observations and interpretations, which provide an understanding of his thought. He gave an overall structure to the work by dividing it into six sections, focusing on a range of themes of Pure Land teaching. His motives for writing are not entirely clear, nor is the date. However, it seems to have been a work in progress and was revised at various times.

We know little of Shinran's activities beyond the fact that he managed in the course of the years to develop a community of faith. We know nothing of his methods of propagation or the response to it by other groups. Perhaps the story of the conversion of Myōhōbō in the *Godenshō* gives a suggestion of Shinran's approach. According to this story, a Shingon priest, a mountain ascetic (*yamabushi*), despised Shinran and threatened to kill him. However, once he met Shinran his life transformed.

For some unknown reason Shinran decided to return to Kyoto around 1235. Once in Kyoto he never left again. However, in this final period of his life, Shinran engaged in writing, exchanging letters, and visits with disciples. A major incident in his life was the disowning of his eldest son Zenran in the later period of his life.

Because of misinterpretations of the teaching there was conflict among the disciples in the Eastern provinces. Shinran received disturbing messages involving licensed evil and sent his son Zenran to investigate. While there, Zenran himself became the source of misunderstanding, apparently claiming he had received special teaching from his father. The issue even reached the point where a court trial took place in Kamakura and threatened to bring persecution on the nascent community. Shinran's leading disciples questioned him concerning the position of Zenran, necessitating drastic action to demonstrate his sincerity. Evaluating the various charges and rumors he received, Shinran decided to disown Zenran. Several letters reflect that decision (see entry 9. Disowning) and the acrimony that went with it. Once the issue was settled, Shinran lived quietly until the ripe age of 90 years, passing away in 1262 attended by his daughter and some disciples.

In Eshin-ni's letters, she responds to Kakushin-ni's question about the certainty of Shinran's salvation. Eshin-ni replied that no matter how he died, he certainly went to the Pure Land. It is suggested that Shinran died an ordinary death with no special supernatural signs, befitting the way he lived. In

Buddhist tradition a great man's death is often accompanied by auspicious signs such as the smell of incense and purple clouds that envelop the individual. Hōnen's death is described in this manner. No signs appeared with Shinran. This is in accord with a famous saying of Shinran that even though people may accuse his followers of being cattle thieves, they should not put on the appearance of seekers of the afterlife. Naturalness or ordinariness is the mark of Shinran's way, and he died in that fashion.

Shinran's life, in its outward or observable features, does not exhibit the dramatic events and supernormal experiences that mark the lives of the other great teachers in the history of religion as means to highlight their greatness. Shinran does not prove his teaching with demonstrations of supernatural power nor does he give magical means to his followers to ease their path. Rather, he gave spiritual insight into human nature and a vision of ultimate reality that transformed the inner life of people and enabled them to endure the "slings and arrows of outrageous fortune." This is the source of his appeal even today among religious thinkers and seekers.

B. Shinran's Legacy: The Shin Path to Enlightenment

Almost 2000 years after Gautama Buddha, in Japan, on the background of the many developments of Buddhist tradition in Asia, Shinran, an exponent of the Pure Land teaching, significantly reinterpreted the nature of Buddhism. He opened wide the door of universal salvation for even the most evil person. He was spurred to alter the assumption of self-perfectibility through discipline and practice that underlay the traditions of India, including Buddhism, as a result of his own experience of failure and despair during twenty years of intense practice in the Tendai monastery on Mount Hiei, a major center of Buddhism in medieval Japan.

Shinran lived during the Kamakura period in Japanese history (1185-1332 C.E.), an age of upheaval and turbulence which rendered the traditional forms of Buddhism in Japan ineffectual in bringing spiritual consolation to ordinary people. In the midst of this turmoil, several creative individuals appeared, such as Hōnen (1133-1212 C.E.) in the Pure Land tradition, Dōgen (1200-1253 C.E.) in the Zen, and Nichiren (1222-1289 C.E.) who focused on the *Lotus Sūtra*. They left Mount Hiei largely because it did not measure up to their spiritual ideals and expectations. However, Shinran differed from his contemporaries because he could not fulfill the high spiritual ideals and disciplines of monastic life.

Shinran's sense of personal failure may, in part, be explained by the fact that he entered the monastery at a young age. Concerned for his future destiny, he became a disciple of Hōnen, then a leading teacher of the Pure Land faith. Encouraged by his teacher, Shinran gained release from his fears and anxieties and received the assurance that Amida Buddha had embraced him unconditionally in his compassion and would bring him to final enlightenment.

When separated from Hōnen by exile Shinran became a more independent thinker, developing an interpretation of Pure Land teaching with more philosophical and psychological depth. He also redefined the nature of religion and the meaning of salvation. His thought was also inspired by his life among the peasants, farmers, and townspeople in the distant provinces of Eastern Japan. He acquired a wife and raised a family of six children. After many years he retired to Kyoto where, through various writings, he left his teachings for future generations.

The hallmark of Shinran's teaching is essentially "salvation by faith alone." This teaching has attracted Western scholars because of its similarity to the Apostle Paul and Martin Luther's understanding of religious faith. Taking seriously his inability to gain enlightenment on his own, Shinran interpreted faith as a gift of Amida Buddha's compassion that secures salvation and spiritual liberation for even the most evil person.

Though this teaching may appear similar to ideas in Western religion, there is a world of difference resulting from its root in Mahāyāna Buddhist philosophy. Mahāyāna teaching distinguishes between conventional thought and belief and the truth of the absolute realm. The level of conventional thought denotes thinking based on naïve realism and objectivity. Such knowledge informs our egocentrism and perpetuates our ignorance of our true nature and of the world. The absolute truth, while inconceivable and inexpressible, exposes the unreality and distortions created by our delusory, self-centered knowledge and interests. The Mahāyāna perspective on religion rejects the literalism, dogmatism, objectivism, and moralism found in many religious traditions. Mahāyāna Buddhism recognizes that all people are at differing stages of spiritual development and affirms people as they are. It is a more accepting, compassionate teaching.

Shinran imbibed the spirit of Mahāyāna Buddhism. His Pure Land teaching is an inclusive, humane faith. It is non-authoritarian, non-dogmatic, egalitarian, non-superstitious religious faith. Through deepening religious understanding it liberates people from religious intimidation and oppression, which trade on the ignorance of people and their desire for security. Shinran's teaching does not encourage blind faith at the expense of one's reason and understanding.

Gratitude for the Buddha's compassion is the basis for life and human relations. It expresses deep gratitude to all those who support our lives whether ancestors, family, community, or Nature. Though seemingly otherworldly, it is really a faith for living with resolution and commitment in this life.

Shin Buddhism focuses on the central problem of the ego as the source of our many problems, personal and social, even as we engage in religious practices. The practice of "deep hearing" and self-reflection increase spiritual sensitivity in our day-to-day affairs. It affirms ordinary everyday life, enabling the individual to discover meaning and depth in all aspects of experience. It sanctifies ordinary life as the sphere of personal fulfillment. Rather than material benefits from faith, Shinran's teaching offers us realistic self-understanding which is the greatest benefit of all.

Religious devotion and commitment are expressed in the recitation of Amida Buddha's Name, *Namu-amida-butsu,* understood as an act of gratitude and spiritually as the call of Amida to our hearts. Amida calls us to reflect on the nature of our lives and our entanglements in blind passion and ignorance. As a bright light sharpens the shadows, Amida's compassion and wisdom illuminate the inner recesses of our consciousness and empower and transform us within the process of our daily living. Shinran indicates that in trusting faith the true mind of Amida works within our lives to bring the Buddha's wisdom and compassion to bear on our daily activities and our relations to others.

Shinran's understanding of Buddhism is all-embracing and comprehensive, offering a way of life that can be realized in the workaday world, as well as the religious experience that we are accepted and destined for enlightenment, despite the limitations we encounter constantly in our struggle for existence.

In its historical development in Japanese tradition, Shin Buddhism became a powerful religious and social institution energized by the strong commitment and devotion of its followers to the present day. Nevertheless, it now faces an uncertain future. Rapidly changing societies throughout the world, higher levels of education, the rise of technocracy and the information age, a highly competitive religious environment, advancing threats to the environment, and widespread poverty and violence in the modern world present a challenge, as well as opportunity, for the spiritual legacy of Shinran to illuminate the travail of the human spirit and offer a path of liberation from egoistic bondage.

II. WHAT DO WE KNOW OF SHINRAN IN THE ANCIENT SOURCES?

A. *From Mount Hiei to His Entry into Hōnen's Community*

1. Eshin-ni's Letter #3

I received your letter, dated the 1st day of the twelfth month of last year, shortly after the 20th of the same month. There is no doubt that your father was born in the Pure Land, and there is no need for me to repeat this.

Your father left Mt. Hiei, remained in retreat for one-hundred days at Rokkakudo, and prayed for salvation in the afterlife. Then, on the dawn of the ninety-fifth day Prince Shotoku appeared in a vision, revealing the path to enlightenment, after reciting a verse. Thus, he immediately left Rokkakudo before dawn, and called on Honen Shonin to be shown the way of salvation in the afterlife. And just as he had confined himself for one-hundred days at Rokkakudo, he visited Honen daily, rain or shine, for one-hundred days, regardless of the obstacles that he confronted. He heard the Master teach that when it came to the matter of salvation in the afterlife, there was no difference between a good person or evil person, for only the single-hearted nembutsu was necessary in order to become liberated from the suffering of birth-and-death. He carefully kept these words close to his heart, and when people would say various things about the nembutsu, he would say, "Wherever my Master Honen goes, I shall follow him, no matter what others may say—even if he says he would go to hell, I will accompany him. The reason is that I am such a person, floundering in the world of delusion from the beginningless beginning of time, that I would have nothing to lose, even if I did so."

Furthermore, when we were at a place called Sakai-no-go in Shimotsuma of Hitachi province, I saw the following dream. The scene appeared to be a dedication ceremony for a recently completed temple. The temple faced the east, and it must have been an evening festival, for the light from the candle stands was burning brightly in the front. But to the west of the candle stands and in front of the temple there was a piece of wood placed horizontally, as if it were a torii on which were hung the images of Buddha.

One did not even have the ordinary face of the Buddha—all was light and the center seemed to emanate from the head of the Buddha—and I could not see any figure. There was nothing but rays of light. The other image clearly showed the face of Buddha, so I asked, "What is the name of this Buddha?" I didn't know who answered, but there was a reply, "That one which shows only rays of light is Honen Shonin. He is none other than Seishi Bosatsu (Mahasthamaprapta Bodhisattva)." So I asked again, "Who then is the other image?" "That is Kannon Bosatsu (Avalokitesvara Bodhisattva). He is none other than Zenshin (Shinran)."

As soon as I heard these words, my eyes opened and I realized that it was all a dream. But I had heard that such dreams should never be revealed to others, and I also thought that no one would believe it, even if I had related it, so I did not tell anyone. I did tell your father, however, about Honen Shonin in my dream, and he said, "There are various kinds of dreams, but this is a very telling dream which reveals what is true and real. The dream that reveals Honen Shonin to be an incarnation of Seishi Bosatsu is frequently reported from various places. Seishi Bosatsu is *unexcelled wisdom* itself, and that wisdom is manifested in the form of light."

Although I never told your father about the dream in which I saw him as an incarnation of Kannon Bosatsu, since then I never regarded him as just an ordinary person and continued to serve him. I hope that you too will appreciate him in the same way. Thus, regardless of how he died, I firmly believe that there is no doubt about his birth in the Pure Land. And I understand also that Masukata was at the bedside of father's death—even though they are bound karmically as father and son, this is an especially significant karmic happening, and when I think of this, I am very pleased and happy.

(Postscript) This letter certifies that your father was a *doso* (monk of lower rank) at Mt. Hiei, left the mountain and confined himself at Rokkakudo for one-hundred days, and that Prince Shotoku appeared and showed him the way, when he prayed for salvation in the afterlife, on the dawn of the 95th day. I have written this down, so that you may read it for yourself. . . [Ohtani, Yoshiko, *The Life of Eshinni: Wife of Shinran Shonin* (Kyoto: Jodo Shinshu Hongwanji-ha, 1970, 1990), pp. 91-94].

Note: Eshin-ni is the historically attested wife of Shinran, though tradition suggests that there were other alleged wives such as Tamahi, the reputed daughter of Lord Kujō Kanezane, a well-known Imperial Minister and disciple of Hōnen. There are texts implying yet another possible wife, the mother of one Sokushōbō, as also a possible wife mentioned in a letter of Shinran. (*Collected Works of Shinran* [hereafter CWS] (Kyoto: Jōdo Shinshū Hongwanji-ha, 1997), *Uncollected Letters*, 4. I, p. 581.)

Her letters were written to her daughter Kakushin-ni, who attended Shinran in his last years and lived in Kyoto. Here she evidences her high regard for Shinran.

It was the discovery of Eshin-ni's letters in 1921 that proved beyond doubt that Shinran was an authentic disciple of Hōnen. It further shows that rather than the legendary high status of Shinran on Mount Hiei, he was a low-ranking serving priest, probably in the Hall of Continuous Nembutsu. Nobles would sponsor services of recitation of the *nembutsu* or chanting of sūtras for the benefit of ancestors.

2. Shinran's Dream in the Rokkakudō

The Rokkakudo's World Savior Bodhisattva appeared to me in the form of a holy sage of stern demeanor. Sitting on a magnificent white lotus blossom and dressed in a flowing white robe with kesa, the sage made this announcement to me, Zenshin:

> O Practicer, if it is in your karma to violate a woman, I shall assume the body of the woman you would so violate, And throughout your life together I will adorn it with wonders, Till at life's end I can lead you to birth in the Land of Ultimate Bliss.

Having thus spoken, the World Savior Bodhisattva turned to me, Zenshin, and said,

> This is my solemn vow, Zenshin. You must spread this message for all to hear.

Note: *Shinran's Dream Record* (*Shinran Muki*), translated by Mr. Wayne S. Yokoyama. Two copies of this dream are held by the Takada branch of the Shin tradition. There are two early forms: one is in Shinran's handwriting, undated, and the second is a copy made by a close disciple of Shinran, Shimbutsu. It is included in Kakunyo's *Godenshō* narrative (ch. 3) of Shinran's dream-vision in the Rokkakudo. However, in variant versions of the *Godenshō* the date of the event differs (See below H. *Godenshō*, p. 35). See also James C. Dobbins, *Jōdo Shinshū: Shin Buddhism in Medieval Japan*. (Bloomington, Indiana: Indiana University Press, 1989), p. 80, note 19 on Shinran's dreams.

3. Shinran's Account of His Relation to Hōnen

I, Gutoku Shinran, disciple of Śākyamuni, discarded sundry practices and took refuge in the Primal Vow in 1201. In 1205 Master Genkū, out of his benevolence, granted me permission to copy his Passages on the Nembutsu Selected in the Primal Vow. In the same year, on the fourteenth day of the fourth month, the master inscribed [the copy] in his own hand with an inside title, "Passages on the Nembutsu Selected in the Primal Vow," with the words, "Namu-amida-butsu: as the act that leads to birth in the Pure Land, the nembutsu is taken to be fundamental," and with [the name he had bestowed on me,] "Shakkū, disciple of Śākyamuni." That day, my request to borrow his portrait was granted, and I made a copy. During that same year, on the twenty-ninth day of the seventh intercalary month, the master inscribed my copy of the portrait with "Namu-amida-butsu" and with a passage expressing the true teaching:

> If, when I attain Buddhahood, the sentient beings of the ten quarters say my Name as few as ten times and yet are not born, may I not attain the supreme enlightenment. The Buddha has now actually attained Buddhahood. Know that the momentous Primal Vow is not in vain, and that when sentient beings say the Name, they unfailingly attain birth.

Further, since my name "Shakkū" had been changed in accord with a revelation in a dream, on the same day he wrote the characters of my new name [Zenshin] in his own hand. At that time, the master was seventy-three years of age.

Passages on the Nembutsu Selected in the Primal Vow was compiled at the request of the Chancellor, an ordained layman (Lord Tsukinowa Kanezane, Buddhist name Enshō). The crucial elements of the true essence of the Pure Land way and the inner significance of the nembutsu have been gathered into this work, which is easily understood by those who read it. It is a truly luminous writing, rare and excellent; a treasured scripture, supreme and profound. Over the days and years, myriads of people received the master's teaching, but whether they were closely associated with him or remained more distant, very few gained the opportunity to read and copy this book. Nevertheless, I was in fact able to copy it and to paint his portrait. This was the virtue of practicing the right act alone, and the manifestation of the decisive settlement of birth.

Thus, suppressing tears of both sorrow and joy, I record the circumstances that have resulted [in my compilation of this work].

How joyous I am, my heart and mind being rooted in the Buddha-ground of the universal Vow, and my thoughts and feelings flowing within the dharma-ocean, which is beyond comprehension! I am deeply aware of the Tathāgata's immense compassion, and I sincerely revere the benevolent care behind the master's teaching activity. My joy grows even fuller, my gratitude and indebtedness ever more compelling. Therefore, I have selected [passages expressing] the core of the Pure Land way and gathered here its essentials. Mindful solely of the profundity of the Buddha's benevolence, I pay no heed to the derision of others. May those who see and hear this work be brought—either through the cause of reverently embracing the teaching or through the condition of [others'] doubt and slander of it—to manifest shinjin within the power of the Vow and reveal the incomparable fruit of enlightenment in the land of peace [*The Collection of Passages Revealing the True Teaching of the Pure Land Way* (the abbreviated title is: *The True Teaching, Practice, and Realization* (hereafter KGSS), VI. I, pp. 290-291, #118].

Note: Genkū is another Buddhist name for Hōnen. *Passages on the Nembutsu Selected in the Primal Vow* is the title of Hōnen's major work *Senchaku hongan nembutsu shū.*

4. An Incident Shinran Recalls

Simply achieve your birth, firmly avoiding all scholarly debate. I recall hearing the late Master Hōnen say, "Persons of the Pure Land tradition attain birth in the Pure Land by becoming their foolish selves." Moreover, I remember him smile and say, as he watched humble people of no intellectual pretensions coming to visit him, "Without doubt their birth is settled." And I heard him say after a visit by a man brilliant in letters and debating, "I really wonder about his birth." To this day these things come to mind [*Letters: Lamp for the Latter Ages*, Letter 6, p. 531].

5. A Disciple's Account of Shinran's Relation with Hōnen

Every one of the assertions discussed above appears to arise out of divergences from shinjin. As the late Master once related, in Master Hōnen's day, among his many disciples there were few who were of the same shinjin as Hōnen, and because of this, Shinran became involved in a debate with some fellow practicers. It happened in this way.

Shinran remarked, "My shinjin and the Master's are one."

Seikan-bō, Nembutsu-bō, and others among his fellow practicers strongly argued, "How can your shinjin be the same as the Master's?"

Shinran responded, "The Master possesses vast wisdom and learning, so I would be mistaken if I claimed to be the same in those respects, but in shinjin that is the cause of birth, there is no difference whatever. The Master's shinjin and mine are one and the same."

The others remained skeptical, however, asking how that could be. So finally they all decided that the argument should be brought before Hōnen to determine which side was right.

When they presented the details of the matter, Master Hōnen said, "My shinjin has been given by Amida; so has that of Zenshin-bō [Shinran]. Therefore they are one and the same. A person with a different shinjin will surely not go to the Pure Land to which I will go" [*A Record in Lament of Divergences*, p. 678, Postscript].

6. On the Persecution of Hōnen's Community

Reflecting within myself, I see that in the various teachings of the Path of Sages, practice and enlightenment died out long ago, and that the true essence of the Pure Land way is the path to realization, now vital and flourishing.

Monks of Śākyamuni's tradition in the various temples, however, lack clear insight into the teaching and are ignorant of the distinction between true and provisional; and scholars of the Chinese classics in the capital are confused about practices and wholly unable to differentiate right and wrong paths. Thus, scholar-monks of Kōfuku-ji presented a petition to the retired emperor in the first part of the second month, 1207.

The emperor and his ministers, acting against the dharma and violating human rectitude, became enraged and embittered. As a result, Master Genkū—the eminent founder who had enabled the true essence of the Pure Land to spread vigorously [in Japan]—and a number of his followers, without receiving any deliberation of their [alleged] crimes, were summarily sentenced to death or were dispossessed of their monkhood, given [secular] names, and consigned to distant banishment. I was among the latter. Hence, I am now neither a monk nor one in worldly life. For this reason, I have taken the term Toku ["stubble haired"] as my name. Master Genkū and his disciples, being banished to the provinces in different directions, passed a period of five years [in exile].

On the seventeenth day of the eleventh month, 1211, during the reign of the emperor Sado-no-in, Genkū received an imperial pardon and returned to Kyoto. Thereafter, he lived in the capital, at Ōtani, north of Toribeno in the western foothills of Higashiyama. In 1212, during the midday hour of the twenty-fifth day of the first month, he passed away. The auspicious signs [that occurred then], too numerous to record here, may be found in his biography [*KGSS*,VI. I, pp. 289-290, #117].

B. The Journey to Eastern Japan (Kanto): Shinran's Realization of Other-Power

7. Eshin-ni's Letter #5

From about the noon of the 14th day of the fourth month, 3rd year of Kangi, Zenshin (Shinran) felt a cold coming on and went to bed in the evening. He became quite ill, but he did not let anyone massage his back or legs and would not let anyone nurse him. He just lay quietly, but when I touched his body, it was burning with fever. He also had a severe headache, something beyond the normal. On the dawn of the fourth day, passed in such a condition, he said in the midst of his great discomfort, "It must be truly so." So I asked him, "What is the matter? Did you say something in your delirium?"

Then he replied, "No, it's not delirium. Two days after I came to bed, I read the Larger Pure Land Sutra continuously. Even when I closed my eyes, I could see each character of the sutra very clearly. How strange, I thought. Thinking that there should be nothing on my mind beside true entrusting, born out of the joy of nembutsu, I carefully thought about the matter. Then I remembered an incident which occurred seventeen or eighteen years ago, when I began reading the Triple Pure Land Sutras faithfully a thousand times for the benefit of sentient beings. I suddenly realized the grave mistake I was making, for while I truly felt that the repayment of the Buddha's blessing is to believe the teaching for one-self and then teach others to believe, as in the saying, 'To believe the teaching oneself and make others believe, this is the most difficult of all difficulties,' yet I attempted to read the sutra as if to complement the saying of nembutsu which should have been sufficient by itself. Thus, I stopped reading the sutra. A similar thought must have still remained, lingering in my mind. Once people begin thinking like this, it's difficult to change. When I realized how difficult it is to get rid of self-generated faith and vowed to be constantly alert about it, there was no longer any need to read the sutra. And so on the dawn of the fourth day in bed, I said, 'It must be truly so.'" Soon after he explained all this, he perspired profusely and he became well.

(Postscript) Your father began to re-read the Triple Pure Land Sutras faithfully a thousand times, when Shinrenbo was four years old. He began reading them at a place called Sanuki in the province of Musashi, or was it Kozuke, but four or five days later he decided to stop reading. This was the time that he moved to Hitachi. Shinrenbo was born at noon on the 3rd day of the third month (5th year of Shogen, year of Kanoto-hitsuji); therefore, he must be 53 years old this year.

10th Day of the Second Month, 3rd Year of Kocho from Eshin. [Eshin-ni's Letter #5 *Lady Ohtani*, pp. 95-96; See also *Kudenshō* below p. 17]

C. *Shinran's Account of His Spiritual Development*

8. Turning through the Three Vows

Thus I, Gutoku Shinran, disciple of Śākyamuni, through reverently accepting the exposition of [Vasubandhu,] author of the Treatise, and depending on the guidance of Master [Shan-tao], departed everlastingly from the temporary gate of the myriad practices and various good acts and left forever the birth attained beneath the twin Śāla trees. Turning about, I entered the "true" gate of the root of good and the root of virtue, and wholeheartedly awakened the mind leading to the birth that is non-comprehensible.

Nevertheless, I have now decisively departed from the "true" gate of provisional means and, [my self-power] overturned, have entered the ocean of the selected Vow. Having swiftly become free of the mind leading to the birth that is non-comprehensible, I am assured of attaining the birth that is inconceivable. How truly profound in intent is the Vow that beings ultimately attain birth!

Having entered forever the ocean of the Vow, I now realize deeply the Buddha's benevolence. To respond with gratitude for the supreme virtues, I collect the crucial passages expressing the true essence of the Pure Land way, constantly saying, out of mindfulness [the Name that is] the inconceivable ocean of virtues. Ever more greatly rejoicing, I humbly receive it [KGSS, VI. I, p. 240, #68].

Note: Vasubandhu (Tenjin/Seshin, fourth century) is one of Shinran's select Great Teachers. He is credited with establishing the "Consciousness Only" school. Shan-tao (Zendō, 613-681) is a major Chinese Pure Land teacher.

The term *Gutoku* is Shinran's self-designated title. It signified a foolish short-haired monk who had broken precepts without repentance. A term of derision. (Yoshifumi Ueda and Dennis Hirota, *Shinran: An Introduction to His Thought* (Kyoto: Hongwanji International Center, 1989), p. 34). Here Shinran refuses the government's name given to the defrocked monk and selects his own with deeper meaning, confessing his spiritual condition.

D. Shinran Disowns His Eldest Son

9. Disowning

To begin, I have never heard such statements as Jishin's or even the ter-minology he uses, much less learned them; hence, what he says cannot be something I taught him privately. Further, I have not instructed Jishin alone, whether day or night, in a special teaching, concealing it from other people. If, while having told Jishin these things, I now lie and conceal it, or if I have taught him without letting others know, then may the punishment, first, of the Three Treasures, and of all the devas and benevolent gods in the three realms of existence, of the naga-gods and the rest of the eight kinds of transmundane beings in the four quarters, and of the deities of the realm of Yama, the ruler of the world of death—all be visited on me, Shinran.

From this moment on, I cease to regard Jishin as my son. He is spreading incomprehensible lies and absurd statements about secular matters as well; hence, not only regarding religious matters, but regarding secular matters also, there are a countless number of appalling statements. Among them, these statements concerning the teaching are particularly incomprehensible to hear. I have never heard or learned such things. It is utterly astounding and saddening. In abandoning Ami-da's Primal Vow, people have followed [Jishin], and they have asserted me to be a person who tells lies. It is lamentable and deplorable [*Letters of the Tradition. Letter 2*, pp. 575-576. A number of letters provide background to this event: *A Collection of Letters*, 5, 6, 7; *Letters of the Tradition*, 2; *Uncollected Letters*, 6. I, pp. 559-584].

Note: Jishin is the Buddhist name for Zenran, Shinran's eldest son whom he had to disown.

E. Shinran and Other Disciples of Hōnen

10. Variant Views-1

In recent years the teaching of nembutsu has undergone so many alterations, it is hardly necessary for me to comment on them; nevertheless, for people who have carefully received the teaching of the late Master it is still as it originally was, undergoing no change at all. This is well known, so I am sure you have heard about it. Although people who teach variant views of the Pure Land teaching are all disciples of the Master, they rephrase the teaching in their own ways, confusing themselves and misleading others. This is truly deplorable. Even in the capital there are many who are going astray; how much more this is so in the provinces I have little desire to know. It is impossible to say everything in this letter; I will write again [*Letters: Lamp for the Latter Ages*, Letter 19, p. 551].

11. Variant Views-2

In the past, however, some of those desiring birth failed to understand certain things. It seems that this is still the case. Even in Kyoto there are people who do not understand and who stray in confusion, and I hear of many such people in the various provinces. And even among Hōnen's disciples those who take themselves to be remarkable scholars make various changes in expressing the teaching, confusing others as well as themselves so that all suffer together [*Lamp for the Latter Ages*, Letter 20, p. 552].

F. Stories from Early Tradition: Kakunyo's Treatise of Oral Tradition (Kudenshō)

Note: The *Kudenshō* (Treatise of Oral Tradition) purports to be a record of incidents and teachings from the life of Shinran transmitted to Kakunyo, the third Abbot, by Nyoshin, Shinran's grandson. Nyoshin reputedly studied with Shinran in his youth. He is the son of Zenran (Jishin) whom Shinran disowned. (See above entry 9. Disowning)

The text is a major resource in 21 chapters for information on early Shin Buddhism. It also provides alternative accounts for incidents found in Eshin-ni's letters and the *Record in Lament of Divergences* (*Tannishō*). The stories exalt the status of Shinran in Hōnen's community or as founder of the Hongwanji branch of Shin Buddhism. The text also presents issues in Shinran's thought. We are grateful to Mr. Wayne Yokoyama who graciously permitted us to use his unpublished translation. The numbering of the stories follows that of the text for easy reference to the original. Translated from *Jōdo Shinshū Seiten. Annotated Edition* (Kyoto: Hongwanji Shuppansha, 1988, rev. ed. 2004), pp. 870-914.

12. Kudenshō Incidents

(1) On the envoy to Seikaku Hōin

On one occasion Shinran related the following episode: When the Kuro-dani Shōnin Genkū's efforts to promote the Pure Land as a true school were beginning to flourish, he noticed incipient signs that there were those in society, from the man at the top (the Emperor) on down, who were decidedly set against it. As a result, his critics, in order to strike down the principle of establishing the Pure Land school as an independent entity, arranged to have an imperial decree issued, stating: "That the Pure Land school should not be regarded as a school independent from the various schools of the Sage Path," this on the occasion of a seven-day mock funeral in the Forbidden Palace [the date of this event is unknown, but it possibly took place during the reign of Tsuchimikado, r. 1198-1210], to which Seikaku Hōin of Ango-in was the officiant. While Seikaku tried to conform to that decree, he interceded on Genkū Shōnin's behalf and sought to deflect criticism from his teacher's basic intent, reiterating it in a way that would not cause further disturbance, saying: "We must recognize that, apart from the Sage Path, there is a Pure Land school that exists independent from it, that offers the ordinary person the great benefit of entering the Pure Land directly."

When Genkū Shōnin heard what happened in the imperial court, the thought occurred to him, "What if our critics had succeeded in having the principle of our school rejected at that time, how could we ever lay the foundation for the Pure Land school?" Thus he decided to send a messenger to get advice from Ango-in (Seikaku). The Shōnin scanned the faces around him trying to decide whom to send, and finally said, "Brother Zenshin (Shinran)—he's the man for the job!" The brethren also agreed, saying, "Yes, he is the one most suited."

When I, Zenshin (Shinran), heard this, I firmly declined, even doing so several times. But in the end, as this request was being made by such an esteemed personage as my master, I was obliged to make my way to the residence of Ango-in, in the capacity of a messenger charged with a mission. But first I made a request, saying, "This mission I am charged with is one of the gravest importance, and it is better that I have someone to accompany me." The person selected to accompany me was Brother Zenshaku, of Saii.

When the two of us arrived at Ango-in's residence, we were shown in. Ango-in (Seikaku) was bathing at the time. "Messengers? Who could they be?" Seikaku said. "Zenshin has arrived, sir," a servant announced. When Seikaku heard this, he was greatly surprised and said, "It is most unusual that such a messenger should have business with me! This is truly most extraordinary!" and he hurried out of the bathhouse to greet us. I immediately launched into a long and detailed explanation of the higher values that our master Genkū stood for and wished to promote.

Hōin (Seikaku) had this to say, "Those are the very thoughts that I have entertained for years. How could I stand by and watch them be put down. Even if an imperial decree were made, I would never let our master's lifework be destroyed. Before we pull the hood of imperial decree over our eyes, we must never confuse the two gates of the Sage Path and the Pure Land—indeed, I stand ready to declare to the world the principle of the Pure Land. The reason is, I place far greater value on our wise teacher than on any imperial decree, and so please tell him to rest assured."

Seikaku told me about the events of the other day, talking in rapid succession without stopping for a break. When I, Zenshin, returned, I presented myself to Genkū and explained what the Hōin told me was his role as the officiant, and the gist of his emphatic talk, all this without leaving out a single word. At that time the Shōnin asked Brother Zenshaku who had accompanied me, "Is there anything missing in his account?" Zenshaku answered, "I, Saii, sat in on both sessions, and now I have just heard the preaching of the Dharma twice—what can I say, I am speechless."

[Kakunyo comments:] Thus, of the 380-some disciples, Zenshin was by far the best; he was the one with the best understanding, and was already regarded as the best choice for the role of envoy, as Saii's words well attest. Is this scenario not like that of Prabhūtaratna Tathāgata coming to give testimony [in the *Lotus Sūtra*]. Such honors were frequently conferred on Zenshin during the lifetime of the great master Genkū Shōnin.

Zenshin had long ago sworn off taking the role of officiant of ceremonies, and even made a vow before Genkū Shōnin to the effect that he would desist from the role of instructing others and observing precepts. He did not want patrons fawning over him, nor did he comply with the requests of others to assume that role. Around that time, Jōshin, as the novice Jirō was known, who was a descendant of Genzo Nakatsukasa no-jo, went through a great deal of trouble to have a temple built out of earth and wood, and humbly submitted a request that Zenshin take the role of officiant at the *pūjā* ceremony. At this point Zenshin Shōnin had to interrupt and firmly explain to him that his code of values prevented him from doing so. At that time Zenshin Shōnin was cast in the role of a *gonja* (a manifestation of higher powers), and while he may have appeared no different from any other confused ordinary person, he pointed out the gravity of making a sermon with an impure heart.

Translator's Notes: Genkū refers to Hōnen (1133-1212), teacher of Shinran and founder of the Jōdo-shū. Ango-in refers to Seikaku (1165-1235). Shinran made copies of Seikaku's *Yuishinshō* (On Faith Alone) for distribution and even wrote a brief commentary on it. Little is known about Zenshaku. According to the historical note attached to the *Tannishō* in the Hongwanji version, Zenshaku was one of four persons executed in the nembutsu persecution of 1207.

(6) On the quarrels among disciples and fellow seekers, and their taking back one another's *Honzon* scroll and sacred writings, with a warning that such things should never be done

Once, Shingyō-bō, of Hitachi-no-kuni-Niitsutsumi, was in the audience when he heard Shinran Shōnin explain the doctrinal principle of a scriptural passage. For the infraction of not paying his respects to the Shōnin, he was reprimanded and sent back to his home country in disgrace. The disciple Renni-bo said, "Since Shingyō-bō has violated the code of the brotherhood and is being sent back to his country, he should be asked to return the *Honzon* scroll and sacred writings he has in his possession. This is especially the case since these are sacred teachings with the name of Shinran Shōnin inscribed on the title page. Not only did his action result in his expulsion from the brotherhood, does it not clearly show his lack of respect for these items?" The Shōnin said, "Demanding the return of the *Honzon* scroll or sacred writings is something we should never do. The reason is, there is not a single disciple that I, Shinran, have, for what have I ever taught anyone to call them my disciple. As we are all the disciples of the Tathāgata, all of us stand on a par as fellow seekers. When we gain an insight into how we receive the true entrusting of birth through nembutsu, it becomes apparent to us it arises out of the skillful means of the two honored ones, Śākyamuni and Amida. When seen in this way, we come to understand this is exactly what I, Shinran, have been saying all along. When differences of opinion arise in this world, the land becomes raucous with complaints to return the *Honzon* scroll and sacred writings, to return the titles, to return the true entrusting they've gotten. But the more you think about it, the more you realize that such things should never be done. The *Honzon* scroll and sacred writings are forms of skillful means meant to benefit sentient beings. Even if someone were to decide to cut their ties with me and to enter someone else's community, I have no special monopoly on these sacred writings, for what the Tathāgata teaches has currency throughout all communities. Even if someone were filled with dislike for the items inscribed with my name, feeling, "How I hate that priest and hate the kesa he wears," and were to take the sacred writings and dump them in the mountains, the living beings in that area are certain to be saved by those sacred writings meant to benefit all beings everywhere. Thus, the long-held wish to benefit sentient beings would be fulfilled at that time. So too with the treasure of the true entrusting the ordinary person possesses; we should never insist it be returned. Take this point well to heart."

(8) On the Issaikyō compilation project

When Shurinosuke Tokiuji, the father of the Zenmon of Saimyōji (Hōjō Tokiyori, 1227-1263), held the reins of political power, he initiated a project to transcribe the entire Issaikyō Buddhist sūtra collection. For the work of compiling this edition, he extended an invitation to wise and learned monks, and while calling on the two celebrated priests, Muto Saemon Nyūdō and Yadoya no Nyūdō, to urge them to participate, as chance would have it he also called on Shinran Shōnin as well.

The Shōnin accepted his invitation to take part in the Issaikyō compilation. In the midst of the work, the vice-shogun and retinue were in the vicinity, and at times he held banquets serving all kinds of delicacies, where the various celebrities could meet one another and exchange information. Unlike the priests who were die-hard vegetarians who made sure their demeanor was proper, the Shōnin simply took his place among the ordinary initiates and commoners, and did not hesitate to help himself to the fish and poultry dishes. At one point he stopped in front of the vinaigretted fish and would not budge, helping himself to one serving after another.

As he was wearing a Buddhist kaṣāya all the while, the Zenmon of Saimyōji, Kaiju Dono, who was then nine years old, pointed to it, and secretly whispered in the ear of the Shōnin, "See those initiates over there; whenever *they* eat any fish they remove their kaṣāya. Brother Zenshin (Shinran), how is it that you wear your kaṣāya while eating. It is strange." The Shōnin said, "Those initiates are always conscious of themselves, and are aware that whenever they are eating they should remove their kaṣāya, and so they remove it to eat, it seems. When I, Zenshin, suddenly come across food like this, I am in such a hurry to eat, that I completely forget to remove it."

Kaiju Dono again said, "There is something about your reply that doesn't sound right. There must be a deeper side to this. Or are you just trying to humor me because you think that I, Kaiju, am still a child," and so saying he withdrew. On another occasion, the Shōnin was again helping himself to some fish while wearing his kaṣāya. Once again, Kaiju Dono came up to him to ask him the same question, and the Shōnin again said he simply forgot. This time Kaiju Dono said, "It is hardly likely that you have again let it slip your mind. Or then again, you might think that a child's mind is simply too foolish to understand anything deep, and so it is pointless to try. All that I am asking is that you tell me the truth," a curt request that he expressed repeatedly.

At that point the Shōnin could not easily slip out of answering, and facing the young child he said, "Rare is it to be born into human form, yet we take the lives of other living things to satisfy our craving for the taste of flesh, this being something that we should never do, and even the Tathāgata thus sets forth strict precepts against it. However, the sentient beings of the present age of the defiled world of the latter dharma live in a precept-less time, such that there are neither those who hold them nor those who violate them. As a result, although my head is shaved and I wear the dyed robes of a priest, because my heart is identical to those of the ordinary worldly masses, I eat things like this. Ah, if only this massive urge to eat were instead translated into the work of liberating these living things. Although I bear the title of Shaku-shi (an ordained disciple of Śākyamuni) it is of little consequence; with a heart steeped in the dust of this worldly life, with my wisdom naught and my merits none, what I can possibly do to save these sentient beings? In this regard there is this kaṣāya I wear, the holy vestment symbolic of the liberation of all buddhas in the triple world. When I don this vestment while eating, through the use of this meritorious kaṣāya it exerts its influence of the vow's intent to save living beings, and thus I wear this while I eat. When you believe that invisible forces watch over us, there is no need to be concerned over how we appear in the eyes of others, however utterly shameless and unconscionable we may appear to them. And so this is the reason I do so."

(9) An incident with Shōkō of Chinzei

Once, when Shinran Shōnin was on his way to the residence of the Kurodani Shōnin (Genkū), he met a lone practicer who asked his servant for directions, saying, "Be so good as to tell me the living quarters of the Shōnin said to be the wisest of all the famous names of all the eight schools in the capital." The servant relayed the request to Shinran who sat inside a carriage. Shinran said, "The residence of the wisest of the Shōnin—now could that be Genkū Shōnin whom you are referring to. Then you must be on your way to visit him, am I right?" The practicer said, "That is so. I have a matter to discuss with Genkū Shōnin." Shinran said, "That's where I'm headed, so let me give you a lift." The practicer was wary and said, "Well, I'm not sure, I don't think I can do that." Shinran Shōnin said, "If it's the Dharma you seek, you need not be so reserved. After all, we're bound together as disciples of Śākyamuni, why make it hard on yourself, just get in." Although the practicer tried to refuse several more times, Shinran could at last instruct his servant,

"Carry the practicer's box, would you," and had the practicer ride in the carriage with him. Thus when they arrived at the hermitage, and were in the presence of Genkū Shōnin, Shinran Shōnin announced, "I have a practicer with me, from Chinzei (Kyushu), who wants to call on your hermitage to seek the Dharma. He is a fellow companion I met on the road leading here, please receive him." Genkū Shōnin said, "Please extend my welcome to this person." Thus, Shinran Shōnin showed the practicer inside and brought him before Genkū.

At this point, Genkū Shōnin stared at the practicer, and the practicer stared back at Genkū Shōnin, and then a long silence ensued. After a while Genkū Shōnin said, "Who then are you, and what business brings you here." The practicer said, "I am a person from Chinzei who, making his way up to the flowery capital (Kyoto) in search of Dharma, seeks to have an interview with you." At that point the Shōnin said, "In search of the Dharma? What kind of Dharma is it you seek?" The practicer said, "I seek the Dharma of the nembutsu." Genkū Shōnin said, "The nembutsu? The nembutsu of the T'ang China or the nembutsu of Japan?" The practicer paused awhile. Then, making up his mind, he said, "I seek the nembutsu of the T'ang." Genkū Shōnin then said, "Well, then, you must be a disciple of Shan-tao." At that point the practicer took out an inkstone from his sleeve and proceeded to write a two-kanji name that he presented to the Shōnin, saying, "Shōkō-bō (Benchō, 1162-1238), of Chinzei."

This hijiri Shōkō-bō, from Chinzei, had all along been scheming, "I will go to the capital to meet the Shōnin known as the wisest in all the world. Once I make my way up to the capital, I will immediately challenge the Shōnin to a mondō (question and answer) session. At that point, if he proves the wiser, then I will become his disciple. But, if I win the mondō session, then he must become my disciple." However, Genkū Shōnin, who was a *gonja* (a manifestation of higher powers), must have seen through the practicer's arrogant mind, hence the reason for the mondō session with him. This hijiri, who thought he had everything in place to make the Shōnin his disciple, at last realized he could not pull it off. His arrogance and conceit came tumbling down, and as a sign of submission to his new teacher, he there and then acknowledged defeat by submitting his name to the Shōnin.

One day, two or three years later, Shōkō-bō put down the box he was carrying, and presented himself before Genkū Shōnin saying, "I miss my homeland and will be returning to Chinzei. I came to bid you farewell." That is, he came to bid farewell and take leave of the brotherhood. Genkū Shōnin said, "New practicers need to take tonsure when they start their practice." These words made Shōkō-bō's ears perk up, and he suddenly said, "It has been some time since I, Shōkō, was ordained as a monk, but now I am admonished to cut my hair, I think this very strange. Because your admonishment remains lodged in my ear,

I am unable to take to the highway. I will make my way home after you tell me what all this is about."

At that point the Shōnin had this to say, "A Buddhist teacher has to deal with three kinds of 'hair,' that is, Supremacy, Profit, and Fame. During the three years you have spent here, I have tried to instill you with the key ideas in the Dharma statements I have compiled. If you return to your homeland only to treat others as inferiors, is this not to strut about with an air of Superiority? No one who saw you sporting this 'hair' of Superiority would ever regard you as a good student of Buddhism; this is what those seeking Fame do. As a result, the only thing they seek in the Buddhist community is Profit for themselves. Only those who have shorn themselves of these three kinds of 'hair' are worthy of being called Buddhist teachers. Thus I have spoken these words to you."

At that time Shōkō-bō showed an air of contrition, and taking out all the writings he had stored in the box he carried with him, proceeded to burn them, and saying his last farewell made his exit. But some residue of the old Shōkō-bō remained, for in the end he set aside the advice Genkū Shōnin offered him, and turning his back on the things he heard the Shōnin speak, he emphasized the idea that our Birth was to be won by various practices, but this orientation becomes a hindrance to self and others when it comes to pursuing the true practice for Birth. He completely forgot the injunctions of our patriarchal teacher Genkū and remembered instead that the hidden forces of the gods are nothing to fear. How sad, and yet how frightening! This story of Shōkō-bō is remarkable since he first received the guidance of Shinran Shōnin and then entered the Kurodani brotherhood, but it shows what happens when our understanding is incomplete.

(11) On setting aside secondary karmic measures

Once, when Shinran Shōnin was touring the eastern countries, he was laid out with a cold for three days and three nights, during which time he couldn't take any liquids. Unlike other times he refused to let anyone nurse him. On the third day he said, "Ah, so that's it," and sat up as if fully recovered. At that time his wife the honorable Eshin asked him, "You were sick for two or three days, so what made you say that?" The Shōnin said, "During the past three years or so I've never been lax in my efforts to read the three Pure Land sūtras, but just when I thought to myself, 'I have to start in on reading them ceremonially a thousand times,' a passage from Shan-tao's *Raisan* appeared to my mind: 'To arrive at your own understanding at last, and then to be stricken with the desire to impart that understanding to others, this, of all the challenges we will ever know, is the one most fraught with difficulty,' and I realized there is meaning to striving to bring others to believe what you yourself believe, but I could not understand why in the world anyone would want to merely pile up reading the three sūtras one after another. When I thought long and hard on why this was so, I realized this yet unresolved problem was presenting itself to me from the time I was laid out in bed. So that was no ordinary illness, and that's why I said, 'Ah, so that's it.'" [Kakunyo writes:] To this I say that when we give this matter careful thought, these words from Shan-tao's *Raisan* were like a message one is imparted in a dream vision, for they clearly show that the principle of the single-direction, sole nembutsu, as the manifestation of the saving grace of Avalokiteśvara, reaches everywhere.

(12) On the Shōnin as Avalokiteśvara in disguise

When in a place called Shimozuke no kuni (Ibaragi ken) Sanuki, Shinran's wife the honorable Eshin had a dream vision: "I remember being at a hall making offerings, and in the garden a beautiful and solemn dance was being performed. Here under the open sky was something like a shrine torii with a horizontal beam from which hung two scrolls with depictions of *Honzon*. I could not make out the figure on one scroll, it was just a radiant light of golden hue, and from the other scroll now I could at length make out a venerable form. The *Honzon* that I could not make out was a person, and so when I asked, someone answered, 'That is Mahāsthāmaprāpta Bodhisattva, that is, Genkū Shōnin.' Then I asked, 'Now a venerable form emerges from the other scroll—what buddha is that?' and I remember someone telling me, 'That is the great compassionate Avalokiteśvara Bodhisattva, who goes by the name of Brother Zenshin.' Then the dream came to an end. When I asked Shinran Shōnin about this, he told me, 'That is the case, the great Mahāsthāmaprāpta Bodhisattva was the avatar of wisdom, thus his wisdom is expressed as radiant light, and that is why his form is just a body of light. People always said that Genkū Shōnin was a transformation body of this Mahāsthāmaprāpta Bodhisattva.' But I just could not bring myself to ask Shinran Shōnin whether he was in fact Avalokiteśvara Bodhisattva in disguise. After this dream vision, in my heart I deeply felt a warm reverence for him that lasted over the months and years. When I learned he passed away after returning to Kyoto, in the announcement I stated, 'Know well that your father was a *gonja* (a buddha in disguise).'" [Kakunyo writes:] This document from the honorable Eshin was sent from Echigo no kuni (Niigata ken) in the spring of Kōchō 3 (1263) to her daughter the honorable Kakushin. To this I say, Genkū Shōnin, as the transformation and manifestation of Mahāsthāmaprāpta Bodhisattva, spread the teaching of our original master Amida in Wakoku (Japan), and Shinran Shōnin, as the manifestation of Avalokiteśvara Bodhisattva, along with bringing the lantern of wisdom of the Tathāgata of unhindered light to shine throughout this land, as a disciple of the master, clearly received the decisive message that he heard from Genkū that he transmitted to posterity. Let us venerate and worship them.

(13) The record of Renni-bo's dream vision

Kenchō 8 (1256), second month, ninth day, at the hour of the tiger (4:00 to 6:00 a.m.), in a dream Shaku Renni was served an imperial proclamation by Shōtoku Taishi. The noble form of this Crown Prince appeared, and facing the Dharma teacher Shaku Shinran, he read a document and respectfully paid reverence to Shinran Shōnin. The text of that proclamation read, . . . "I pay reverence to the great compassionate Amida Buddha. Thanks to the spread of the wonderful teaching we will come to be born in the Pure Land. Even in the midst of this evil time of the five defilements in this wicked world, it is certain that we shall attain the highest enlightenment." Renni especially honored and paid reverence to the Crown Prince, and when he awoke from the dream he wrote down this passage. [Kakunyo writes:] To this I say, when we turn the pages of this record of his dream vision, it becomes clear that our patriarchal teacher Shinran Shōnin emerges as the manifestation of Avalokiteśvara, as well as being indicated as the manifestation of our original teacher Amida. The names Amida and Avalokiteśvara are different names for the same body, and there is no difference between them whatever. But as to the transmission and the explanation of the decisive points spoken by him preserved among the latter branches of his school, his formulations stand apart from the rest and must be said to be without peer. Make careful note of this point.

(14) On Birth with or without bodily loss

Shinran Shōnin told us that during the time of the late teacher Genkū Shōnin there were countless dharma disputes. Zenshin (Shinran) said, "For the person seeking Birth through nembutsu, Birth is achieved without bodily loss," while Zenne-bō of Kozaka (Shōku, 1177-1247) said, "It is only through loss of body that Birth is possible"—this was the nature of the dispute. At this point, the brotherhood demanded that a decision be made as to who was winner and loser, and so a number of them went to the great master Genkū Shōnin and said, "We must have a dharma debate between Brother Zenshin and Brother Zenne," and after having each of them present their thoughts on the matter the great master Shōnin announced his decision, affirming Brother Zenshin's view of Birth without bodily loss, saying, "It is as you say," and then affirming Zenne-bō's view that bodily loss itself is what makes Birth possible, saying, "It is as you say." Thus, with both parties affirmed, it was impossible to make heads or tails of the situation, and so the brotherhood asked for a further clarification of this decision, to which

Genkū Shōnin said, "Zenne-bō's rationale for his view that bodily loss is what makes Birth possible is based on a model of the person who performs multiple practices leading to Birth. Zenshin-bō's rationale for Birth without bodily loss is based on a model of person who does nembutsu leading to Birth." While "the dharma the Tathāgata teaches cannot be two" (Shan-tao's *Hōjisan*), if "in fact the persons who are the sentient beings are not the same" (*Hōjisan*), the corollary to this is we must resign ourselves to whatever our basic personhood is, since everything now turns on the thickness or thinness of the good karma to our name. Nembutsu leading to Birth is the result of the Buddha's Original Vow, whereas the notion of multiple practices leading to Birth has nothing to do with the Original Vow. In nembutsu leading to Birth, the seekers do not need to concern themselves as to their good or bad karma on deathbed. When the single mind of taking refuge in joy and sincerity is settled in us through tariki, we come to hold to the principle of instant Birth with no reversion to transmigration through hearing of it from a good teacher while settled into this groove of ordinary life; although there is no death and loss of our defiled body, our Birth takes place without loss of this body even though we continue to produce karma. The text of the Original Vow clearly states that such people will be looked after. Next, for the person who pursues multiple practices leading to Birth, when they are lying on their deathbed, if they do not receive the welcome of the Buddha that they are waiting for, they will not even be born in the womb palace of the hinterlands. For this reason, since the moment of the death and loss of this defiled body is an important factor, without which this scheme does not work, they emphasize this point. This is seen in the Nineteenth Vow. As to the difference in superiority and inferiority, nembutsu leading to Birth is connected to the Original Vow, that broadly embraces all sentient beings in the ten directions; multiple practices leading to Birth, by contrast, is a non-Original Vow notion limited to the person who engages in concentration and dispersion. Between the Birth without bodily loss of the person of the nembutsu of the Original Vow, and the Birth with bodily loss of the person of the non-Original Vow notion of multiple practices leading to Birth, there is no vast unbridgeable gap; either one of these explanations stands out as self-evident."

(16) On saying the Name out of the core of faith

Shinran Shōnin had a disciple named Kakushin-bō, of Takada. When he was stricken with severe illness and about to face the final curtain, Shinran returned to the residence and saw his critical condition, with breathing so aggravated and already failing him that it left him virtually no leeway to say the Name. At that time the Shōnin said, "It is wonderful to put all your strength into the nembutsu while suffering, but how are you holding up in your condition." Kakushin-bō answered, "That joyful moment is rapidly approaching, that moment that must arrive in all our lives draws near. All this comes to pass in an instant, they say, but as long as the breath remains to me, I know I must express my gratitude to the Buddha's benevolence for letting me receive the great benefit of Birth, thus to express my thanks I catch at every chance to say the Name." At this time Shinran Shōnin said, "Your words evidence the effects of our long years of constantly working together," as tears of joy burst from his eyes in a thousand streams.

However, it is a question to me whether it is essential in Shinshū, or in the conditions for anjin, that we hold to some certain thing or have some certain idea. There are those of our comrades who whip themselves into a frenzy to say the Name out of self-power, and who even lash the bottom of their feet to the lotus dais of the altar as death approaches. It is because it is impossible to determine the karmic cause of our past lives, that we cannot predict what condition of death awaits us. Whether a person is to be burned by fire, drowned in water, pierced by swords, or even dies during sleep, all of these are conditions that have their cause in our past karma, this without exception.

If a person is thus invested with a certain condition of death, as long as this is part of their karmic makeup, there is no way they can avoid it. If a person is to be fatally wounded by their mortal enemy, in that one instant what the ordinary person is thinking is of the hate that bonds them to their enemy, there is no other thought. If a person is to die in his sleep, with his basic mind unaware he is breathing his last; with that last moment behind him, it is already too late for him to make the effort he intended; there is nothing they can do to say the nembutsu. Again, with regard to the person who is to be killed by someone, in addition to the hateful thoughts that fill their mind that crowd out all other thoughts, there is no time left to do the nembutsu. It is unrealistic to count on much leeway as we meet our end. For instance, everyone thinks that, if a person has one of these conditions of death that forces them to diverge from the ordinary pattern of life, they will not be born in the Pure Land; or, for instance, that there are also those people who are prime candidates for the true Vow; such mistaken views as these, however, are virtually impossible to cure.

How much less so, then, can those who are basically saying the Name out of self-power, not avoid thinking that way at the last stage, and by that token end up being born in the periphery of the Pure Land. Indeed it is because it is most difficult for them to avoid the karmic conditioning of their past, that people are bound to run into these problems, and of all the difficulties they face at their station in life, this is the most difficult. In addition, even if they were to wish for Birth in the realm of sloth or hinterlands, it is uncertain whether that wish will be granted. These things are all because they turn their back on the true Vow.

[Kakunyo writes:] Such views are also to be seen in Shinran's commentary *Jōdo Monrui* [*Kyōgyōshinshō*] where it says, "The moment a person recalls Amida's true Vow, / He is naturally allowed to enter therein and definitely decided for Birth. / By simply saying the Tathāgata's Name over and over again, / He repays the kindness of the universal Vow of great compassion." [*Shōshinge*, See *CWS* version, p.71.] And, "Simply by completely giving oneself over to saying the Tathāgata's Name, a person returns the kindness of the universal Vow of great compassion." Thus, for those who have been instructed by a good teacher during ordinary life, and have opened up the true entrusting at this time to dwell in the ranks of the truly settled, there should be no need to wait until the time of death for a second chance to receive the benefit of Birth. As the texts clearly reveal, the saying of the Name after that experience of the true entrusting is what fulfils the great practice of Other power reminding us to be grateful to the kindness of the Buddha. Thus, in the final moments of this disciple's life, there was no difference in their views, and so Shinran was moved to tears. Make careful note of this.

(18) On those in mourning

[This is what Shinran taught:] When you meet someone distraught over the loss of someone dear, recommend to them the medicine of Buddha Dharma, instruct and guide them in what Buddhism has to tell us at this impasse in life: that of the eight sufferings of the human realm, there is nothing more painful than that of having to leave our loved ones behind. First, tell them the plain truth: that in this world of birth and death there is no one who lives forever; next, explain to them the condition of the world of peace and sustenance: that though we are caught in misery and suffering, if we do not wish for the Pure Land where there is no misery and suffering, in the future we shall again meet with grief and sorrow. On the other hand, when we leave behind the six paths where "only the screams of suffering are heard" (Shan-tao's *Jōzengi* chapter) and turn to Amida's Pure Land where "we enter his Nirvana palace" (*Jōzengi* chapter), in this new orientation to our life, the grief and sorrow of the darkness enshrouding us is cleared away, and without knowing it we find ourselves being taken up and brought to benefit from the Light. Next, when you meet someone who is in mourning, the last thing that you want to do is to add more sadness to their existing sadness. When you do this, not only are they in mourning, now you are forcing them to become ever lonelier by the minute. Another name for wine is *bō-yū*, meaning "to forget your troubles." Comfort the mourners by having them partake of some wine, leaving them once their smiles have returned. This, then, is how we should treat those in mourning. Keep these points well in mind.

(19) On the Tathāgata's true Vow originally being for the sake of the ordinary person, and not for the saintly

The Hongwanji Shōnin, Shinran, once told his grandson Nyoshin Shōnin something that his late teacher of Kurodani, Genkū Shōnin, once told him, that people ordinarily think, "If the evil-ridden person attains Birth, how much more so the good person." This view, on the far end, turns it back on Amida's true Vow, and on the near end, contradicts the golden words of Śākyamuni's appearance in this world. For that reason, Amida's five kalpas of laboring in contemplation and the myriad practices that he endured on the six paths, were all necessary for the sake of obtaining the release of the ordinary person, and none of it was for the sake of the saintly. Thus, the ordinary person is the main person who is supposed to ride on the true Vow and arrive at Birth in the reward land. If the ordinary person was incidental to Birth, it was all for nothing that the Buddha made the vows, and all the efforts he made to realize them would simply have dissipated. However, by matching up and loading on the power of the Vow, he was able to achieve great and far-reaching benefit for sentient beings in every direction. As a result, ten kalpas have now passed since his attainment of true enlightenment was praised by all buddhas. This testimony of all buddhas who number as many as the sands of the Ganges—how can such testimony be empty and false? Moreover, even in the commentary (Shan-tao's *Gengibun*) there are statements such as, "All ordinary persons good and evil attain Birth." This too regards the evil-ridden ordinary person as main and the good ordinary person as incidental. For that reason, if the good ordinary person, who is cast in the incidental role, can attain Birth, how can it be possible that the evil-ridden ordinary person, who is cast in the main role, will not attain Birth? Thus, I was told, "If the good people can attain Birth, how much more so does this apply to the evil-ridden ones."

G. *A Word from Kakunyo's* Treatise on Correcting Errors (Gaijashō)

13. *Gaijashō*

(3) That we should never choose to make ourselves stand out by donning pleatless robes and owning black kesa (Skt., *kaṣāya*) in the manner of those who retire from the world to live a Buddhist reclusive life.

... However, in the turn of events that resulted from the decree of Cessation of the Sole Practice of Nembutsu, when the exclusive nembutsu movement was abolished from the capital, and Shinran was ordered by the authorities to be defrocked and go to Echigo, from that time on he used the name Gutoku for his signature. In the use of this name is expressed the dimension of his being neither a monastic nor a layman, as was the case with Kyōshin Shami. From this experience he was heard to say, "It's one thing if other people accuse you of being a cow thief, but it's inexcusable if you go around putting on airs of being a good man, or an afterworlder, or a so-called Buddhist—that you should never do." In this case the thoughts and actions of that league of Buddhist afterworlders who ply the pleatless robes and black kesa are as far apart as the clouds above and the mud below. While our school may well go beyond the teachings and methods of the hidden and revealed schools of the larger and smaller vehicle, shut away the cardinal point of Amida's Other power in the depths of your heart and to all outward appearances keep that merit hidden from view [*Gaijashō* 3, translated by Mr. Wayne Yokoyama, unpublished; text from the *Jōdo Shinshū Seiten*, pp. 920-922].

Note: Kakunyo refers in this passage to the persecution of Hōnen's community, including Shinran. The name Gutoku, assumed by Shinran at the time, signaled his intention to model his life on that of Kyōshin Shami (ninth century) who was a type of lay monk, living unostentatiously, while pursuing a life of *nembutsu* devotion. However, the statement that one might better be called a "cow thief" than an "afterworlder," displaying piety by one's robes and demeanor, was a criticism of the religious style of Ippen and his followers. This movement was known as Jishu. Rennyo took up this theme, urging Shin followers not to display piety outwardly. In our modern parlance we would say not to wear our religion on our shirtsleeves or as an epaulet for all to admire. (See also Minor L. Rogers and Anne T. Rogers, *Rennyo: The Second Founder of Shin Buddhism* (Berkeley: Asian Humanities Press, 1991), *Letter* II-2, pp. 174-175, also *Letter* II-13, p. 189, and *Letter* III-11, pp. 212-213.)

H. The Earliest Biography of Shinran: Kakunyo's Godenshō

14. Traditional Biography: The Life of Shinran Shōnin

Note: Kakunyo Shōnin, the third Abbot of the Hongwanji (1270-1351) is credited with the first effort to provide an overall view of Shinran's life. Because most people at the time were illiterate the text was combined with a series of pictures known as the *Denne* or Pictorial Biography. *Godenshō* refers to the written text. Kakunyo drew on stories from the developing tradition which he learned from Nyoshin, Shinran's grandson, as well as passages from the *Kyōgyōshinshō* and Eshin-ni's letters. The text has been recited at Hōonkō services commemorating Shinran's death.

The text is from the *Collected Writings on Shin Buddhism* (Kyoto: Shinshū Ōtaniha, 1973), pp. 165-190. We want to express our appreciation to the Matsugaoka Library and the Ōtani Headquarters office for permission to use Drs. Gesshō Sasaki and Daisetz T. Suzuki's translation in this publication. For the general reader we have not included the detailed notes and annotations of the translators. Scholars may refer to the original editions.

(Original) Editors' Note

The literary works in which Shinran's thought and faith are transmitted are numerous. They include, besides the *Kyōgyōshinshō*, his *Wasan* (The Songs of Shinran), and the *Tannishō*, compiled by his disciple Yuiembō. Materials relating to his life, however, are few. In spite of a vigorous literary activity that continued until the year before his death at age 90, there is almost nothing to relate concerning his personal affairs that would be based on firm historical evidence. In 1911, at the time this translation of Shinran's traditional biography, *Godenshō*, was made by Gesshō Sasaki and D.T. Suzuki, some historians even advocated the view that Shinran had never really existed at all. They charged that Kakunyo wrote the *Godenshō* in disregard of historical fact in order to further his aim of establishing the Hongwanji order.

Since then, thanks to the appearance of such new material as the holograph letters of his wife Eshin-ni, which were discovered in 1921, and the great advance in scientifically-based research, today Shinran's existence has been established beyond any doubt. These developments have brought about a new recognition of the historical significance of the *Godenshō* as well, as the earliest biography we now possess. Nonetheless, even today there are many varying theories concerning different aspects of his life: his youth, his mother, the motives behind his entering the priesthood, the life of religious practice he led during his twenty years on Mt. Hiei, his marriage, his life during the five year exile in Echigo, the reason he went to the Kanto area after his release from exile instead of returning directly to Kyoto, the outcome of his twenty years of teaching there, the reason he finally returned to the capital from the Kanto area in his later years—such questions as these have yet to be satisfactorily answered.

Although traditions that were current in the Hongwanji order at the time of the translation are introduced in the notes appended to the work, along with soundly based historical fact, we have chosen to reprint the entire work here in its original form. Romanization of proper nouns have usually been left as they appeared in the original 1911 edition.

Kyoto, 1972

Translators' Preface

The death of Shinran Shōnin took place on the twenty-eighth of November, 1262, and ever since, this day has been commemorated by followers throughout the country. The services of the commemoration go on generally over a space of seven days, at the close of which falls the death-day of the Shōnin. During this week consecrated to the memory of the great founder of the True Sect, subjects for sermons are mostly taken from "The Life," and on the night of the middle day of the commemoration "The Life" (*Godenshō*) itself is recited amid most solemn surroundings. The recitation is listened to with the utmost reverence, and kindles afresh the faith of the devotees. The scene is extremely inspiring.

The author of this Life is Kakunyo Shōnin (1270-1351), the third Hosshu (Master of the Law) of the Hongwanji. He was the great-grandson of Shinran Shōnin. From the time he was eight years old, he studied the Confucian classics under Fujiwara Narinori and the Buddhist literature belonging to the Kusha and the Tendai schools under Chōkai of the Chōrakuji temple. During the Kō-an era, he was instructed by Jōchin, high priest of the Nanryu-in, in all the esoteric as well as the exoteric philosophy of Buddhism. When seventeen years old, he was ordained as a monk by Shinshō who then held a very high priestly position at Nara. His study of the Yogācārya philosophy was carried on under Gyōkwan Hōin. Thus thoroughly equipped with the knowledge of all the schools of Buddhism, he finally embraced the faith of the True Sect under the guidance of Nyoshin Shōnin, who was the grandson of Shinran Shōnin and was then holding the second patriarchal chair at the Hongwanji.

In the third year of Shōwō, when he was twenty-one years old, he began to be deeply moved by the life of his great-grandfather. He made earnest inquiries among the personal disciples of Shinran who were still surviving, as to the details of his earthly-career. Not quite satisfied with this, he made a pilgrimage himself, visiting every landmark left by the Shōnin and traveled even up to the northern extremes of the country. The result of this trip lasting three years appeared as "The Life of Shinran Shōnin," as we have it here. On the trip he was accompanied by Jōga of the Kōrakuji, and it was he who illustrated for the first time each chapter of this biographical record.

This *Life* was completed about the middle of October in the third year of Yeinin when the author was twenty-six years of age, and it was the thirty-fourth year since the passing of Shinran Shōnin. After this, many biographical works have been compiled, but none surpasses the present one, not only in antiquity but in reliability.

The second patriarch Nyoshin died in the second year of Shōan, and after some discussions about the rightful successor to the chair,

Kakunyo, the author of the present work, was called upon to fill the vacancy as third patriarch of the Hongwanji. His death took place during the reign of Emperor Murakami, at age eighty-two; he had held the office for forty-two years. The prosperity of the True Sect and the development of its teachings owe much to this untiring priest-scholar. For his other works still extant, see the *Principal Teachings of the True Sect* (Kyoto: The Eastern Hongwanji, 1928), pp. 29-30.

Many commentaries have been written on *Godenshō*, and some of the most important ones are enumerated in Gesshō Sasaki's *The Life of Shinran Shōnin* (Appendix Nos. [Tokyo, 1910]), pp. 2-4. The fourth and the eighth chapters of the present translation are missing in the old manuscript copies preserved in the Senjuji temple, of Ise, and in the Hōonji temple, Bandō, and on this account these two chapters are sometimes considered later additions. But they appear in the manuscripts copied by the author himself which are still in existence in the Jōkōji temple and the Shōgwanji temple, of Hidachi, and, therefore, Kakunyo himself must have added these while later revising his first manuscript, between the third year of Kōyei and the second year of Teiwa.

The Life of Shinran Shōnin

PART I

1

The Shōnin in his worldly relation was a scion of the Fujiwara family. The twenty-first descendant of Prince Amatsu Koyane was the Grand Minister Kamatari, and after five generations there was Lord Uchimaro, of the first court rank, junior grade, who was General of the Imperial Guards and a state minister; and six generations after him there was Lord Saishō Arikuni, Police General; and when five more generations passed there was Lord Arinori, who was a high court officer belonging to the service of the Empress Dowager of the time; and the Shōnin was born (1173 A.D.) as son of this noble personage. In consequence of his distinguished birth, his earthly prospects were full of promise. If he desired, he could have become a high dignitary at the Imperial court and enjoyed whatever prosperity he would have aspired to the end of his life. But his heart was inclined towards things unworldly; for he wished to devote himself to the holy cause of Buddhism and to increase the spiritual welfare of all beings. This looked-for opportunity came when he was nine years old. Accompanied by his uncle Lord Noritsuna, of the third court rank, junior grade, he went to the monastery of the venerable Jiyen. Jiyen had held till then a high ecclesiastical position called Daisōjō. The Shōnin had his head shaved by this noble priest and was given the Buddhist name, Hanyen. After this he applied himself most earnestly to the study of the deep philosophy of the Tendai schools concerning the three aspects of the mind and especially to the mastery of a profound system expounded by Yeshin who used to live at the Ryōgon-in, Yokawa. There was thus nothing in the Tendai philosophy which escaped his penetrating insight, including the doctrine of the four grades in perfect harmony which are distinguished in the teaching of the Buddha.

2

During the first year of Kennin (1201 A.D., when he was twenty-nine years old) his earnest heart, ever intent on spiritual and unworldly things, induced him to call on Genkū Shōnin at his Yoshimidzu monastery; for he wished to walk in the high way of Easy Practice, finding it very uncertain to plod along the narrow path of Difficult Practice in these later days when humanity is so degraded. The Venerable Genkū (i.e., Hōnen) in whom the True Sect finds a most illustrious transmitter of its doctrine, took special pains to explain to him in a most exhaustive manner the essentials of his teaching and their ultimate signification. As soon as this was done, the Shōnin instantly came to realize the inmost meaning of the doctrine of salvation through Amida and his all-embracing love for sentient beings; and to his heart's fullest content, he found his faith firmly established in the truth that leads every sentient being, however ignorant, to the direct path of the Pure Land.

3

On the fifth day of the fourth month in the third year of Kenrin, the Shōnin had a vision at night in the hour of the Tiger. According to the *Record,* "Bodhisattva Avalokiteśvara of the Rokkakudō manifested himself before the Shōnin in the form of a holy monk whose serene countenance was awe-inspiring. He was clad in a white robe (kaṣāya), sitting quietly in a huge white lotus flower, and spoke to Zenshin (i.e., Shinran) in an authoritative voice: 'When the devotee finds himself bound by his past karma to come in contact with the female sex, I will incarnate myself as a most beautiful woman and become his object of love; and throughout his life I will be his helpmeet for the sake of embellishing this world, and on his death I will become his guide to the Land of Bliss.' 'This,' continued the Bodhisattva, 'is my vow. Thou, Zenshin, shalt announce the signification of this my vow to the world and make all sentient beings know of it.' At this time, Zenshin still in a state of trance looked eastward facing directly the Rokkakudō, and descried a range of high mountains, on the highest peak of which was found congregating an immense number of people. He addressed them as commanded by the Bodhisattva, and when he imagined that he had come to the end of his address, he awaked from the dream."

When we think of the purport of this vision as described in the *Record*, we notice herein symbolized an auspicious opening for the establishment of the True Sect and the propagation of its doctrine of salvation. Thus says the Shōnin later on: "Buddhism was founded first in the West, and that we have its sacred books in this country now is altogether due to the auspicious virtue of Prince Jyōgū [Shōtoku], which was higher than a mountain and deeper than the ocean. It was during the reign of the Emperor Kimmei of our Imperial House that Buddhist literature was brought here over the sea, and with it came those Sūtras and Śāstras on which the doctrine of the Pure Land Sect is based; if in those days the Imperial Heir were not disposed to spread his benevolence far and wide, how could the poor and ignorant become acquainted with the Buddha's vows for universal salvation? As Bodhisattva Avalokiteśvara is the original abode of the Imperial Heir, Jyōgū, he revealed in himself his august original abode in order to make known his vows, that is, to incarnate himself in a human form and thereby to advance the cause of Buddhism.

"And again, if my Great Teacher, the Venerable Genkū, were not sent away into a remote province by the authorities, how should I ever live a life of banishment? And if I did not live a life of banishment, how could I hope to have the opportunity to convert the people living far away from the center of culture? This too must be ascribed to the virtue of my Venerable Teacher.

"My Great Teacher, the Venerable Genkū, was no other personage than an incarnation of Bodhisattva Mahāsthāmaprāpta, while Shōtoku, the Imperial Heir, was an earthly manifestation of Avalokiteśvara. It devolves upon me under the guidance of these two Bodhisattvas now to proclaim far and wide the Original Vow of the Tathāgata, through which it is that the True Sect has arisen and the doctrine of *Nembutsu* (recitation of the Buddha's name) is gaining ground. This, however, is all due to the instructions of the holy ones altogether independent of the achievements of my humble self. The weighty vows as offered by these two august beings are to recite the name of the One Buddha with singleness of heart. The followers of Buddhism these days ought not to go astray and pay their reverence to those two personages who stand by the Buddha; let them adore the One only." Thus, the reason why the Shōnin Shinran pays his respect to the Imperial Heir along with the Buddha himself is that he is grateful for his greatest deed of benevolence which made it possible for Buddhism to spread all over this land.

4

On the ninth day of the second month in the eighth year of Kenchō (1256 A.D.), at the Tiger's hour at night, Shaku Renni had a vision in which he was told of the Imperial Heir, Shōtoku, who, prostrating himself before the Shōnin Shinran, said: "I must reverently bow to the Great Merciful Buddha Amida, who has revealed himself on earth in order to propagate the doctrine full of spiritual meaning; for it is through him that I, born in a world of evils and at the age of the five defilements, was enabled most assuredly to attain the highest wisdom." According to this, it is evident that the Shōnin, the founder of the True Sect, was no other personage than an incarnation of Amida Tathāgata.

5

While the Venerable Teacher, Genkū, was yet on earth, he was so kindly disposed towards the Shōnin that the latter was graciously allowed to have access to the writings of the Teacher and even to copy them, and again that the Teacher himself condescended to write the name of the Shōnin and gave him the inscription. Thus, we read in one of the Shōnin's writings, entitled *Passages Collected to Show the Truth of the Pure Land Doctrine* [*Kyōgyōshinshō*]: "Thus, I, Shinran, the simple-hearted man with a shaven head, during the era of Kennin abandoned the practice of unessential work and found the home in the Original Vow of Amida. During the era of Genkyū, I was permitted through the gracious consideration of the Teacher to copy his work, *Selected Passages*, while in the same year, on the fourteenth day of the first summer month, he inscribed in my copy the inside title of the book, which is, *Selected Passages Concerning the Original Vows of the Pure Land*, and together with it: '*Na-mu-A-mi-da-bu-tsu*: for those who wish to be born in the land of Amida, the one thing needed is to recite the name of the Buddha. Given to Shaku Shakkū.' This was written by the Teacher's own hand. On the same day I was permitted to carry his portrait home in order to make a copy of it.

"In the second year of the same era, which was a leap year, on the twenty-ninth of the seventh month, I was given his own portrait with an autograph inscription: '*Na-mu-A-mi-da-bu-tsu*: Upon my attainment of Buddhahood, if sentient beings in the ten quarters of the world, who recited my name once or repeated it up to ten times, were not to be born in my land, then I would not embrace the supreme wisdom. This Buddha is at present abiding in Buddhahood; therefore let it be known that his Original Vows, his grand vows, have already been fulfilled, and whoever recites his name will assuredly be born in his land.'

"Again, according to a vision, my Teacher had my name, Shakkū, changed to Zenshin, and on the same day with his own hand he inscribed my new name.

"My Venerable Teacher, Shōnin Genkū, is seventy-three years old this year. His *Selected Passages Concerning the Original Vows of the Pure Land* was compiled in compliance with the request of the devout Buddhist Prime Minister, Tsukinowa Kanezane, and it comprises all the essential teaching of the True Sect and the inmost signification of *Nembutsu*, which will readily be comprehended by those who study them. The work is the efflorescence of faith so rare and unsurpassable; it is the holy treasure of Buddhism unfathomably deep. Though there have been hundreds of thousands of people who come to receive instructions from the Teacher—the period of their discipleship ranging from days to years—and whatever relationship to the Teacher, distant or near, they may have had, still they have all found it quite a rare occurrence to be permitted to see and copy his work; whereas I have had all these privileges granted, that is, the copying of his literary production as well as his own portrait. This I must ascribe to the merit of engaging myself in the orthodox work with singleness of heart. It is symbolic of the assurance of one's rebirth in the country of Amida. And for this reason, restraining my tears of sadness and gratitude, I have hereby recorded all these circumstances."

6

While the Venerable Genkū was still alive, he was always devoted to the propagation of the doctrine of salvation through "Other-Power" and rebirth in Amida's country, and the entire world was then anxious to listen to his teaching. Not only were Imperial personages ready to pluck the golden-colored flowers of the Pure Land, but noble lords of the highest ranks were glad to gaze at the silvery moon shining on the Forty-eight Vows of Amida. Nay, even people, remote and humble, were glad to come to the Venerable Teacher and pay him homage. Thus, his followers, noble and lowly, coming thick upon him, converted his residence into a sort of prosperous market. Those who were in constant attendance on him numbered about three hundred and eighty. In spite of this, however, those who were personally cared for by the Teacher and who earnestly followed his instructions were not many, hardly numbering more than five or six.

The Shōnin Zenshin once said to his Teacher: "Since my abandonment of the Path of Difficult Practice for that of Easy Practice and my entrance into the Gate of the Pure Land away from that of Holy Path, I have ever been under your wise guidance whereby I was made to hoard up the good seeds of release and emancipation. If not for you, what would become of me? For that reason, I know not how to

give vent to my feeling of happiness and gratitude. There are, however, many fellow-believers of mine, all of whom are enjoying the
friendship of belonging to the same company under one director, and
yet we know not one another well as regards our inner faith, whether
it is such as to enable us to be born in the country of Amida or not.
Besides, I have a desire to know who among us could be real spiritual friends in our coming lives, and also to have a sort of meeting
to test our faith while still living here. Will you kindly permit me to
say a few words to my fellow-believers on such an occasion as seems
proper?"

To this the Teacher replied, "Your request is most reasonable. You
shall speak to them when they all come here tomorrow."

The next day when they were assembled, the Shōnin requested
them to arrange themselves into two groups according to their views
on what constitutes the stage of steadfastness, that is, whether it is
attained by faith or by work. Some three hundred fellow-believers
of his, who were present at this meeting, seemed not to comprehend fully the sense of this request. There were two, however, who
declared themselves as belonging to the group of those who believed
in the all-importance of faith: they were Seikaku who was a Hōin,
Daikwashō-i, and Shaku Hōren called Shinkū Shōnin.

Later came in Hōriki, Kumagai Naozane, a lay-disciple of the
Teacher and asked, "My venerable Zenshin, what are you engaged
in?" Replied the Shōnin, "Sir, we are trying to make a distinction
between those who believe in the all-importance of faith and those
who believe in work as most essential." Said Hōriki, "If this be the
case, I must not be left out, for I will join the rank of those who
believe in the all-importance of faith." Thereby, Zenshin took down
his name as requested, while the rest of those present numbering
several hundreds had not a word to say concerning the matter in
question. Perhaps this silence was due to their inability to free
themselves from the bondage of "self salvation" and to their minds
still being dark as regards the true diamond-like faith. Thus, as they
remained silent, the Shōnin who was acting as recorder, put his own
name down. After a while, the Venerable Teacher said, "I also will
take a seat with those who believe in the all-importance of faith."
Then among his disciples, some humbly and devoutly expressed their
willingness to follow his example while others felt dejected over
their weakness of faith.

7

Said the Shōnin, "When we were once gathered in the presence
of the Teacher, the Venerable Genkū, including such personages as
Shōshimbō, Seikwambō Nembutsubō, and many others, we entered

unexpectedly into a heated discussion. This was raised by my remark to the effect that the faith entertained by the Teacher and myself so completely coincided that there could not be any distinction whatever between his and mine. The others present did not agree with me and raised an objection, saying, 'We cannot see any reason in your remark that the faith of the Teacher and your own are one and the same. How could they be one?' I then said, 'Why should I not say that they are one? Of course, I am not so presumptuous as to imagine for a moment that I am equal to the Teacher in deep wisdom and wide learning; but as far as my faith in the Pure Land of Amida is concerned, it has been firmly established since my listening to the doctrine of salvation by "Other-Power" and I have been free from the notion of "by myself." Now, the faith of the Teacher is based upon a power other than the Self, and so is mine. Hence my declaration that they are both one and the same.'

"Thereupon, the Venerable Teacher truly observed: 'Faith varies so long as it is based on "Self-Power," for we all have different intellectual capacities, and the faith based upon them cannot be identical; whereas the faith based upon a power other than the Self is one that is given by the Buddha to us, ignorant beings, regardless of our moral attainments; and therefore, what makes up my faith cannot in any way differ from the faith embraced by Zenshin, they are identical. My faith is not the outcome of my ingenuity. Those who entertain a faith other than that which has just been referred to, may not go to the same Pure Land where I am bound for. Let this be thoroughly understood by all.'

"With this, they held their tongues and did not speak a word."

8

Nyūsaibō, one of the disciples of the Shōnin, was wishing for some time to have his portrait painted, and the Shōnin reading his thought told him to engage the artist, Jōzen Hokkyō, for the purpose, who was living near Shichijō. Feeling grateful for his kind insight, Nyūsaibō sent for the Hokkyō, who immediately responded to the invitation.

As soon as he came to the presence of the Shōnin, he said, "Last night I had a wonderful dream and the holy personage who appeared in it had exactly the same features as those of the one whom I now confront." Saying this, he was instantly moved with the feelings of deep gratitude and adoration, and related the story of the dream: "Two holy-looking monks came in, and one of them requested me to draw a portrait of the spiritual personage here. I asked him who that spiritual personage was, and the reply was: He is the venerable monk who is enshrined at the Zenkōji temple as its founder. Though in a dream, I folded my hands together and knelt down most reverently before him. I was awestruck and trembled all over, for I realized that I was facing Amida himself. The monk told me that the portrait might be simply that of his head. After this dialogue I awoke from the dream. On coming here, as I looked up at the venerable features before me, I perceived their perfect identity with the holy monk in my vision." Saying this, he was in tears from excess of his grateful feelings.

Then he painted, according to the miraculous advice given in the vision, the head only of the Shōnin. The vision is said to have taken place on the night on the twentieth day of the ninth month in the third year of Ninji (1242 A.D.).

When we weigh the significance of this singular incident, it is evident that the Shōnin was a manifestation of Amida Nyorai. Therefore, his teaching must be regarded as the direct communication of Amida, which is on the one hand to dispel the darkness of this defiled world by means of the pure light of wisdom, and on the other to give the necessary moisture by sending down the spiritual rain of nectar, to us who are ignorant and confused and dying of dryness of heart. So let us adoringly believe this.

PART II

1

There were many Buddhist scholars, then, living in the South and the North of Kyoto, who were greatly irritated to see the rise of the Pure Land Sect at the expense of the Holy Path teaching, which was steadily losing ground. They attributed this to the baneful influence of the Venerable Genkū, and wished to have him incriminated without delay.

We read in the [Kyōgyōshinshō], "Passages Relating to the Land of the Transformed Body, VI": "All the schools, I observe, belonging to the Holy Path, have long been on the decline, as far as their practical discipline and spiritual attainment are concerned; while the True Sect of the Pure Land is now making it possible for every one to come to spiritual attainment. The Buddhist monks belonging to the various other schools, however, have no adequate understanding of their doctrine and are unable to distinguish truth from falsehood. Even so with the learned scholars of the Imperial capital, they have no definite ideas concerning practical morality, they are at a loss how to discriminate between right and wrong. The Buddhist monks of the Kōfukuji naturally took advantage of this fact, and early in the mid-spring of the first year of Jyōgen (1207) during the present reign, they maliciously denounced us to the Ex-emperor as well as to the reigning Emperor. In consequence of this, Genkū the Teacher, the great illustrious founder of the True Sect, and several of his disciples were charged with crimes, of which they were quite innocent; some were summarily condemned to death, while others were deprived of their ecclesiastical orders, given secular names, and banished to the remote countries. Of the latter, I was one. Thenceforth, I am neither a monk nor a layman, and for my family name I have adopted the title 'Toku' (bald-headed). Since the banishment of the Teacher, Genkū, and his disciples into various remote parts of the Empire, five years have now passed. . . ."

The Venerable Genkū was given the criminal name Fujii Moto-hiko and banished to Hakata in the province of Tosa; while the criminal name of Shinran Shōnin was Fujii Yoshizane and he was banished to Kokubu in the province of Echigo. As to the execution and banishment of other disciples of his, no details will be given here.

During the enlightened reign of the Emperor, in the first year of Kenryaku (1211), or the twenty-seventh day of the eleventh month, Lord Norimitsu Okazaki, a high court official, delivered the Imperial message of pardon to the Shōnin, and to his receipt of the order he signed "Toku" (bald-headed man) as aforementioned.

Though thus pardoned, the Shōnin remained yet for some time in his place of banishment, for he wished to continue his religious work already started there.

2

After Echigo, the Shōnin transferred his abode to Hidachi, where he settled at the village of Inada in the county of Kasama. Though his cottage was a lonely one far from town, there was always a large number of anxious truth seekers, noble and lowly, lay and monkish, who knocked at his rustic gate. His long cherished desire to see the Buddha's Law widely propagated, as well as his ever-abiding desire for the welfare of all beings, were thus satisfactorily brought to a consummation. "This," said the Shōnin then, "fully coincides with what in my former days I was given to understand in a vision through the order of Bodhisattva Avalokiteśvara."

3

When the Shōnin was thus engaged in the propagation of the doctrine of *Senju Nembutsu* (recitation of the Buddha's name with singleness of purpose) in the province of Hidachi, few reviled him, and many there were who faithfully followed his instructions. There was however one monk (said to be a *yamabushi*) who at times harbored a deep hatred against the Buddha's Law, and this hatred finally ripened into an evil intention upon the person of the Shōnin. He was occasionally seen looking for a timely chance. As the Shōnin was wont to travel a mountain-pass called Itajiki-yama, the man frequently waited for him coming up that way, but could never have an opportunity to meet the Shōnin. He pondered this, and considering it altogether extraordinary, a desire was awakened in him to see the Shōnin, and he visited him at his residence. The Shōnin without much ado bade him enter. As soon as the man came to the personal presence of the Shōnin the evil intention he harbored at once vanished, and overcome by repentance, he could not forbear weeping bitterly. After a while he frankly confessed all the evil desires that had been possessing him. But the Shōnin remained perfectly collected. Thereupon, the man broke his bow and arrows, threw away his sword, took off his headgear, and changing his persimmon-colored garment, embraced the Buddha's teaching. It is said that he finally came to realize the faith. It was a miracle, indeed. The man was no other personage than Myōhōbō, the name given him by the Shōnin.

4

The Shōnin, now leaving his abode beyond the eastern frontier, was on his way to the capital. When one day towards the evening he was laboring up the long weary pass of Hakone, along the track beaten only by a few travelers, he at last came to a solitary house. It was now past midnight, and the moon was about to wend her way down behind a neighboring hill. The dawn was already approaching when the Shōnin walked towards the house and knocked at the door. In response, a man far advanced in years and in full dress, came out of it, betraying not the least sign of surprise, and said to the Shōnin: "Living as I am near a Shinto shrine, I was spending the whole night in the company of the priests, when I thought I fell asleep just for a few seconds. I was not exactly dreaming, or seeing a vision; but the god of the shrine addressed me, saying, 'A visitor whom I revere is just coming up this way, and you shall serve him most faithfully and hospitably, and prepare for him an especial feast. . .' I had hardly recovered from this divine revelation when all of a sudden you appeared at the door. How could you then be an ordinary personage? The divine words leave no room for doubt, and their instant actualization commands my utmost respect." So saying, he treated the Shōnin most worshipfully both in heart and body, serving him with various foods and some rare delicacies.

5

After returning to his native town, the Shōnin reflected upon the past, and realizing how years come and go like a dream or a vision, he came to look upon his earthly abode in the metropolis as a thing not worth troubling his mind. He moved from one place to another, sometimes in the west and sometimes in the east. And there was a house near Gojō and Nishi-no-Tōin, to which he took a fancy for a while as he considered the site fine. Here were gathered those disciples of his, coming from various quarters, who had in former days received his personal instructions, and renewed their friendship.

In those days there was living a commoner called Heitarō of an unknown family in the village of Ōbu, Naka-no-sai county, in the province of Hidachi, who embraced the doctrine of the Shōnin with singleness of heart. The Heitarō was on one occasion obliged on account of his profession to pay homage to the Kumano shrine and came to the Shōnin to get enlightened on the matter. The Shōnin then said to him: "Now, the Holy Teaching has many forms, and each one is productive of great benefits when it is in full accordance with the character of a believer. In these latter days, however, the practice of the Holy Path is by no means to be recommended. For we read: 'In the time when the Law begins to decay, not one among myriads of beings could be found who could gain the Path, however much they might discipline themselves [according to the Path] and try to observe the Law'; and again, 'But there is one gate of the Pure Land through which only we may all enter the way.' These are the words unmistakably set forth in our sacred books and commentaries as uttered by the golden mouth of the Tathāgata himself.

"It was upon this true doctrine of the Pure Land, the only reality, that those venerable patriarchs in the three countries founded their teachings; so what I, simple-hearted and ignorant, advise you is not from my selfish will. Absolute single-heartedness as they expound it constitutes the essence of the doctrine of rebirth in the Pure Land, and is the backbone of our religion. While this doctrine is sometimes esoterically and sometimes exoterically set forth in each of the three canonical books, we cannot fail to recognize everywhere in an unmistakable manner where the context and the general meaning tend. In the *Larger Sūtra*, the three classes of believers are mentioned, and yet they are all urged to accept the 'absolute single-heartedness,' and in the concluding part of the *Sūtra* this doctrine is committed to Maitreya. In the *Meditation Sūtra*, the threefold heart is mentioned in connection with the nine grades of rebirth, and the *Sūtra* is entrusted to the hands of Ananda. Finally, the one heart referred to in the *Smaller Sūtra* is testified by all the Buddhas. Therefore, the author of the *Discourse [on the Pure Land]* treats of the one heart and Donran comments on the doctrine of absolute single-heartedness. Whatever texts we thus resort to, they are all one in upholding this doctrine, which teaches to think of the Buddha with absolute oneness of thought.

"The original abode of Shōjōden is no other than Amida, the ever-present master of our faith, who, desiring to come in contact with all sentient beings in every possible relation, has left his earthly trace [in

Kumano]. The ultimate signification of this—his leaving an earthly trace here—is to let in all such sentient beings to the seas of the Original Vows as have come in touch with him in whatever way. Therefore, whoever, believing in the Vows of Amida, the original abode, are engaged in the recitation of the name of the Buddha with singleness of purpose, are entirely free from the workings of a selfish heart, even when, in conformity to their public duties or to their master's instructions, they tread on the grounds of a god to pay homage to his shrine or temple. This being so, it is not necessary to put on any outward form of wisdom or morality or purity, though we are holding within ourselves all manners of falsehood and unreality; only let the Vows of Amida, the original abode, work themselves out. O, be thou ever reverent! Never think that this is slighting the dignity of a god; and there will be no divine wrath whatever visiting upon thy own person."

Accordingly, Heitarō on his way to the Kumano Shrine did nothing special towards the formal observation of the ceremonial rules; but as an ordinary mortal drowned in the mire of ignorance, he did not trouble himself much about the purification of his person. As to the Original Vows of Amida, however, he always kept them in deep reverence, not for a moment forgetting the instructions of his teacher. At last he arrived at his destination in safety. While in a dream that night he was visited by a layman who in full dress came out by opening the doors of the Shōjōden. He said to the man, "Why dost thou hold me in disrespect by not cleansing thyself from impurities?" When this was said, lo, all of a sudden there appeared the Shōnin directly confronting the layman, and said. "He is one who spends his days in the recitation of the name of the Buddha as instructed by me, Zenshin." Thereupon, the layman holding his *shaku*, respectfully bowed to him and did not utter another word. Heitarō awoke from his dream, and his wonderment at the incident was beyond description.

On his way home from the shrine, he stopped at the Shōnin's residence and told him every detail of his experience. To this, the Shōnin simply said, "That was what I meant." What a remarkable event!

6

Towards the latter part of mid-winter in the second year of Kōchō (1262), the Shōnin showed the symptoms of a slight indisposition, and after that, his talk never referred to earthly things, dwelling only on how deeply grateful he was to the Buddha; he uttered nothing but the name of Amida, which he constantly repeated. On the twenty-eighth of the same month, at noon, he laid himself on his right side with his head towards the north and his face towards the west; and when at last his recitation of the name of Amida was no more heard, he expired. He was then just completing his ninetieth year.

His abode was then in the western part of the capital, (south of Oshikōji and east of Madenokōji), and his remains were carried along the road east of the river, to Yenninji, on the western slope of Higashiyama and south of Toribeno. His ashes were gathered there and then deposited at Ōtani, which is situated north of Toribeno at the foot of Higashiyama. Not only those disciples who were present at his death-bed, but all other people, young and old, who received his instructions, unanimously mourned the passing of the Shōnin, recalling the days of his earthly life and lamenting his disappearance from their midst.

7

In the ninth year of Bunyei (1272), the tomb at Ōtani, north of Toribeno, on the western slope of Higashiyama, was removed sometime during the winter to the western part of the same grounds north of Yoshimidzu, where the remains of the Shōnin were deposited. A temple was built and his image enshrined there. In those days, the religion transmitted from the Shōnin was flourishing with more vitality than ever, and the teaching bequeathed by him found a wider acceptance than during his lifetime. His disciples filled every province and every county, and his followers increased all over the land, numbering many millions. Those who kept his instructions in deep reverence and felt sincerely grateful to him, monks as well as laymen, the old as well as the young, year after year, all came here to pay their homage at the shrine.

As to the many wonderful things which happened in his lifetime, I cannot begin to enumerate them now, and it is to my great regret that I have to omit them.

III. SHINRAN INTERPRETS PURE LAND TEACHING

A. Shinran's Self-Understanding: The Human Condition

1. "Hell is decidedly my abode": The Personal Dimension

Note: The following passages reveal Shinran as one of the most confessional of all Buddhist teachers, exposing his inmost spiritual condition as a foolish being to his disciples. His declarations are consistent with the spirit of his teaching and his relations with his disciples in not putting himself above others. His personal expressions show his capacity to identify with all those entangled in the chains of ego and passion, making his teaching attractive to ordinary people as it became increasingly known beyond his lifetime.

He declares his true humanity as it was illuminated by Amida's compassion and wisdom. His deep personal awareness of imperfection shaped his teaching, highlighting the all-embracing character of Amida's Vow, which promises ultimate Enlightenment to even the most evil person. It is often said that the brighter the light, the sharper the shadows.

15. Confession-1

Although I take refuge in the true Pure Land way,
It is hard to have a true and sincere mind.
This self is false and insincere;
I completely lack a pure mind.

Each of us, in outward bearing,
Makes a show of being wise, good, and dedicated;
But so great are our greed, anger, perversity, and deceit,
That we are filled with all forms of malice and cunning.

Extremely difficult is it to put an end to our evil nature;
The mind is like a venomous snake or scorpion.
Our performance of good acts is also poisoned;
Hence, it is called false and empty practice.

Although I am without shame and self-reproach
And lack a mind of truth and sincerity,
Because the Name is directed by Amida,
Its virtues fill the ten quarters.

Lacking even small love and small compassion,
I cannot hope to benefit sentient beings.
Were it not for the ship of Amida's Vow,
How could I cross the ocean of painful existence?

With minds full of malice and cunning, like snakes and
    scorpions,
We cannot accomplish good acts through self-power;
And unless we entrust ourselves to Amida's directing of
    virtue,
We will end without knowing shame or self-reproach
[*Gutoku's Hymns of Lament and Reflection*, I, pp. 421-422, #94-99].

Note: "Directing" in this verse refers to the transfer of Amida's true mind and virtue embodied in his Name. It is bestowed on, or given to, beings, and manifested in their trust in Amida's Vow.

16. Confession-2

I know truly how grievous it is that I, Gutoku Shinran, am sinking in an immense ocean of desires and attachments and am lost in vast mountains of fame and advantage, so that I rejoice not at all at entering the stage of the truly settled, and feel no happiness at coming nearer the realization of true enlightenment. How ugly it is! How wretched! [*KGSS*, III. I, p. 125, #113].

Note: Gutoku was the surname Shinran adopted for himself when he was exiled. It means foolish, ignorant, stubble-headed, or untonsured monk who does not keep precepts.

17. Confession-3

Through hearing the shinjin of the wise, the heart of myself,
Gutoku ("foolish/stubble-haired"), becomes manifest:
The shinjin of the wise is such that they are inwardly
    wise outwardly foolish.
The heart of Gutoku is such that I am inwardly foolish
[*Gutoku's Notes*, I, p. 587].

18. Confession-4

While persons ignorant of even the characters for "good" and
    "evil"
All possess a sincere mind,
I make a display of knowing the word "good" and "evil";
This is an expression of complete falsity.

I am such that I do not know right and wrong
And cannot distinguish false and true;
I lack even small love and small compassion,
And yet, for fame and profit, enjoy teaching others
[*Hymns of the Dharma-Ages*, I, p. 429, #115-116].

19. Confession-5

The Master would often say,

When I consider deeply the Vow of Amida, which arose from
five kalpas of profound thought, I realize that it was entirely
for the sake of myself alone! Then how I am filled with gratitude for the Primal Vow, in which Amida resolved to save
me, though I am burdened with such heavy karma [*A Record in
Lament of Divergences*, I, p. 679, Postscript].

Note: This is a very famous passage highlighting the deep personalization marking the
experience of *shinjin* or true entrusting. It is not simply an event in some mythical
past, but an event in "my" life, as I awaken to Amida's Vow in true entrusting and
my life is transformed through deep gratitude. The phrase resounds in Japanese:
"*Shinran hitori ga tame ni.*"

20. Confession-6

*We should not express outwardly signs of wisdom, goodness, or
    diligence*
People who aspire for the Pure Land must not behave outwardly as though wise or good, nor should they act as though
diligent. The reason is stated, *for inwardly we are possessed of
falsity* (literally, *that which is empty and transitory*) [*Notes on
"Essentials of Faith Alone,"* I, p. 466].

21. Confession-7

Although I say the nembutsu, the feeling of dancing with joy is faint with me, and I have no thought of wanting to go to the Pure Land quickly. How should it be [for a person of the nembutsu]?

When I asked the master this, he answered, "I, too, have had this question, and the same thought occurs to you, Yuiembō. When I reflect deeply on it, by the very fact that I do not rejoice at what should fill me with such joy that I dance in the air and dance on the earth, I realize all the more that my birth is completely settled. What suppresses the heart that should rejoice and keeps one from rejoicing is the action of blind passions. Nevertheless, the Buddha, knowing this beforehand, called us 'foolish beings possessed of blind passions'; thus, becoming aware that the compassionate Vow of Other Power is indeed for the sake of ourselves, who are such beings, we find it all the more trustworthy.

"Further, having no thought of wanting to go to the Pure Land quickly, we think forlornly that we may die even when we become slightly ill; this is the action of blind passions. It is hard for us to abandon this old home of pain, where we have been transmigrating for innumerable kalpas down to the present, and we feel no longing for the Pure Land of peace, where we have yet to be born. Truly, how powerful our blind passions are! But though we feel reluctant to part from this world, at the moment our karmic bonds to this saha world run out and helplessly we die, we shall go to that land. Amida pities especially the person who has no thought of wanting to go to the Pure Land quickly. Reflecting on this, we feel the great Vow of great compassion to be all the more trustworthy and realize that our birth is settled.

"If we had the feeling of dancing with joy and wishing to go to the Pure Land quickly, we might wonder if we weren't free of blind passions" [*A Record in Lament of Divergences*, I, pp. 665-666, #9].

Note: This is a very significant chapter in the *Record in Lament of Divergences* (*Tannishō*) indicating Shinran's deep identification with, and sympathy for, his disciple. The text also reveals the disjunction between scripture and experience. The *Contemplation Sūtra* declares that when a devotee is about to be born into the Pure Land because of dedicated practice (here, entrusting) he/she is described as "[rejoicing] so greatly as to dance" (Hisao Inagaki, *The Three Pure Land Sutras* [Kyoto: Nagata Bunshodo, 1994], p. 340). In the *Notes on Once-Calling and Many-Calling*, Shinran comments: "Leap and dance (*yuyaku*) means to dance in the air (*yu*) and to dance on the ground (*yaku*); it is the form of boundless joy and manifests the state of gladness and delight. 'Gladness' is to rejoice upon attaining what one shall attain and 'delight' is happiness. Attaining the stage of the truly settled expresses itself in this form" (*Notes on Once-Calling and Many-Calling*, pp. 480-481; See also *Notes on "Essentials of Faith Alone,"* pp. 463-464). Yuiembō, despite his entrusting, did not have joy in the prospect of his birth in the Pure Land, due to the continuing bondage of passion that attends foolish beings in Shinran's understanding: "Attaining what one shall attain" refers to birth into the Pure Land. Yuiembō felt quite the opposite because of his worldly attachments and passion and Shinran acknowledges he did also. See above 16. Confession-2.

22. Confession-8

> This is a statement of one who doubts the Primal Vow and fails to understand the influence of good and evil karma of past lives.
>
> Good thoughts arise in us through the prompting of good karma from the past, and evil comes to be thought and performed through the working of evil karma. The late Master said, "Knowing that every evil act done—even as slight as a particle on the tip of a strand of rabbit's fur or sheep's wool—has its cause in past karma."
>
> Further, the Master once asked, "Yuiembo, do you accept all that I say?" "Yes I do," I answered.
>
> "Then will you not deviate from whatever I tell you?" he repeated.
>
> I humbly affirmed this. Thereupon he said, "Now, I want you to kill a thousand people. If you do, you will definitely attain birth."
>
> I responded, "Though you instruct me thus, I'm afraid it is not in my power to kill even one person."
>
> "Then why did you say that you would follow whatever I told you?"
>
> He continued, "By this you should realize that if we could always act as we wished, then when I told you to kill a thousand people in order to attain birth, you should have immediately done so. But since you lack the karmic cause inducing you to kill even a single person, you do not kill. It is not that you do not kill because your heart is good. In the same way, a person

may not wish to harm anyone and yet end up killing a hundred or a thousand people."

Thus he spoke of how we believe that if our hearts are good, then it is good for birth, and if our hearts are evil, it is bad for birth, failing to realize that it is by the inconceivable working of the Vow that we are saved.

The Master further stated:

"For those who make their living drawing nets or fishing in the seas and rivers, and those who sustain their lives hunting beasts or taking fowl in the fields and mountains, and those who pass their lives conducting trade or cultivating fields and paddies, it is all the same. If the karmic cause so prompts us, we will commit any kind of act" [*A Record in Lament of Divergences*, I, pp. 670-671, #13].

Note: This is a very significant passage in which Shinran expresses a view of the power of karma that approaches fatalism. However, his intention is not to promote fatalism, but to recognize that we all have given conditions, dispositions, or tendencies that are part of our lives from our birth on. Consequently, we cannot be proud of our virtue nor should we lament our limitations. They are all elements in our karmic stream from past lives and our present experience. The point is that Amida's compassion embraces us all despite our virtue or our evils. He is implying that we are really more complex beings and simply not free to do as we wish. Shinran is stressing the complete sufficiency of Amida's Vow to overcome all hindrances. It is a message of humility and hope.

23. Confession-9

Inquiring on what is essential for rebirth, he (Shinran) had this thought: "Although I immerse myself in the still water of meditation, the waves of consciousness are constantly surging. Although I contemplate the moon of the mind, I am covered constantly by clouds of delusion. Nevertheless, without catching my breath, a thousand years have passed. Why do I envy the transitory sangha and vainly exhaust myself in provisional studies? I must abandon power and profit and immediately aspire for release from (births and deaths)" [Zonkaku, *Tandokumon*, in *Jōdo Shinshū Seiten* (Kyoto: Hongwanji Shuppansha, 1988, revised), p. 1077].

Note: Zonkaku (1290-1373) is the eldest son of the 3rd Abbot, Kakunyo. He was very scholarly. *Tandokumon* is "Words in Praise of (Shinran's) Virtue." The text praises Shinran and includes this quotation from him, expressing his reflections of his disappointing experience on Mount Hiei. The translation is by Alfred Bloom.

2. The World of Foolish Beings

24. Human Condition-1

However, since the beginningless past, the multitudes of beings have been transmigrating in the ocean of ignorance, sinking aimlessly in the cycle of all forms of existence and bound to the cycle of all forms of pain; accordingly, they lack the entrusting that is pure. In the manner of their existence, they have no entrusting that is true and real. Hence, it is difficult for them to encounter the unexcelled virtues, difficult to realize the supreme, pure shinjin. In all small foolish beings, at all times, thoughts of greed and desire incessantly defile any goodness of heart; thoughts of anger and hatred constantly consume the dharma-treasure. Even if one urgently acts and urgently practices as though sweeping fire from one's head, all these acts must be called "poisoned and sundry good," and "false and deceitful practice." They cannot be called "true and real action." To seek to be born in the land of immeasurable light through such false and poisoned good is completely wrong.

Why? Because when the Tathāgata was performing bodhisattva practices, there was not a moment—not an instant—when his practice in the three modes of action was tainted by the hindrance of doubt. Because this mind is the Tathāgata's mind of great compassion, it necessarily becomes the truly decisive cause of attaining the fulfilled land. The Tathāgata, turning with compassion toward the ocean of living beings in pain and affliction, has given unhindered and vast pure shinjin to the ocean of sentient beings. This is called the "true and real shinjin that is [Amida's] benefiting of others" [*KGSS*, II. I, p. 98, #28; See also II, p. 103, #39 and *Passages on the Pure Land Way*, I, pp. 311-312].

Note: Generally, Pure Land tradition has maintained the concept of *mappō*, the last Dharma age when the teaching declines and disappears. It is used to explain the gradual decline of Buddhism over time and must have been evident when the Sūtras were composed. It was promoted by early Pure Land teachers in China such as T'an-luan and Tao-ch'o. However, though Shinran also employs that concept (see below), he also stresses that this is the human condition from its very beginnings. It transcends the process of history. His graphic descriptions are amplified by those in the *Larger Pure Land Sūtra*, which describes the people of the world and the five evils (Inagaki, *The Three Pure Land Sutras*, pp. 282-287, pp. 291-301).

3. The Evil World of the Last Dharma Age

25. Last Age-1

Thus, the multitudes of this evil, defiled world, ignorant of the distinctive characteristics of the latter age, revile the behavior and attitude of monks and nuns, but all people of the present, whether monk or lay, must take measure of their own capabilities.

Considering the teachings concerning the three dharma-ages, we find that the date of the Tathāgata's parinirvana falls on the fifty-third year (the year water/monkey) of the reign of King Mu, the fifth emperor of the Chou dynasty. From that year of water/monkey to the first year of our Gennin era (the year wood/monkey) it is 2,173 years. Based on the *Auspicious Kalpa Sūtra*, the *Benevolent Kings Sūtra*, and the *Nirvāna Sūtra*, we find that we are already 673 years into the last dharma-age [*KGSS*,VI. I, p. 244, #78-79; *KGSS*, VI. I, p. 242, #73].

26. Last Age-2

Truly we know that the teachings of the Path of Sages were intended for the period when the Buddha was in the world and for the right dharma-age; they are altogether inappropriate for the times and beings of the semblance and last dharma-ages and the age when the dharma has become extinct. Already their time has passed; they are no longer in accord with beings.

The true essence of the Pure Land way compassionately draws all of the innumerable evil, defiled beings to enlightenment without discrimination, whether they be of the period when the Buddha was in the world, of the right, semblance, or last dharma-ages, or of the time when the dharma has become extinct [*KGSS*, VI. I, pp. 240-241, #69].

27. Last Age-3

It is now more than two thousand years
Since the passing of Śākyamuni Tathāgata.

The right and semblance ages have already closed;
So lament, disciples of later times!

Now, amid the five defilements in the last dharma-age,
Sentient beings are incapable of practice and realization;
Hence the teachings that Śākyamuni left behind
Have all passed into the naga's palace.

During the right, semblance, and last ages,
Amida's Primal Vow has spread.
At the end of the semblance and in this last dharma-age,
Good practices have all gone into the naga's palace.

* * *

As the time of kalpa-defilements advances,
The bodies of sentient beings gradually grow smaller;
Their evil and wrongdoing amid the five defilements increase,
So that their minds are like poisonous snakes and evil dragons.

Ignorance and blind passions abound,
Pervading everywhere like innumerable particles of dust.
Desire and hatred arising out of conflict and accord
Are like high peaks and mountain ridges.

Sentient beings' wrong views grow rampant,
Becoming like thickets and forests, bramble and thorns;
Filled with suspicion, they slander those who follow the
      nembutsu,
While the use of violence and the poison of anger spread
      widely.

* * *

We may think that these times belong to the right
      dharma-age,
But in us—the lowest of foolish beings—
There is no mind that is pure, true, or real;
How could we awaken the aspiration for enlightenment?
[*Pure Land Hymns on the Right, Semblance, and Last Dharma Ages*,
I, pp. 399-400, #2-4; 7-9; 15].

Note: Shinran's reference to the theory of *mappō* or decline of the Dharma serves the purpose of stressing the deteriorating spiritual condition of the age he lived in. His computations of the stages in this decline employ the figures that indicate longer onset of the final stage.

In the traditional *mappō* theory there are varying numbers given for each stage, right Dharma, semblance Dharma, and final Dharma. According to some theories the final stage begins 2000 years after the death of the Buddha. In others it is 1500 years after his death. Yet other theories divide history into 5 periods of 500 years each with the last being an age of corruption and conflict. We have already entered into the final period which lasts 10,000 years. Shinran based his computations on the 1500 years theory to give the longest time for decline in *mappō*. Traditionally *mappō* is thought to begin in either 552 C.E. or 1052 C.E. in Japan.

According to Mahāyāna tradition, the Buddha, foreseeing the decline of the Dharma after his death, hid the teachings in the palace of the Dragon (*naga*) King in the ocean. He prophesied that the teacher-philosopher Nāgārjuna would recover particularly the Wisdom literature at a later time, when people were ready to understand it. However, all the major schools of Mahāyāna claim Nāgārjuna as the founder of their tradition and for some he is a second Buddha because of the important philosophy of the Middle Way that he developed from the Wisdom texts. In some iconography he is portrayed with a halo composed of a many-headed serpent. His name means "Noble Serpent." Shinran extolled Nāgārjuna for dispelling wrong views of being and non-being, a major point in his philosophy. However, the 84,000 teachings of the Path of the Sages, or self-power practices, were all stored there. Among them Nāgārjuna distinguished the difficult from the easy practice, particularly the recitation of Amida's Name, preparing the path for the development of the Pure Land teaching.

28. Last Age-4

As a mark of increase in the five defilements,
All monks and laypeople of this age
Behave outwardly like followers of the Buddhist teaching,
But in their inner thoughts, believe in non-buddhist paths.

How lamentable it is that monks and laypeople
Select "fortunate times" and "auspicious days,"
And paying homage to gods of the heavens and earth,
Engage in divination and rituals of worship.

Although "monk" and "teacher of dharma"
Were taught to be titles of respect,
Like "dharma" used by Devadatta for his fivefold wrong
    teaching,
They are now applied to the lowly.

Monks are no different, in their hearts, from non-buddhists,
Brahmans, or followers of Nirgrantha;
Always wearing the dharma-robes of the Tathāgata,
They pay homage to all gods and spirits.

How lamentable it is that at present
All the monks and laypeople of Japan,
While following the Buddhist rules of conduct,
Venerate gods and spirits of the heavens and earth.

A mark of the evil of the five defilements
Is that the titles "monk" and "teacher of dharma"
Are used for serfs and servants
And have become derogatory terms.

Although monks are so in name only and keep no precepts,
Now in this defiled world of the last dharma-age
They are the equals of Śāriputra and Maudgalyāyana,
And we are urged to pay homage to and revere them.

Karmic evil is from the beginning without real form;
It is the result of delusional thought and invertedness.
Mind-nature is from the beginning pure,
But as for this world, there is no person of truth.

The sorrow of this evil world of the last dharma-age
Is that Buddhists of the southern capital and the northern
    peak
Call servants "palanquin-carrier monks" and "serving
    dharma-teachers"
To show deference to the high-ranking priests.

A mark of contempt for the Buddhist teaching
Is that "bhiksu" and "bhiksuni" are terms for serfs;
The titles "teacher of dharma" and "monk"
Are now used for servants
[*Gutoku's Hymns of Lament and Reflection*, I, pp. 422-424, #100-
109].

29. Last Age-5

Concerning this, we find that even if the multitudes of this defiled world, the sentient beings of corruption and evil, have abandoned the ninety-five wrong paths and entered the various dharma-gates—imperfect or consummate, accommodated or real—those who are authentic [in their practice] are extremely difficult to find, and those who are genuine are exceedingly rare. The false are extremely numerous; the hollow are many. For this reason, Śākyamuni Buddha guides the ocean of beings by disclosing the store of merit [for birth in the Pure Land], and Amida Tathāgata, having established the Vows, saves the ocean-like multitude of beings everywhere [*KGSS*, V. I, p. 207, #2].

30. Last Age-6

The time has come when the five defilements increase;
Those who doubt and revile Amida's Vow are numerous.
Both monks and laypeople despite the Nembutsu
And harm any they see engaging in it.

Those who revile and attack the Primal Vow
Are termed "persons completely blind to dharma" or "persons lacking the seed of Buddhahood."
Passing kalpas numerous as the particles of the great earth,
They long sink in the three evil courses
[*Hymns of the Pure Land Masters*, I, p. 382, #83-84].

31. Last Age-7

For this reason, in the Tathāgata's teaching this world is called the defiled world of the corrupt dharma. All beings lack a true and sincere heart, mock teachers and elders, disrespect their parents, distrust their companions, and favor only evil; hence, it is taught that everyone, both in the secular and religious worlds, is possessed of "heart and tongue at odds," and "words and thoughts both insincere." The former means that what is in the heart and what is said are at variance, and the latter means that what is spoken and what is thought are not real. Real means "sincere." People of this world have only thoughts that are not real, and those who wish to be born in the Pure Land

58

have only thoughts of deceiving and flattering. Even those who renounce this world have nothing but thoughts of fame and profit. Hence, know that we are not good persons, nor persons of wisdom; that we have no diligence, but only indolence, and within, the heart is ever empty, deceptive, vainglorious, and flattering. We do not have a heart that is true and real [*Notes on "Essentials of Faith Alone,"* I, p. 466].

32. Last Age-8

In distinguishing the sutras that will remain in the world from those that will disappear, we must consider that all the teachings of Śākyamuni's lifetime will last through the five hundred years of the right dharma-age and the thousand years of the semblance dharma-age; during the ten thousand years of the last dharma-age, sentient beings will diminish in number, and the sutras will all disappear. The Tathagata, out of pity for the sentient beings in the various forms of pain and torment, will have this sutra in particular survive, remaining for a hundred years [Tao-ch'o. *KGSS*, VI. I, p. 243, #76].

Note: This passage is from the text, *Passages on the Land of Happiness* by Tao-ch'o, an important Chinese Pure Land teacher in Shinran's lineage. He stressed the Last Age in advocating the centrality of Pure Land teaching for this age. The sūtra which endures for a hundred years is the *Larger Pure Land Sūtra*. The passage has significance for highlighting the importance of the *Larger Sūtra* for the age of *mappō* and implying that the Pure Land teaching is the sole basis of salvation in this age. See Inagaki, *Three Pure Land Sutras*, p. 312 for the sūtra text.

33. Last Age-9

With the advent of the semblance and last dharma-ages, and
    this world of the five defilements,
The teachings left by Śākyamuni entered into concealment.
Only the compassionate vow of Amida becomes widely
    known,
And attainment of birth through the Nembutsu spreads
[*Hymns of the Dharma-Ages*, I, p. 403, #18].

B. Shinran's Experience of True Entrusting (Shinjin)

Note: In this section we focus on Shinran's distinctive teaching of True Entrusting. We have avoided the use of the terms "belief" or "faith" in this context in order to highlight his significant contribution to understanding religious faith as a human experience and concern. *Shinjin* may be translated as the "believing mind," or the "trusting mind." However, those general English expressions do not convey sufficiently the nature of the faith-experience in Shinran or its implications. Some teachers advocate keeping the term in the Japanese, but the Japanese term itself does not necessarily express Shinran's peculiar perspective. We have adopted True Entrusting, following Dr. Taitetsu Unno, to set Shinran's understanding from the general view of belief and faith. There is probably no term that fully clarifies Shinran's meaning, but we hope that True Entrusting will facilitate understanding. [See Taitetsu Unno, trans., *Tannishō: A Shin Buddhist Classic* (Honolulu: Buddhist Study Center Press, 1996), pp. 49-55.]

1. Shinran's Unfaltering Trust

34. Trust-1

Mindful solely of the depth and vastness of the Buddha's benevolence, I am unconcerned about being personally abused. Let companions who aspire for the Pure Land and all who abhor this defiled world accept or discard what they will of this work, but let them not ridicule the teaching [*KGSS*, III. I, p. 77, Preface].

35. Trust-2

Such is the benevolence of Amida's great compassion,
That we must strive to return it, even to the breaking of our
    bodies;
Such is the benevolence of the masters and true teachers,
That we must endeavor to repay it, even to our bones
    becoming dust
[*Hymns of the Dharma-Ages*, I, p. 412, #59].

Note: This passage is the *Ondokusan* (*Hymn of Repaying Virtue*), used in services and expressing dedication and commitment to the teaching.

The following passages are quoted below by Shinran from Hōin Seikaku (1167-1235), whom he admired greatly. It is perhaps the basis for Shinran's *wasan* (hymn, poem).

36. Trust-3

In reflecting fully, I realize that the benevolence of his teaching and guidance is truly one with the compassionate Vow of

Amida. Even to your bones becoming dust, then, should you repay it; even to the breaking of your body should it be returned [Seikaku, *Notes on the Inscriptions on Sacred Scrolls,* I, p. 514].

37. Trust-4

Realizing the vastness of the benevolence of the great master's teaching, you should endeavor to repay it, even to your bones becoming dust; strive to return it, even to the breaking of your body. Carefully study this teaching of Master Seikaku [*Notes on the Inscriptions on Sacred Scrolls,* I, pp. 516-517].

38. Trust-5

Each of you should attain your birth without being misled by people and without faltering in shinjin. However, the practicer in whom shinjin has not become settled will continue to drift, even without being misled by anyone, for he does not abide among the truly settled [*Lamp for the Latter Ages,* I, p. 531].

39. Trust-6

Each of you has come to see me, crossing the borders of more than ten provinces at the risk of your life, solely with the intent of asking about the path to birth in the land of bliss. But if you imagine in me some special knowledge of a path to birth other than the nembutsu or of scriptural writings that teach it, you are greatly mistaken. If that is the case, since there are many eminent scholars in the southern capital of Nara or on Mount Hiei to the north, you would do better to meet with them and inquire fully about the essentials for birth.

As for me, I simply accept and entrust myself to what my revered teacher told me, "Just say the nembutsu and be saved by Amida"; nothing else is involved.

I have no idea whether the nembutsu is truly the seed for my being born in the Pure Land or whether it is the karmic act for which I must fall into hell. Should I have been deceived by Master Hōnen and, saying the nembutsu, were to fall into hell, even then I would have no regrets.

The reason is, if I could attain Buddhahood by endeavoring in other practices, but said the nembutsu and so fell into hell, then I would feel regret at having been deceived. But I am incapable of any other practice, so hell is decidedly my abode whatever I do.

If Amida's Primal Vow is true, Shakyamuni's teaching cannot be false. If the Buddha's teaching is true, Shan-tao's commentaries cannot be false. If Shan-tao's commentaries are true can Hōnen's words be lies? If Hōnen's words are true, then surely what I say cannot be empty.

Such, in the end, is how this foolish person entrusts himself [to the Vow]. Beyond this, whether you take up the nembutsu or whether you abandon it is for each of you to determine [*A Record in Lament of Divergences*, I, p. 662, #2].

Note: The background of this passage suggests issues raised by Zenran, Shinran's eldest son, who claimed that his father had given him special teaching one night and sent him to Kanto in the east with the authority as his father's representative to resolve problems among the disciples. Shinran, however, denied giving any special teaching to Zenran secretly, or any such authority. (On Zenran's disowning see passage 9. Disowning; also *A Collection of Letters*, 7, I, pp. 568-569; *Letters of the Tradition*, 2, I, p. 575; *Uncollected Letters*, 6, pp. 582-584 give further information on the issue.) However, a visit by a delegation of followers, who came to inquire of Shinran about his teaching, gave rise to this eloquent chapter.

40. Trust-7

It appears that disputes have arisen among followers of the sole practice of nembutsu, who argue that "these are my disciples" or "those are someone else's disciples." This is utterly senseless.

For myself, I do not have even a single disciple. For if I brought people to say the nembutsu through my own efforts, then they might be my disciples. But it is indeed preposterous to call persons "my disciples" when they say the nembutsu having received the working of Amida.

We come together when conditions bring us to meet and part when conditions separate us. In spite of this, some assert that those who say the nembutsu having turned from one teacher to follow another cannot attain birth. This is absurd. Are they saying that they will take back the shinjin given by Amida as if it belonged to them? Such a claim should never be made.

If one comes to be in accord with the spontaneous working of the Vow (*jinen*), one will awaken to the benevolence of the

Buddha and of one's teachers. Thus were his words [*A Record in Lament of Divergences*, I, p. 664, #6].

41. Trust-8

Concerning the nature of shinjin, I have learned from the Master of Kuang-ming temple that after true shinjin has become settled in us, even if Buddhas like Amida or Śākyamuni should fill the skies and proclaim that Śākyamuni's teaching and Amida's Primal Vow are false, we will not have even one moment of doubt [*Letters of the Tradition*, 2, I, p. 575].

42. Trust-9

Even when the world is filled with a great fire,
Pass through it and seek to hear the dharma;
Then you will unfailingly become a world-honored one
And free all beings from birth, aging, and death
[*KGSS*, II. 10, I, p. 17. From the *Sutra of the Immeasurable Pure Enlightenment of Equality*].

2. Shinran's Joy in True Entrusting

43. Joy-1

How joyous I am, Gutoku Shinran, disciple of Śākyamuni! Rare is it to come upon the sacred scriptures from the westward land of India and the commentaries of the masters of China and Japan, but now I have been able to encounter them. Rare is it to hear them, but already I have been able to hear. Reverently entrusting myself to the teaching, practice, and realization that are the true essence of the Pure Land way, I am especially aware of the profundity of the Tathāgata's benevolence. Here I rejoice in what I have heard and extol what I have attained [*KGSS*, Preface, I, p. 4; also p. 291; See also *Passages on the Pure Land Way*, I, p. 303].

44. Joy-2

To rejoice (*kyōki*) means to be joyous after being assured of attaining what one shall attain; it is rejoicing after realizing shinjin [*Notes on "Essentials of Faith Alone,"* I, p. 463; See also *A Collection of Letters*, Letter 3, I, p. 562].

45. Joy-3

Joy (*kangi*) means to be gladdened in body (*kan*) and gladdened in heart (*gi*). It means to rejoice beforehand at being assured of attaining what one shall attain [*Notes on Once-Calling and Many-Calling*, p. 474; See also I, p. 480-481].

Note: Shinran uses two terms for Joy. The term *kyōki*, used in this passage, refers to what one has received in trust in Amida's Vow. It is present religious experience. *Kangi* is directed to the future in the prospect of birth in the Pure Land.

46. Joy-4

Thus, when one attains the true and real practice and shinjin, one greatly rejoices in one's heart. This attainment is therefore called the stage of joy. It is likened to the first fruit: Sages of the first fruit, though they may give themselves to sleep and to sloth, will still never be subject to samsaric existence for a twenty-ninth time. Even more decisively will the ocean of beings of the ten quarters be grasped and never abandoned when they have taken refuge in this practice and shinjin. Therefore the Buddha is called "Amida Buddha." This is Other Power [*KGSS*, II. I, pp. 54, #71].

47. Joy-5

Know that when the true and real shinjin that is one thought-moment of joy unfolds, you will be born without fail in the land fulfilled by the Primal Vow. Joy is joy upon realizing shinjin. . . [*Notes on the Inscriptions on Sacred Scrolls*, I, p. 518].

48. Joy-6

The light of compassion illumines us from afar;
Those beings it reaches, it is taught,
Attain the joy of dharma,
So take refuge in Amida, the great consolation
[*Hymns of the Pure Land*, I, p. 327, #10].

3. Shinran on His Limitations

Note: Shinran is unusual in never claiming to be a spiritually realized saint, with supernormal experience, though he had dreams or visions on various occasions. He acknowledged his limitations and ignorance in many areas. He did not claim to be a proficient scholar, though he had studied diligently, as his writings show. He was a *bombu*, a foolish being, like others, except that he relied on Amida's Vow as his ultimate refuge. Shinran, in his humanity, experiencing strong passion, comes through in his humanness and for that reason has been one of the most attractive religious figure in Japan, even among those with no professed interest or involvement with religion.

49. Limits-1

Thus I record these categories. Please ask about them of any knowledgeable person; it is not possible to present them in detail in this letter. My eyes fail me, and besides being utterly forgetful about everything, whatever it may be, I am hardly the person to clarify these matters for others. Please inquire fully of the Pure Land scholars about them [*Lamp for the Latter Ages*, Letter 8, I, p. 535].

50. Limits-2

Among Master Shinran's words were: I know nothing at all of good or evil. For if I could know thoroughly, as Amida Tathāgata knows, that an act was good, then I would know good. If I could know thoroughly, as the Tathāgata knows, that an act was evil, then I would know evil. But with a foolish being full of blind passions, in this fleeting world—this burning house—all matters without exception are empty and false, totally without truth and sincerity. The nembutsu alone is true and real [*A Record in Lament of Divergences*, I, p. 679, Postscript].

51. Limits-3

It is truly hard to continue cultivating merits through myriads of kalpas;
  In each moment, blind passions intrude a hundred or a thousand times; Though some may hope to realize dharma-insight in this Sahā world,

They will pass kalpas countless as the Ganges' sands in the
six courses,
And still the time of realization will not come
[Genshin, *KGSS*, VI. I, p. 219, #26].

4. Shinran on His Death

52. Death-1

On the issue of funerals (*Gaijashō* 16 *Treatise on Correcting
Errors*) Kakunyo, the third abbot, discusses that the sangha is
not to make them the primary activity. In making this point,
he quotes Shinran who said: "When I die, put my body in the
Kamo river as food for the fish" [*Jōdo Shinshū Seiten. Chushakuban*
(Kyoto: Hongwanji Publishing Dept., 1988) pp. 936-937].

53. Death-2

My life has now reached the fullness of its years. It is certain
that I will go to birth in the Pure Land before you, so without
fail I will await you there [*Lamp for the Latter Ages*, Letter 12, I,
p. 539].

54. Death-3

Now then, concerning Kakushin-bo, I was deeply saddened
by his death, but also felt great esteem for him, for he never
deviated from shinjin. I asked him many times how his realization of shinjin was. Each time he answered that he had not
digressed from shinjin and that his realization became stronger
and stronger. On his way to Kyoto after he left his own province, he became ill at a place called Hitoichi, and although his
companions advised him to return, he replied, "If it is a fatal illness, I will die whether I return or not. If I am to be sick, I will
be sick whether I return or whether I stay. If it is all the same,
I wish to die at the side of the Shōnin." His shinjin was truly
splendid—so splendid and enviable that it reminds me of Shan-
tao's parable of the two rivers. At the point of death he uttered
*Namu-amida-butsu, Namu-mugekō-nyorai, Namu-fukashigikō-
nyorai* (Tathāgata of light that surpasses understanding), and
putting his hands together, quietly met his end.

Whether one is left behind or goes before, it is surely a sorrowful thing to be parted by death. But the one who first attains nirvana vows without fail to save those who were close to him first and leads those with whom he has been karmically bound, his relatives, and his friends. It should be so, and since I have entered the same path of the teaching as Kakushin, I feel strongly reassured. Since it is said that being parent and child is a bond from a previous life, you too must feel reassured. It is impossible to express how moving and impressive it all was, so I will stop here. How can I speak of it further? I hope to say much more later.

I read this letter to the Shōnin in order to see if there were any errors; he told me that there was nothing to be added, and that it was fine. He was especially moved and wept when I came to the part about Kakushin, for he is deeply grieved by his death [Written by Ren'i for Shinran] [*Lamp for the Latter Ages*, Letter 14, I, p. 545; See Section III, C, 4, d on the White Path, p. 122-125].

55. Death-4

I have carefully read your letter of the first day of the inter-calary tenth month. I am truly sad to hear about Kakunenbō. I had expected that I would go first [to the Pure Land], but I have been left behind; it is unutterably saddening. Kakushinbō, who left us last year, has certainly gone [to the Pure Land] and is awaiting us there. Needless to say, I will surely meet them there; it is beyond words. Kakunenbō's words did not differ at all from what I have said, so we will certainly go to the same place [the Pure Land]. If I am still alive in the tenth month of next year, it will undoubtedly be possible to meet again in this world. Since your mind of entrusting also does not differ at all from my own, even if I go first, I will await you in the Pure Land [*Uncollected Letters*, Letter 2, I, pp. 579-580].

C. *Shinran on the Meaning of True Entrusting*

1. Scriptural Foundation

a. Why Buddhas Appear in the World

56. Appear-1

In his boundless compassion, the Tathāgata is filled with com-
miseration for the beings of the three realms. I have appeared
in the world and expounded the teachings of the way to
enlightenment, seeking to save the multitudes of living beings
by blessing them with the benefit that is true and real [*KGSS*, I,
p. 8, #3. From the *Larger Sūtra*].

57. Appear-2

The fundamental intent for which the Buddha appeared in the
    world
Was to reveal the truth and reality of the Primal Vow.
He taught that to encounter or behold a Buddha
Is as rare as the blossoming of the udumbara
[*Hymns of the Pure Land*, I, p. 340, #54].

58. Appear-3

The true and real benefit is Amida's Vow. Thus, the reason that
the Buddhas appear in the world age after age is that they desire
to bless and save all sentient beings by teaching the power of
Amida's Vow. Since they take this as their fundamental intent,
the Vow is called *the true and real benefit*. Further, it is termed
"the direct teaching for which all Buddhas appear in the world"
[*Notes on Once-Calling and Many-Calling*, I, p. 485].

Note: The concept of the reason for the Buddha's appearing in the world is a major
Mahāyāna teaching. It contrasts with the "Hīnayāna" view that Gautama initially
sought his own deliverance and only later, at the request of the gods, offered it to all
people. Here it was the Buddha's primary intention to deliver all beings. The story of
the Bodhisattva Dharmākara in the *Larger Pure Land Sūtra* illustrates the outgoing,
altruistic nature of Mahāyāna Buddhism. In the Tendai and Nichiren interpretations
of the *Lotus Sūtra* this concept was a major principle distinguishing traditions. Therefore, Shinran highlights this principle in order to establish the Pure Land teaching on
the highest level of Mahāyāna teaching.

b. The Major Vows: The Basis of Shinran's Teaching

Note: For the convenience of the reader we are including the major Vows from the
Larger Pure Land Sūtra that structure and provide the scriptural basis for Shinran's
thought. The *Bodhisattva Dharmākara* made Forty-Eight Vows in establishing the

spiritual realm of the Pure Land and the way for birth into it. From among these Forty-Eight, the Eighteenth became central in Shinran's thought, together with its completion text, in formulating his teaching of absolute Other-Power. While all Vows are in some sense Primal or fundamental Vows in this process, the Eighteenth is *the* Primal Vow. Those Vows that are the basis for self-power practice (Nineteenth and Twentieth) are termed Provisional Vows. See Inagaki, *The Three Pure Land Sutras,* pp. 242-244.

59. Vows-1

(11) If, when I attain Buddhahood, humans and devas in my land should not dwell in the Definitely Assured State and unfailingly reach Nirvana, may I not attain perfect Enlightenment.

(12) If, when I attain Buddhahood, my light should be limited, unable to illuminate at least a hundred thousand kotis of nayutas of Buddha-lands, may I not attain perfect Enlightenment.

(13) If, when I attain Buddhahood, my life-span should be limited, even to the extent of a hundred thousand kotis of nayutas of kalpas, may I not attain perfect Enlightenment.

(17) If, when I attain Buddhahood, innumerable Buddhas in the land of the ten quarters should not all praise and glorify my Name, may I not attain perfect Enlightenment.

(18) If, when I attain Buddhahood, sentient beings in the lands of the ten quarters who sincerely and joyfully entrust themselves to me, desire to be born in my land, and call my Name, even ten times, should not be born there, may I not attain perfect Enlightenment. Excluded, however, are those who commit the five gravest offences and abuse the right Dharma.

(19) If, when I attain Buddhahood, sentient beings in the lands of the ten quarters, who awaken aspiration for Enlightenment, do various meritorious deeds and sincerely desire to be born in my land, should not, at their death, see me appear before them surrounded by a multitude of sages, may I not attain perfect Enlightenment.

(20) If, when I attain Buddhahood, sentient beings in the lands of the ten quarters who, having heard my Name, concentrate

their thoughts on my land, plant roots of virtue, and sincerely transfer their merits towards my land with a desire to be born there, should not eventually fulfill their aspiration, may I not attain perfect Enlightenment.

(22) If, when I attain Buddhahood, bodhisattvas in the Buddha-lands of other quarters who visit my land should not ultimately and unfailingly reach the Stage of Becoming a Buddha after One More Life, may I not attain perfect Enlightenment. Excepted are those who wish to teach and guide sentient beings in accordance with their original vows. For they wear the armor of great vows, accumulate merits, deliver all beings from birth-and-death, visit Buddha-lands to perform the bodhisattva practices, make offerings to Buddhas, Tathāgatas, throughout the ten quarters, enlighten uncountable sentient beings as numerous as the sands of the River Ganges, and establish them in the highest, perfect Enlightenment. Such bodhisattvas transcend the course of practice of the ordinary bodhisattvas, manifest the practices of all the bodhisattva stages, and cultivate the virtues of Samantabhadra.

(35) If, when I attain Buddhahood, women in the immeasurable and inconceivable Buddha-lands of the ten quarters who, having heard my Name, rejoice in faith, awaken aspiration for Enlightenment and wish to renounce womanhood, should after death be reborn again as women, may I not attain perfect Enlightenment.

Note: The clause at the end of the Eighteenth Vow which excludes people who are guilty of certain evils appears to contradict the principle of Amida Buddha's unconditional compassion. As a consequence, Pure Land teachers, such as Shan-tao, explained it away in the passage offered below as a warning for believers not to commit such evils. Shinran follows Shan-tao's view. It is even more important for Shinran in view of his statement in *The Record in Lament of Divergences* (*Tannishō*), that "even a good person attains birth in the Pure Land, so it goes without saying that an evil person will" (*A Record of Lament of Divergences*, I, ch. 3, p. 663).

60. Exclusion-1

Excluded are those who commit the five grave offenses and those who slander the right dharma. Excluded means that those who commit the five grave offenses are rejected and reveals how grave the evil of slandering the dharma is. By showing the gravity of these two kinds of wrongdoing, these words make us realize that all the sentient beings throughout the ten quarters, without a single exception, will be born in the Pure Land [*Notes on the Inscriptions on Sacred Scrolls*, I, p. 494].

61. Exclusion-2

The Master of Kuang-ming temple states:

Question: According to the Forty-eight Vows, only those who commit the five grave offenses and those who slander the right dharma are excluded and cannot attain birth. Here, according to the passage on the lowest grade of the lowest rank in the *Contemplation Sutra*, those who slander the dharma are set apart and those who commit the five grave offenses are grasped. What does this mean?

Answer: The intent may be understood as a teaching to make us desist from evil. As stated in the Forty-eight Vows, those who slander the dharma and those who commit the five grave offenses are excluded; this means that these two kinds of action are the gravest of hindrances. When sentient beings commit them, they plunge directly into Avici hell, where they undergo long kalpas of terror and panic without any means of emerging. The Tathāgata, fearing that we would commit these two kinds of faults, seeks to stop us through compassionate means by declaring that we will then not be able to attain birth. This does not mean that we will not be grasped.

It is taught, concerning the lowest grade of the lowest rank, that those who commit the five grave offenses are taken up but those who slander the dharma are excluded; this is because beings [of the lowest grade] have already committed the five grave offenses, but must not be abandoned to endless transmigration. Thus Amida, awakening great compassion, grasps them and brings them to birth. Since, however, they have yet to commit the karmic evil of slandering the dharma, in order to prevent them from doing so it is stated that if one slanders the dharma one will not attain birth. This is to be understood as relevant to those who have not committed this evil. Even if one has committed it, one will nevertheless be grasped and brought to attainment of birth. Although one attains birth in the Pure Land, however, one must pass many kalpas enclosed in a lotus bud. Such people of karmic evil, while they are within the lotus, are possessed of the three kinds of obstructions: first, they cannot see the Buddha and the noble assemblies; second, they cannot hear the right dharma; third, they cannot travel to the lands of the Buddhas to make offerings. But apart from these obstructions, they do not undergo any form of pain. In the sutras, it is taught that their state is like that of a bhiksu who has entered the bliss of the Third Dhyana Heaven. Reflect on this. Although they are confined within the flower that is closed for many kalpas, is this not better than to suffer all the torments for endless kalpas in Avici hell? Thus, this passage should be understood as a teaching to make us desist from evil [*KGSS*, III. I, p. 148, #121].

Completion Text of the Eighteenth Vow

62. Vow-Completion text-Chinese-1

All sentient beings who having heard his Name, rejoice in faith, remember him even once, and sincerely transfer the merit of virtuous practices to that land, aspiring to be born there, will attain birth and dwell in the Stage of Non-retrogression. But excluded are those who have committed the five gravest offenses and abused the right Dharma [Inagaki, *The Three Pure Land Sutras*, p. 268].

63. Vow-Completion text-Shinran's reading-2

All sentient beings, as they hear the Name, realize even one thought-moment of shinjin and joy, which is directed to them from Amida's sincere mind, and aspiring to be born in that land, they then attain birth and dwell in the stage of non-retrogression. Excluded are those who commit the five grave offenses and those who slander the right dharma [*KGSS*, III. I, p. 80, #4].

Note: Above we have given two translations of the Fulfillment text of the Eighteenth Vow. In the first passage, we have the translation according to the original Chinese version. The second gives the translation following the way Shinran read this passage. Comparison of the two passages is useful to see clearly Shinran's fundamental insight that true entrusting (*shinjin*) is given by Amida Buddha, as the Buddha's true mind is manifested in the mind of the person as trust in the Vow and aspiration for birth into the Pure Land. Shinran made this point in this passage, which he read in such a way so that the portion that originally indicates the devotee's transfer of merit toward birth becomes in Shinran's interpretation an act of Amida Buddha. He was able to do this because of the flexibility of Chinese and Japanese grammar and the use in Japanese of honorific verb forms which were applied alongside the Japanese and showing the direction of the action. Japanese *kambun* is a way of translating Chinese texts into Japanese through a system of markings alongside the Chinese that enables the reader to understand them in Japanese.

c. The Primal Vow

64. Primal-1

Universal means wide, to spread. Bhiksu Dharmākara established the supreme, unexcelled Vow and spread it widely. "Supreme" means that it goes beyond the vows of other Buddhas. It connotes transcendent, unequalled. . . [*Notes on "Essentials of Faith Alone,"* I, p. 456].

65. Primal-2

The late Master said, "According to the true essence of the Pure Land way, one entrusts oneself to the Primal Vow in this life and realizes enlightenment in the Pure Land; this is the teaching I received" [*A Record in Lament of Divergences*, I, p. 675, #15].

66. Primal-3

I reflect within myself: The universal Vow difficult to fathom is indeed a great vessel bearing us across the ocean difficult to cross. The unhindered light is the sun of wisdom dispersing the darkness of our ignorance [*KGSS*, Preface, I, p. 3].

67. Primal-4

Hence, whether with regard to the aspect for going forth to the Pure Land or to the aspect for return to this world, there is nothing whatever that has not been fulfilled through the Tathāgata's directing of virtue to beings out of the pure Vow-mind. Reflect on this [*Passages on the Pure Land Way*, I, p. 302].

68. Primal-5

Truly we know, then, that the crucial matter for which the Great Sage, the World-honored one, appeared in this world was to reveal the true benefit of the compassionate Vow and to declare it to be the direct teaching of the Tathāgatas. The essential purport of this great compassion is to teach the immediate attainment of birth by foolish beings. Thus, looking into the essence of the teachings of the Buddhas, we find that the true and fundamental intent for which all the Tathāgatas, past, present, and future, appear in this world, is solely to teach the inconceivable Vow of Amida.

When, through Amida's directing of virtue to them by the power of the Vow, the foolish beings ever floundering in birth-and-death hear the true and real virtues and realize supreme shinjin, they immediately attain great joy and reach the stage of non-retrogression, so that without being made to sunder their blind passions, they are brought quickly to the realization of great Nirvana [*Passages on the Pure Land Way*, I, p. 317].

69. Primal-6

It is a great torch in the long night of ignorance;
Do not sorrow that your eyes of wisdom are dark.
It is a ship on the vast ocean of birth-and-death;
Do not grieve that your obstructions of karmic evil are heavy
[*Hymns of the Dharma-Ages*, I, p. 407, #36].

70. Primal-7

The power of the Vow is without limit;
Thus, even our karmic evil, deep and heavy, is not oppressive.
The Buddha's wisdom is without bounds;
Thus, even those of distracted minds and self-indulgence are not abandoned
[*Hymns of the Dharma-Ages*, I, p. 408, #37].

71. Primal-8

This is being protected in the present life means that Amida protects us in this world. This karmic power of the Buddha, fulfilled through the Primal Vow, is the strong cause of the attainment of birth by the person of shinjin; hence it is called *the decisive cause.* The person who rejoices in realizing shinjin is taught in a sutra to be the equal of the Buddhas [*Notes on Once-Calling and Many-Calling*, I, p. 480].

72. Primal-9

Amida's Vow is a great torch in the long night of ignorance. We should reflect that, although our wisdom-eyes are dark, we need not despair. . . . The power of Amida's Vow is a great ship upon the vast ocean of birth-and-death. Seikaku states that we should not grieve that our existence is one of greatest evil, deep and heavy [*Notes on the Inscriptions on Sacred Scrolls*, I, p. 516].

73. Primal-10

Once you simply realize that the Vow surpasses conceptual understanding and with singleness of heart realize that the Name surpasses conceptual understanding and pronounce it, why should you labor in your own calculation? . . .

. . . Once you have simply come to realize that Vow and Name surpass conceptual understanding, you should not calculate in this way or that. There must be nothing of your calculation in the act that leads to birth [*Lamp of the Latter Ages*, Letter 9, I, p. 536].

74. Primal-11

Once you have come simply to believe that it surpasses conceptual understanding, there should be no struggle to reason it out. . . .

. . . If you realize that the wisdom of the Buddhas surpasses conceptual understanding, there should not, in addition, be any calculating. You simply should not fall into doubts over the different things that people say. Simply give yourself up to Tathāgata's Vow; avoid calculating in any way [*Lamp for the Latter Ages*, Letter 10, I, p. 537].

75. Primal-12

Contemplating the power of Tathāgata's Primal Vow,
One sees that no foolish being who encounters it passes by
    in vain.
When a person single-heartedly practices the saying of the
    Name alone,
It brings quickly to fullness and perfection [in that person] the
    great treasure ocean of true and real virtues
[*The Hymns of the Two Gateways of Entrance and Emergence*, I, p.
624; See also *Hymns of the Pure Land Masters*, I, p. 364, #13].

76. Primal-13

Concerning "blossoms from the muddy ponds," the
    [*Vimalakīrti*] *Sutra* states:
"The lotus does not grow in the solid ground of lofty plateaus,
But in the muddy ponds of lowland marshes."
This is an analogy meaning that foolish beings, while in the
    mud of blind passions,

Put forth the blossoms of the Buddha's perfect enlightenment;
This indicates the inconceivable power
Of the Tathāgata's universal Primal Vow.
Thus, the two gates of entrance and emergence are taught as
    Other Power
[*The Hymns of the Two Gateways of Entrance and Emergence*, I, p.
627].

77. Primal-14

"Saved by the inconceivable working of Amida's Vow, I shall
realize birth in the Pure Land": the moment you entrust yourself thus to the Vow, so that the mind set upon saying the
nembutsu arises within you, you are immediately brought to
share in the benefit of being grasped by Amida, never to be
abandoned.

Know that the Primal Vow of Amida makes no distinction
between people young and old, good and evil; only shinjin is
essential. For it is the Vow to save the person whose karmic evil
is deep and grave and whose blind passions abound.

Thus, for those who entrust themselves to the Primal Vow, no good acts are required, because no good surpasses the nembutsu. Nor need they despair of the evil they commit, for no evil can obstruct the working of Amida's Primal Vow [*A Record in Lament of Divergences*, I, p. 661, #1].

78. Primal-15

When I have fulfilled the Buddha-way,
My Name shall pervade the ten quarters;
If there be any place it is not heard,
I vow not to attain the supreme enlightenment.
For the sake of all beings I will open forth the treasure-store

And give away universally its treasure of virtues.
Among the multitudes of beings
I will always preach the dharma with a lion's roar
[*KGSS*, II. I, pp. 13-14, #3. From the *Larger Sūtra, Juseige* [*Hymn of Weighty Vows*].

79. Primal-16

The ocean of birth-and-death, of painful existence, has no
     bound;
Only by the ship of Amida's universal Vow
Can we, who have long been drowning,
Unfailingly be brought across it
[*Hymns of the Pure Land Masters*, I, p. 363, #7].

d. *The Larger Sūtra of the Buddha of Immeasurable Life*: the Supreme Truth

i. The Significance of the *Larger Sūtra* for Shinran

80. Sūtra-1

To reveal the true teaching: It is the *Larger Sutra of the Buddha of Immeasurable Life*. The central purport of this sutra is that Amida, by establishing the incomparable Vows, has opened wide the dharma-storehouse, and full of compassion for small, foolish beings, selects and bestows the treasure of virtues. [The sutra further reveals that] Śākyamuni appeared in this world and expounded the teachings of the way to enlightenment, seeking to save the multitudes of living beings by blessing them with this benefit that is true and real. Thus, to teach the Tathāgata's Primal Vow is the true intent of this sutra; the Name of the Buddha is its essence [*A Collection of Passages Revealing the True Teaching of the Pure Land Way*, I, p. 7, #2; See also *Passages on the Pure Land Way*, I, pp. 295-296].

ii. The True Intent of the *Larger Sūtra*

81. Sūtra-2

Birth in accord with the *Larger Sutra* is [brought about by] the Tathāgata's selected Primal Vow, the inconceivable oceanlike vow. This is Other Power. In other words, by the cause of the Vow of birth through the nembutsu, we gain the fruit of the Vow of necessary attainment of nirvana. In this life we dwell in the stage of the truly settled and we necessarily attain the true and real fulfilled land. Thus, because of the true cause—Amida Tathāgata's directing of virtue for our going forth—we realize the enlightenment of supreme Nirvana. This is the true intent of the *Larger Sutra*. Hence, it is termed "birth in accord with the *Larger Sutra*," and also "birth that is inconceivable" [*A Collection of Passages on the Types of Birth in the Three Pure Land Sutras*, I, p. 639].

iii. The Ultimate Teaching of the "One Vehicle"

82. Vehicle-1

Thus, these passages give clear testimony that the Larger Sutra reveals the true teaching. It is indeed the right exposition for which the Tathāgata appeared in the world, the wondrous scripture rare and most excellent, the conclusive and ultimate exposition of the One Vehicle, the precious words disclosing perfect, instantaneous fulfillment, the sincere words praised by all the Buddhas throughout the ten quarters, the true teaching in consummate readiness for the beings of this day. Let this be known [*KGSS*, I. I, p. 10, #7].

83. Vehicle-2

"One Vehicle" here refers to the Primal Vow. "Perfect" means that the Primal Vow is full of all merits and roots of good, lacking none, and further, that it is free and unrestricted. "Unhindered" means that it cannot be obstructed or destroyed by blind passion and karmic evil. "True and real virtue" is the Name. Since the wondrous principle of true reality or suchness has reached its perfection in the Primal Vow, this Vow is likened to a great treasure ocean. True reality-suchness is the supreme great nirvana. Nirvana is dharma-nature. Dharma-nature is Tathāgata. With the words, "treasure ocean," the Buddha's non-discriminating, unobstructed, and non-exclusive guidance of all sentient beings is likened to the all-embracing waters of the great ocean [*Notes on Once-Calling and Many-Calling*, I, p. 486].

84. Vehicle-3

Know that because the One Vehicle of the Primal Vow is the ultimate sudden teaching, the teaching of sudden and instantaneous attainment, the perfectly fulfilled teaching, and the consummate teaching, it is the absolute and incomparable teaching, the path of true reality or suchness. It is the single within the single, the sudden within the sudden, the true within the true, the consummate within the consummate. The One Vehicle that is true reality is the ocean of the great Vow. It is the supreme, rare practice [*Gutoku's Notes*, I, p. 592].

85. Vehicle-4

Know that the ocean of the One Vehicle of the Primal Vow is the ultimate sudden teaching, the teaching of sudden and instantaneous attainment, the perfectly fulfilled teaching, the consummate teaching [*Gutoku's Notes*, I, pp. 592-593].

86. Vehicle-5

Master Shan-tao explains:

Attaining Buddhahood through the nembutsu: this is the true essence of the Pure Land way.

It is called the ocean of the One Vehicle;
It is also called the bodhi[sattva]-pitaka
[*Hymn of the Two Gateways*, I, p. 629].

87. Vehicle-6

In the expression, "gateways . . . and more," "gateways" refers
to the eighty-four thousand provisional gateways. "More" refers
to the ocean of the One Vehicle, the Primal Vow [*KGSS*, VI. I,
p. 222, #34].

iv. Sūtras of Provisional Practice: *Sūtra of Contemplation, Smaller Amida Sūtra*

88. Provisional-1

Concerning birth in accord with the *Contemplation Sutra*,
through the Vow of performing meritorious acts, one is brought
to awaken sincere mind and aspiration and, directing one's own
good accumulated through the myriad good acts and practices,
to aspire for the Pure Land. Thus, in the *Sutra of Contemplation
on the Buddha of Immeasurable Life*, the various kinds of good
acts—meditative and non-meditative good, the three types of
meritorious conduct and the good acts done by the nine grades
of beings—and the saying of the nembutsu in self-power are
expounded, and the ways of birth of the nine grades of beings
are taught. The sutra takes self-power within the Other Power
teaching as its central purport. For this reason, the kinds of
birth in accord with the *Contemplation Sutra* are all birth into
the provisional transformed lands. This is called "birth attained
beneath twin Śāla trees" [*A Collection of Passages on the Types of
Birth in the Three Pure Land Sutras*, I, p. 645].

89. Provisional-2

Concerning birth in accord with the *Amida Sutra*, through the
Vow of cultivating the root of virtue, one enters the "true" gate
of ultimate attainment of birth in the Pure Land; choosing the
Name that is the root of good or of virtue, one leaves aside the
small good of the myriad good acts and practices. Nevertheless,
the practicers of meditative and non-meditative good by self-

power doubt the inconceivable wisdom of the Buddha and do not accept it. Taking the Name of the Tathāgata as their own root of good, they direct their own merit toward birth in the Pure Land and rely on the Vow that beings ultimately attain birth. While saying the inconceivable Name, they doubt the Vow of great compassion which is indescribable, inexplicable, and inconceivable. Their offense being grave and heavy, they are chained in a prison made of the seven precious materials, where they pass five hundred years. During that time, they are unable to act freely and do not see or devote themselves to the three treasures; this Śākyamuni has taught. But because they say the Tathāgata's Name, they are still able to remain in the womb-palace. Because it comes about through the virtuous Name, it is called "birth that is non-comprehensible." Know that, because of the offense of doubting the inconceivable Vow, it is not called "birth that is inconceivable" [*A Collection of Passages on the Types of Birth in the Three Pure Land Sutras*, I, p. 649].

e. Amida and Śākyamuni

90. Amida-Śākyamuni-1

As I reflect, I find that our attainment of shinjin arises from the heart and mind with which Amida Tathāgata selected the Vow, and that the clarification of true mind has been taught for us through the skilful works of compassion of the Great Sage, Śākyamuni. . . . Here I, Gutoku Shinran, disciple of Śākyamuni, reverently embrace the true teaching of the Buddhas and Tathāgatas and look to the essential meaning of the treatises and commentaries of the masters. Fully guided by the beneficent light of the three sutras. . . [*KGSS*, III. I, p. 77, #1].

91. Amida-Śākyamuni-2

Śākyamuni as Teacher

The true words are extraordinarily subtle and excellent.
They are skilful in expression and content;
They are a store of profound secrets.
For the sake of the multitudes,
He explains extensively with many words;

For the sake of the multitudes, he teaches in summary.
Possessing such words,
He perfectly heals sentient beings.
If there are sentient beings
Who are able to hear these words,
Whether they entrust themselves or not,
They know with certainty that these are the Buddha's
    teaching.
The Buddhas always possess gentle words,
But for the multitudes they teach in rough words.
Rough words or gentle,
All have their basis in the highest truth.
For this reason, I now
Take refuge in the World-honored one.
The words of the Tathāgata are of one taste;
They are like the waters of the broad ocean.
It is called the highest truth.
For this reason, there are no meaningless words;
What the Tathāgata now teaches—
The various innumerable teachings—
Men and women, old and young, hear
And all alike are made to attain the highest truth.
Without cause, without effect;
With no arising, no perishing—
This is termed great nirvana.
Those who hear break all their bonds.
The Tathāgata, for the sake of every being,
Always acts as one's loving father and mother.
Know that all sentient beings
Are the Tathāgata's children
[*KGSS*, III. I, pp. 138-139, #115].

92. Amida-Śākyamuni-3

Reverently I say to fellow practicers who aspire for birth:
You should all deeply repent! Śākyamuni Tathāgata is
    truly our compassionate father and mother.
With a variety of compassionate means
    he leads us to awaken the supreme shinjin
[*Hymns of the Dharma-Ages*, I, p. 396; See also *Hymn of the Two
Gateways of Entrance and Emergence*, 4, I, p. 629].

93. Amida-Śākyamuni-4

Śākyamuni and Amida are our parents of great compassion; using many and various compassionate means, they awaken the supreme shinjin in us. Thus the settling of true shinjin is the working of Śākyamuni and Amida. Persons become free of doubt about their birth because they have been grasped. Once grasped, there should be no calculation at all. . . .

Since true shinjin is awakened through the working of the two honored ones, Śākyamuni and Amida, it is when one is grasped that the settling of shinjin occurs. Thereafter the person abides in the stage of the truly settled until born into the Pure Land. Other Power means above all that there must not be the slightest calculation on our part [*Lamp for the Latter Ages*, Letter 13, I, p. 540].

94. Amida-Śākyamuni-5

Śākyamuni and Amida are our father and our mother,
Full of love and compassion for us;
Guiding us through various skillful means,
They bring us to awaken the supreme shinjin
[*Hymns of the Pure Land Masters*, p. 380, #74; See also *Notes on "Essentials of Faith Alone,"* I, pp. 454, 464].

95. Amida-Śākyamuni-6

Truly we know that without the virtuous Name, our compassionate father, we would lack the direct cause for birth. Without the light, our compassionate mother, we would stand apart from the indirect cause of birth. Although direct and indirect causes may come together, if the karmic-consciousness of shinjin is lacking, one will not reach the land of light. The karmic-consciousness of true and real shinjin is the inner cause. The Name and light—our father and mother—are the outer cause. When the inner and outer causes merge, one realizes the true body in the fulfilled land [*KGSS*, II. I, p. 54, #72; See also *Lamp for the Latter Ages*, Letter 22, I, p. 555].

2. Shinran's Style of Interpreting Scripture: Hidden and Manifest Meanings

Note: Shinran's perspective on scripture is distinctive among Pure Land teachers. With his particular understanding of the experience of true entrusting as the transfer or directing of Amida's true mind to persons, Shinran had to integrate that understanding with the traditional scriptures. They all teach essentially that the believer directs his/her merit from faith and practice or good deeds toward birth into the Pure Land.

In order to harmonize his view with tradition, Shinran developed two levels of interpretation of scripture. There was the surface or manifest level which recognizes the traditional understanding. The second is the implicit or hidden meaning in which all Sūtras are unified with the meaning of the Fulfillment text where true entrusting is the expression of Amida's sincere mind (See 63. Vow-Completion text-2 Shinran's reading).

On the implicit level, despite differences among the texts, they all teach trust in Amida's Vow. Consequently, all apparently self-power teachings in Pure Land texts can be used as compassionate means to guide people in attaining true entrusting. As example, note *KGSS*, VI. I, pp. 212-213, #15, where Shinran gives examples of his interpretation of the *Contemplation Sūtra*.

96. Interpreting-1

Question: Are the three minds taught in the *Larger Sutra* and those taught in the *Contemplation Sutra* the same or different?

Answer: When I consider the *Sutra of Contemplation on the Buddha of Immeasurable Life*, taking into account the interpretation of the commentator [Shan-tao] I find there is an explicit meaning and an implicit, hidden, inner meaning.

"Explicit" refers to presenting the meditative and non-meditative good acts and setting forth the three levels of practicers and the three minds. The two forms of good and the three types of meritorious acts, however, are not the true cause of birth in the fulfilled land. Further, the three minds that beings awaken are all minds of self-benefit that are individually different and not the mind that is single, which arises from [Amida's] benefiting of others. They are roots of good with which to aspire for the Pure Land that Śākyamuni] Tathāgata taught as a distinct provisional means. This is the import of the sutra; it is its "explicit" meaning.

"Implicit" refers to disclosing the Tathāgata's universal Vow and revealing the mind that is single, to which [practicers of the three minds] are led through [Amida's] benefiting of others.

Through the opportunity brought about by the grave evil acts of Devadatta and Ajātaśatru, Śākyamuni, with a smile, disclosed his inner intent. Through the condition brought about by the right intention in Vaidehī's selection, Amida's Primal Vow of great compassion was clarified. This is the hidden, implicit meaning of the sutra [*KGSS*, VI, I, p. 212, #15; See also *KGSS*, VI. I, p. 225, #36; VI, pp. 225-227, #37; *Passages on the Pure Land Way*, I, pp. 315-316].

97. Interpreting-2

Although in their general import the three sutras have explicit meanings and an implicit, hidden, inner meaning, they each reveal shinjin to be the basis for entry [into dharma]. Hence, each sutra opens with the words, "Thus [have I heard]." "Thus" (*nyoze*) signifies the aspect of genuine entrusting. Reflecting on the three sutras, I find that they all teach the true, diamond-like mind to be what is most essential. The true mind is great shinjin. Great shinjin is rare, most excellent, true and wondrous, and pure. Why? Because the ocean of great shinjin is extremely difficult to enter, for it arises through the power of the Buddha; because the true land of bliss is extremely easy to go to, for one is born there immediately through the power of the Vow. Here I have sought to discuss the sameness and differences of the "mind that is single" [in relation to the threefold mind of the *Larger* and *Contemplation Sutras*]; the import is as I have clarified above [*KGSS*, VI. I, p. 227, #37].

3. Other-Power: The Fundamental Principle of Shinran's Interpretation

Note: The distinction of Self-Power and Other-Power traces itself back to T'an-luan (476-542 C.E.) the Chinese teacher, who is credited with establishing the popular tradition of Pure Land teaching (Alfred Bloom, *Shinran's Gospel of Pure Grace* [Ann Arbor, MI: Association for Asian Studies, rep. 1991], pp. 10-11). According to his understanding, the *nembutsu* or recitation of Amida Buddha's name was effective because it represented and embodied the Buddha's aspiration for the enlightenment of all beings in the Eighteenth Vow. Thus the Pure Land tradition is generally marked by the belief in Other-Power—that the Buddha participates and assists in the process of liberation of those who rely on and recite the *nembutsu* with sincere faith. This principle also became particularly prominent in Hōnen's teaching and that of his successors.

Shinran is distinctive in this development because of the thoroughgoing way that he applied the concept of Other-Power. In the traditional view based on the *Contemplation Sūtra* and the Chinese teacher Shan-tao (613-681 C.E.), there are three aspects to religious faith in the *nembutsu* required to make it effective. These are deep faith, sincerity, and the intention to direct the merit toward birth in the Pure Land. Hōnen, recognizing one cannot just generate such conditions, indicated that through the recitation, those elements arise naturally. Shinran went further in making clear the textual and buddhalogical basis, as well as the experiential dimension, of these elements as Amida Buddha's true mind or the realization of Buddha-nature.

In our presentation we are calling Shinran's view of Other-Power, *Absolute Other-Power* in order to indicate that the reality, source, and validation of faith and practice lie beyond the empirical self and its volitional determination. Deliverance is totally the work of Amida Buddha as the reality that discloses itself through true entrusting.

The passages of the *Jinen Hōni shō* (107. Uncalculating-6; 108. Uncalculating-7) are very famous and important texts of Shinran written when he was age 86. The text expresses Shinran's thought succinctly in a very short scope. It gives the essence of his teaching on Absolute Other-Power in a more abstract but very clear way. *Jinen* means nature, natural. In modern speech it is *shizen*. Just as a thing in the realm of nature operates spontaneously, following the law of its nature from within itself and not acted on by external forces, Amida Buddha acts from the principle of compassion and wisdom that constitute his nature. He brings about the deliverance of beings, naturally and spontaneously. Deliverance, therefore, transcends human devising or calculation and achievement. The understanding of this principle is mediated through Amida Buddha with form, awakening our religious consciousness as true entrusting in his Vow, and arousing our awareness of the formless, colorless body of truth which is the ground and reality of our deliverance.

a. The Meaning of Other-Power

98. Other-Power-1

The nembutsu, for its practicers, is not a practice or a good act. Since it is not performed out of one's own designs, it is not a practice. Since it is not good done through one's own calculation, it is not a good act. Because it arises wholly from Other Power and is free of self-power, for the practicer, it is not a practice or a good act [*A Record in Lament of Divergences*, I, p. 665, #8].

99. Other-Power-2

Even a good person attains birth in the Pure Land, so it goes without saying that an evil person will.

Though it is so, people commonly say, "Even an evil person attains birth, so it goes without saying that a good person will." This statement may seem well founded at first, but it runs counter to the intent of the Primal Vow, which is Other Power. This is because people who rely on doing good through their self-power fail to entrust themselves wholeheartedly to Other Power and therefore are not in accord with Amida's Primal Vow, but when they overturn the mind of self-power and entrust themselves to Other Power, they will attain birth in the true and fulfilled land.

It is impossible for us, who are possessed of blind passions, to free ourselves from birth-and-death through any practice whatever. Sorrowing at this, Amida made the Vow, the essential intent of which is the evil person's attainment of Buddhahood. Hence, evil persons who entrust themselves to Other Power are precisely the ones who possess the true cause of birth.

Accordingly he said, "Even the good person is born in the Pure Land, so without question is the person who is evil" [*A Record in Lament of Divergences*, I, p. 663, #3].

b. Self-Power-Other-Power

100. Other-Power-3

Self-power is the effort to attain birth, whether by invoking the names of Buddhas other than Amida and practicing good acts other than the nembutsu, in accordance with your particular circumstances and opportunities; or by endeavoring to make yourself worthy through mending the confusion in your acts, words, and thoughts, confident of your own powers and guided by your own calculation.

Other Power is the entrusting of yourself to the Eighteenth among Amida Tathāgata's Vows, the Primal Vow of birth through the nembutsu, which Amida selected and adopted from among all other practices. Since this is the Vow of Tathāgata, Hōnen said: "In Other Power, no working is true working." "Working" [that is negated] is a term connoting calculation. Since the calculation of the person seeking birth is self-power, it is "working." Other Power is entrusting ourselves to the Primal Vow and our birth becoming firmly settled; hence it is altogether without one's own working. Thus, on the one hand, you should not be anxious that Tathāgata will not receive you because you do wrong. A foolish being is by nature possessed of blind passions, so you must recognize yourself as a being of karmic evil. On the other hand, you should not think that you deserve to attain birth because you are good. You cannot be born into the true and real fulfilled land through such self-power calculation. I have been taught that with shinjin of self-power a person can attain birth only in the realm of indolence, the borderland, the womb-palace, or the city of doubt [*Lamp for the Latter Ages*, Letter 2, I, pp. 525-526; See also *The Virtue of the Names of Amida Tathāgata*, I, p. 658].

101. Other-Power- 4

Concerning compassion, there is a difference between the Path of Sages and the Pure Land Path.

Compassion in the Path of Sages is to pity, commiserate with, and care for beings. It is extremely difficult, however, to accomplish the saving of others just as one wishes.

Compassion in the Pure Land Path should be understood as first attaining Buddhahood quickly through saying the nembutsu and, with the mind of great love and compassion, freely benefiting sentient beings as one wishes.

However much love and pity we may feel in our present lives, it is hard to save others as we wish; hence, such compassion remains unfulfilled. Only the saying of the nembutsu, then, is the mind of great compassion that is thoroughgoing [*A Record in Lament of Divergences*, I, p. 663, #4].

c. Uncalculating Trust

102. Uncalculating-1

Even saintly people who observe these various Mahayana and Hinayana precepts can attain birth in the true fulfilled land only after they realize the true and real shinjin of Other Power. Know that it is impossible to be born in the true, fulfilled Pure Land by simply observing precepts, or by self-willed conviction, or by self-cultivated good.

Nor rejecting those who break precepts and whose evil karma is profound

Break precepts applies to people who, having received the precepts for monks or laymen mentioned earlier, break and abandon them; such people are not rejected [*Notes on "Essentials of Faith Alone,"* I, p. 458].

103. Uncalculating-2

Other Power means to be free of any form of calculation [*Lamp for the Latter Ages*, Letter 10, I, p. 537].

104. Uncalculating-3

Because persons of shinjin dwell in the same stage as Maitreya, who will attain Buddhahood after one lifetime, it is certain that they are grasped, never to be abandoned. Hence, what we call Other Power means that there is no room for the slightest particle of calculation on the part of the practicer. For this reason, it is said that no working is true working. The great master [Hōnen] said, "Beyond this, nothing needs to be said. Simply entrust yourself to the Buddha" [*A Collection of Letters*, Letter #7, I, p. 574].

105. Uncalculating-4

In entrusting ourselves to the Tathāgata's Primal Vow and saying the Name once, necessarily, without seeking it, we are made to receive the supreme virtues, and without knowing it, we acquire the great and vast benefit. This is dharmicness, by which one will immediately realize the various facets of enlightenment naturally. "Dharmicness" means not brought about in any way by the practicer's calculation; from the very beginning one shares in the benefit that surpasses conception. It indicates the nature of *jinen*. "Dharmicness" expresses the natural working (*jinen*) in the life of the person who realizes shinjin and says the Name once [*Notes on Once-Calling and Many-Calling*, I, p. 481].

106. Uncalculating-5

[*The Vow and the Name are One*]

I have read your letter very carefully.

I fail to understand why your question should arise, for although we speak of Vow and of Name, these are not two different things. There is no Name separate from the Vow; there is no Vow separate from the Name. Even to say this, however, is to impose one's own calculation. Once you simply realize that the Vow surpasses conceptual understanding and with singleness of heart realize that the Name surpasses conceptual understanding and pronounce it, why should you labor in your own calculation?

It seems to me that with all your attempts to understand by reasoning and by learning you have fallen into confusion. It is completely in error. Once you have simply come to realize that Vow and Name surpass conceptual understanding, you should not calculate in this way or that. There must be nothing of your calculation in the act that leads to birth.

Respectfully,

You must simply entrust yourself to Tathāgata.

Respectfully.

Fifth month, 5th day [*Lamp for the Latter Ages*, Letter #9, I, p. 536].

107. Uncalculating-6

[On *Jinen Hōni*] A writing by Shinran at age eighty-eight

[Concerning "realize" (*gyaku-toku*):] *Gyaku* means to realize in the causal stage, and *toku* means to realize on reaching the resultant stage.

[Concerning "Name" (*myōgō*):] *Myō* indicates the Name in the causal stage, and *gō* indicates the Name in the resultant stage.

Concerning *jinen* [in the phrase *jinen hōni*]: *Ji* means "of itself"—not through the practicer's calculation. It signifies being made so. *Nen* means "to be made so"—it is not through the practicer's calculation; it is through the working of the Tathāgata's Vow.

Concerning *hōni*: *Hōni* signifies being made so through the working of the Tathāgata's Vow. It is the working of the Vow where there is no room for calculation on the part of the practicer. Know, therefore, that in Other Power, no working is true working.

Jinen signifies being made so from the very beginning. Amida's Vow is, from the very beginning, designed to bring each of us to entrust ourselves to it—saying "Namu-amida-butsu"—and to receive us into the Pure Land; none of this is through our calculation. Thus, there is no room for the practicer to be concerned about being good or bad. This is the meaning of *jinen* as I have been taught.

As the essential purport of the Vow, [Amida] vowed to bring us all to become supreme Buddha. Supreme Buddha is formless, and because of being formless is called *jinen*. Buddha, when appearing with form, is not called supreme nirvana. In order to make it known that supreme Buddha is formless, the name Amida Buddha is expressly used; so I have been taught. Amida Buddha fulfills the purpose of making us know the significance of *jinen*.

After we have realized this, we should not be forever talking about *jinen*. If we continuously discuss *jinen*, that no working is true working will again become a problem of working. It is a matter of inconceivable Buddha-wisdom [*Hymns of the Dharma-Ages*, I, pp. 427-428].

108. Uncalculating-7

[On *Jinen-Hōni*]

Concerning *jinen* [in the phrase *jinen hōni*]:

Ji means "of itself"—not through the practicer's calculation. It signifies being made so.

Nen means "to be made so"—it is not through the practicer's calculation; it is through the working of the Tathāgata's Vow.

Concerning *hōni*:

Hōni signifies being made so through the working of the Tathāgata's Vow. It is the working of the Vow where there is no room for calculation on the part of the practicer. Know, therefore, that in Other Power, no working is true working.

Jinen signifies being made so from the very beginning. Amida's Vow is, from the very beginning, designed to bring each of us to entrust ourselves to it—saying "Namu-amida-butsu"—and to receive us into the Pure Land; none of this is through our calculation. Thus, there is no room for the practicer to be concerned about being good or bad. This is the meaning of *jinen* as I have been taught.

As the essential purport of the Vow, [Amida] vowed to bring us all to become supreme Buddha. Supreme Buddha is formless, and because of being formless is called *jinen*. Buddha, when appearing with form, is not called supreme nirvana. In order to make it known that supreme Buddha is formless, the name Amida Buddha is expressly used; so I have been taught. Amida Buddha fulfills the purpose of making us know the significance of *jinen*.

After we have realized this, we should not be forever talking about *jinen*. If we continuously discuss *jinen*, that no working is true working will again become a problem of working. It is a matter of inconceivable Buddha-wisdom.

[Shoka 2 {1258}, Twelfth month, 14th day]

Gutoku Shinran

Written at age 86 [*Letters: Lamp for the Latter Ages*, Letter 5, I, p. 530].

109. Uncalculating-8

Ji also means of itself. "Of itself" is a synonym for *jinen*, which means to be made to become so. "To be made to become so" means that without the practicer's calculating in any way whatsoever, all that practicer's past, present, and future evil karma is transformed into the highest good, just as all waters, upon entering the great ocean, immediately become ocean water. We are made to acquire the Tathāgata's virtues through entrusting ourselves to the Vow-power; hence the expression, "made to become so." Since there is no contriving in any way to gain such virtues, it is called *jinen*. Those persons who have attained true and real shinjin are taken into and protected by this Vow that grasps never to abandon; therefore, they realize the diamond-like mind without any calculation on their own part, and thus dwell in the stage of the truly settled. Because of this, constant mindfulness of the Primal Vow arises in them naturally (by *jinen*). Even with the arising of this shinjin, it is written that supreme shinjin is made to awaken in us through the compassionate guidance of Śākyamuni, the kind father, and Amida, the mother of loving care. Know that this is the benefit of the working of *jinen* [*Notes on "Essentials of Faith Alone,"* I, pp. 453-454].

d. No-working is True-working

Note: This paradoxical statement is attributed by Shinran to Hōnen, his teacher. In context it suggests that the devotee should not involve in calculations of benefit and result in adopting the *nembutsu* nor deal in complicated speculations and theorizing. He calls for a simple faith which recognizes the depravity of human nature and the unconditional compassion of Amida Buddha. It must be observed that Shinran reiterates Hōnen's view, though he gave the teaching a more detailed and substantive interpretation than his teacher had, theoretically and in personal experience.

The Chinese term translated here as "working" has a range of meanings such as reason, principle, meaning, discrimination, calculation. "Working" in this context implies self-working or assertion in the attempt to gain birth through one's own effort. In the context of 114. No-working-5, "Reason of no-reason" might be better insofar as the emphasis of the passage is on conceivability.

110. No-working-1

Further, Other Power means that no working is true working. "Working" [that is negated] is the practicer's calculating and designing. Tathāgata's Primal Vow surpasses conceptual understanding; it is a design of the wisdom of Buddhas. It is not the design of foolish beings. No one can fathom the wisdom of Buddhas, which surpasses conceptual understanding. This includes Maitreya Bodhisattva, who is in [the rank of] succession to Buddhahood. Thus, the great teacher Hōnen said, "No working is true working." My understanding has been that nothing apart from this realization is necessary for the attainment of birth into the Pure Land; therefore, what others may say is of no concern to me [*Letters: Lamp for the Latter Ages*, Letter 7, I, p. 533; See also *Notes on the Inscriptions on Sacred Scrolls*, I, p. 520].

111. No-working-2

If it is understood that the person of shinjin dwells in the stage of the truly settled, there is no calculation on the part of the practicer; hence, we speak of Other Power, in which no working is true working. Since practicers have become free of calculation as to whether they are good or evil, pure or defiled, it is said that no working is true working. . . . Because persons of shinjin dwell in the same stage as Maitreya, who will attain Buddhahood after one lifetime, it is certain that they are grasped, never to be abandoned. Hence, what we call Other Power means that there is no room for the slightest particle of calculation on the part of the practicer. For this reason, it is said that no working is true working. The great master [Hōnen] said, "Beyond this, nothing needs to be said. Simply entrust yourself to the Buddha" [*Letters of the Tradition (Zensho Text)*, I, pp. 573-574].

112. No-working-3

Further, once one has entrusted oneself to Amida's Primal Vow, as the great teacher Master [Hōnen] has said, no working is true working. Thus, it is taught that as long as one's own working remains, it is not Other Power, but self-power.

Further, with regard to Other Power, since it is inconceivable Buddha-wisdom, the attainment of supreme enlightenment by foolish beings possessed of blind passions comes about through the working shared only by Buddhas; it is not in any way the design of the practicer. Thus, no working is true working. "Working" [that is negated] refers to the calculation of the person of self-power. Concerning Other Power, then, no working is true working. I know nothing at all about what these people are saying, so I should not comment on it in any way [*A Collection of Letters*, I, pp. 571-572, #10].

113. No-working-4

Other Power is the entrusting of yourself to the Eighteenth among Amida Tathāgata's Vows, the Primal Vow of birth through the nembutsu, which Amida selected and adopted from among all other practices. Since this is the Vow of Tathāgata,

Hōnen said: "In Other Power, no working is true working." "Working" [that is negated] is a term connoting calculation. Since the calculation of the person seeking birth is self-power, it is "working." Other Power is entrusting ourselves to the Primal Vow and our birth becoming firmly settled; hence it is altogether without one's own working. Thus, on the one hand, you should not be anxious that Tathāgata will not receive you because you do wrong. A foolish being is by nature possessed of blind passions, so you must recognize yourself as a being of karmic evil. On the other hand, you should not think that you deserve to attain birth because you are good. You cannot be born into the true and real fulfilled land through such self-power calculation [*Lamp for the Latter Ages*, Letter #2, pp. 525-526; See also *Notes on the Inscriptions on Sacred Scrolls*, I, p. 520].

114. No-working-5

Concerning the nembutsu, no working is true working. For it is beyond description, explanation, and conceptual understanding [*A Record in Lament of Divergences*, I, p. 666, #10].

e. Shinran's Ranking of Buddhist Teachings (Critical Classification of Teachings)

Note: Classifying or organizing Buddhist teachings was a feature of Chinese Buddhism. It resulted from the fact that Buddhist Sūtras and teachings entered China in an unsystematic way, giving rise to confusion about the order and relationship of the various teachings. Though it was believed that Śākyamuni had taught all these teachings, offered in the Sūtras, there were many contradictions and ambiguities among the very diverse texts. Consequently, Buddhist teachers attempted to organize the texts and teachings based on a principle of progression from simpler to more complex, tracing from the Hīnayāna through the Mahāyāna and within Mahāyāna. Several systems grew up based on the *Hua Yen Sūtra*, the *Lotus Sūtra* of T'ien-t'ai (Tendai), Shan-tao in the Pure Land tradition, Kōbō Daishi in the Shingon sect in Japan, and Shinran.

The Pure Land system grew gradually from the distinctions developed among the early teachers from Nāgārjuna to Shan-tao. Shan-tao set forth the most comprehensive outline, which we have termed here the traditional view. Shinran formulated his own system to highlight absolute Other-Power, though he also employed the traditional system.

In the traditional system there is a basic distinction between the Sage or Saintly Path, which is self power and the Pure Land gate, which is Other-Power. The Sage Path is the way of difficult practices of meditation and morality, while the Pure Land is the easy path of *nembutsu* which came to mean vocal recitation of the Buddha's name. The Sage Path practices may be directed to all Buddhas and Bodhisattvas, as well as Amida, but the easy path of *nembutsu* is directed to Amida. The Sage Path within Pure Land teaching, based on Vasubandhu, employs a variety of practices for birth into the Pure Land such as worship, praise-adoration, aspiration, meditation, and directing merit. Later, with Shan-tao, the system of five right practices was set forth: chanting Sūtras, meditation, worship, reciting *nembutsu*, making offerings. Within this group, reciting *nembutsu* was called correct practice, while the other four were assisting practices. Those devoted to other Buddhas were called sundry practice, while those directed to Amida were correct or true practice. Hōnen later determined that the recitation of the *nembutsu* was the sole practice provided by Amida for the salvation of ordinary people. He set forth the "sole practice of *nembutsu*." His successors varied in emphasis on the use of the supplementary, assisting practices.

Shinran followed Hōnen in stressing the sole practice of *nembutsu*, rejecting completely the assisting practices while focusing on the issue of true entrusting that motivates the *nembutsu*. He shifted attention from the external practice to the inner mind and attitude of trust.

Shinran's system of two pairs and four levels highlights the issue in Mahāyāna of sudden and gradual approaches to Enlightenment. The Sage Path is symbolized by vertical-gradual, while the Pure Land is horizontal-sidewise-sudden. "Going out" by various compassionate means denotes the various practices, and true "transcending" is the way of *shinjin-nembutsu*. Combining the four characteristics make two pairs that include all the many practices of Buddhism.

The distinctions "two pair and four levels" are an important facet of Shinran's classification of teachings. They position Shinran's teaching in relation to the principles of Other-Power and "suddenness" which reflect the inward nature of Shinran's perspective. He goes a step beyond the understanding of Hōnen's successors by rejecting the gradual accumulation of merit through self-striving, while establishing the position of absolute Other-Power marked by the sudden arising of true entrusting in the Vow. Also, he sees a self-power *nembutsu* within Other-Power when the practice of *nembutsu* is used as a source of merit.

Though Shinran is clear that self-power faith and practice does not bring birth into the Pure Land on an equal level with true entrusting, he indicates that those who are of mixed mind or mixed practice are born in an outer region of the Pure Land, termed borderland, womb-palace, or realm of indolence. After a period of time, they will finally enter the Pure Land. Shinran's view is one of universal, positive hope of the attainment for all persons, despite the spiritual limitations he sees in general religious practice.

The four levels and two pairs system that Shinran created may be understood through a set of images. Vertical is self-power, going out is gradual, crosswise is Other-power, and transcending is sudden or instantaneous. The four sets of pairs are: vertical-going out, vertical-transcending, crosswise-going out, and crosswise-transcending. The vertical-going out includes the Hīnayāna and early Mahāyāna such as the Consciousness-only school and Three Treatise school. They illustrate a swimmer going across a stream by his own strength. The vertical-transcending is self-power with direct, immediate attainment and is depicted by Zen with a runner pole-vaulting across a stream. The crosswise-going out compares to Pure Land teaching and meritorious recitation of the Name. It is like a person grasping a life preserver and being hauled to shore. Crosswise-transcending is absolute Other-Power, the instantaneous embrace by the Buddha, and may be likened to a drowning person snatched from the water by a rescuer. Only the last represents Shinran's teaching; all others are provisional and while partially true may lead finally to the experience of true entrusting as devotees become aware of their spiritual incapacity and realize trust in Amida's Vow.

i. The Traditional Pure Land View

115. Classification-1

Among all the teachings that Shakyamuni Buddha taught during his lifetime, those that teach attaining sacred wisdom and realizing the fruit in this world are called the Path of Sages. They are termed the path of difficult practice. Within this path there are Mahayana and Hinayana; gradual attainment and sudden attainment; the One Vehicle, two vehicles, and three vehicles; accommodated and true; exoteric and esoteric; departing lengthwise and transcending lengthwise. These are self-power teachings, the path of the accommodated gate of provisional means recommended [by those] in the state of benefiting and guiding others.

Attaining sacred wisdom and realizing the fruit in the Pure Land of peace is called the Pure Land path. It is termed the path of easy practice. Within this path there are departing crosswise and transcending crosswise; temporary and true; gradual attainment and sudden attainment; auxiliary, right, and sundry practices; mixed praxis and single praxis.

"Right [practices]" refers to the five kinds of right practice. "Auxiliary [practices]" refers to these kinds of practices with the exception of saying the Name. "Sundry practices" refers to all the various practices other than the right and the auxiliary; these are teachings of gradual attainment that expound ways of departing crosswise; they are the temporary gate of self-power, which includes the teachings of meditative and non-meditative practices, the three kinds of meritorious conduct, and the three levels of practicers and nine grades of beings.

"Transcending crosswise" refers to being mindful of the Primal Vow and becoming free of the mind of self-power; this is termed "Other Power of transcending crosswise." It is the single within the single, the sudden within the sudden, the true within the true, the One Vehicle within the [One] Vehicle. It is the true essence [of the Pure Land way] [*KGSS*, VI. I, pp. 222-223, #35].

116. Classification-2

With the expression "sundry practices" and also with "mixed praxis," the term is single, but there are different meanings. "Sundry" embraces all the myriads of practices. In contrast to the five right practices, there are five kinds of sundry practices. The term "sundry" is used because the understandings and practices for birth as human beings, devas, bodhisattvas, and so on are compounded [with aspiration for birth in Amida's land]. Originally, they are not causes resulting in birth in the Pure Land. They are good acts that, with a change of mind, come to be directed toward birth; hence, they are termed "sundry practices within the Pure Land way."

Further, concerning "sundry practices," there is "single practice" and "single mind"; also, there are "combined practices" and "combined mind."

"Single practice" refers to the performance of solely one kind of good act; hence it is termed "single practice." "Single mind" refers to directing merit solely [toward birth in the Pure Land]; hence it is termed "single mind."

Concerning "combined practices" and "combined mind," because one performs various good acts together, the term "combined practices" is used; because minds of meditative good and non-meditative good are combined, the term "combined mind" is used. Further, concerning right and auxiliary, there is single praxis and mixed praxis. Regarding mixed praxis, there is single mind and combined mind. There are two kinds of single praxis: first, only saying the Buddha's Name, and second, the five single [acts]. Concerning these [five] acts, there is single mind and combined mind. The five single [acts] are: 1) solely worshiping [Amida], 2) solely reciting [the Pure Land sutras], 3) solely contemplating [Amida and the Pure Land], 4 solely saying the Name, and 5) solely praising [Amida]. These are termed the five kinds of single praxis.

The term "single praxis" is the same, but it has different meanings. It is meditative single praxis and also non-meditative single praxis.

"Single mind" refers to singly performing the five right practices without double-mindedness; hence, "single mind." This is meditative single mind, and also non-meditative single mind.

"Mixed praxis" is to perform the auxiliary and right acts together; hence "mixed praxis." "Combined mind" refers to mixing the minds of meditative and non-meditative good acts; hence, "combined mind." Reflect on this. . . .

Relying on the teacher of the sutras, [Śākyamuni,] and turning to the commentary of Master [Shan-tao], I find that among "sundry practices" are combined practices performed with a combined mind, combined practices performed with a single mind, and single practice performed with a combined mind. Further, among right practices there is single praxis performed with a single mind, or single praxis performed with a combined mind, and mixed praxis performed with a combined mind; all are causal acts resulting in birth in the borderland, the womb-palace, and the realm of indolence and pride. Hence, although one is born in the land of bliss, one does not see the three treasures. The light of the Buddha's mind does not illuminate and grasp practicers of sundry acts. How truly profound is the intent behind the temporarily guiding Vow! How clear become the teachings of the temporary gate and [Shan-tao's] explanation [that they are for the awakening] of desire for the Pure Land! [*KGSS*, VI. I, pp. 223-225, #36].

117. Classification-3

Attaining Buddhahood through the nembutsu is the true
    essence of the Pure Land way;
The myriad practices and good acts are the temporary gate.
Unless one distinguishes the accommodated and the real, the
    temporary and the true,
One cannot possibly know the Pure Land that is naturalness
    (*jinen*)
[*Hymns of the Pure Land*, I, p. 344, #77].

118. Classification-4

I fear it is hard to be born there by doing sundry good acts according to our diverse conditions

According to our diverse conditions refers to directing the merit of practicing various good acts, which one performs according to one's own particular circumstances and opportunities, toward birth in the land of bliss. There are 84,000 gates of dharma. Since they are all good practices done in self-power, they are rejected as not leading to birth in the true fulfilled land. Thus, *I fear it is hard to be born* [*Notes on "Essentials of Faith Alone,"* I, p. 462].

119. Classification-5

Birth is not attained means that the person is not born. Those of meditative and non-meditative good acts—performing sundry practices, undergoing disciplines, and lacking threefold shinjin—will be born in the true and real fulfilled land, after countless lives in vast ages, after they have realized the threefold shinjin of the *Larger Sutra*. Thus, the person is not born. The sutras state that even if such a person attains birth in the palace of womb or the borderland, he or she must pass five hundred years there; furthermore, out of millions upon millions of beings, scarcely a single one will advance to the true fulfilled land. Thus, we must carefully understand the importance of threefold shinjin and aspire for its realization [*Notes on "Essentials of Faith Alone,"* I, p. 465].

120. Classification-6

Further, those who take up auxiliary good acts are people endeavoring in self-power. "Self-power" characterizes those who have full confidence in themselves, trusting in their own hearts and minds, striving with their own powers, and relying on their own various roots of good [*Notes on Once-Calling and Many-Calling,* I, p. 484].

121. Classification-7

The eighty-four thousand dharma-gates are all good practices of the provisional means of the Pure Land teaching; they are known as the "essential" or provisional gate. This gate consists of the good practices, meditative and non-meditative, taught in the *Sutra of Contemplation on the Buddha of Immeasurable*

Life. Meditative good refers to the thirteen contemplations;
non-meditative good refers to the good acts of the three types
of meritorious behavior and the nine grades of beings. These all
belong to the "essential" gate, which is the provisional means
of the Pure Land teaching; it is also called the provisional gate.
Encouraging and guiding all sentient beings with various means
through this "essential" or provisional gate, the Buddha teaches
and encourages them to enter "the great treasure ocean of true
and real virtue—the Primal Vow, perfect and unhindered,
which is the One Vehicle." Hence, all good acts of self-power
are called provisional ways [*Notes on Once-Calling and Many-
Calling*, I, pp. 485-486].

122. Classification-8

The Path of Sages comprises teachings that people who have
already attained Buddhahood preach in order to encourage us;
it includes such schools as the Busshin, Shingon, Tendai, Kegon,
and Sanron, which are said to be the ultimate developments
of the Mahayana. The Busshin school is the presently growing
Zen school. There are also the accommodated Mahayana and
the Hinayana teachings, such as the Hosso, Jojitsu, and Kusha.
These are all teachings of the Path of Sages. "Accommodated
teachings" are those that Buddhas and bodhisattvas, who have
already attained Buddhahood, promote by temporarily manifesting themselves in various forms; this is the meaning of the
word "accommodated" [*Lamp for the Latter Ages*, Letter 1, I, p.
524].

123. Classification-9

In the Pure Land teaching there are the true and the provisional. The true is the selected Primal Vow. The provisional
teaches the good of meditative and non-meditative practices.
The selected Primal Vow is the true essence of the Pure Land
way; good practices, whether meditative or non-meditative,
are provisional ways. The true essence of the Pure Land way
is the consummation of Mahayana Buddhism; the provisional
gateways of expedience include the other Mahayana and the
Hinayana teachings, accommodated and real [*Lamp for the Latter
Ages*, Letter 1, I, pp. 524-525].

124. Classification-10

Of the conceivable and the inconceivable dharma, the conceivable comprises the 84,000 kinds of good of the Path of Sages. The Pure Land teaching is the inconceivable dharma-teaching [*Lamp for the Latter Ages*, Letter 8. I, p. 535].

125. Classification-11

Know that all the teachings other than solely the selected Primal Vow of Amida Tathāgata, whether Mahayana or Hinayana, accommodated or real, exoteric or esoteric, are the paths of difficult practice, the Path of Sages, or they are the path of easy practice, the Pure Land way, that is termed the directing of merit and aspiration for birth in the Pure Land path, the self-power, provisional gateway of expedience [*Gutoku's Notes*, I, p. 589].

126. Classification-12

Know that the "essential" gate of the Pure Land teaching is the teaching of the two kinds of good acts, meditative and non-meditative, the provisional gate of expedient means, the teaching of the three types of meritorious conduct, and the good acts done by the nine grades of beings [*Gutoku's Notes*, I, pp. 592-593].

127. Classification-13

It is not stated at all that any practicers of various other acts are illumined and embraced: Not one of those who perform sundry practices and disciplines is illumined, taken in, and protected. That such practicers are not illumined and protected means that they are not blessed with the benefit of being grasped, never to be abandoned. Know that this is because they are not practicers who have entrusted themselves to the Primal Vow. Hence it is not stated that such people are grasped and protected, never to be abandoned [*Notes on the Inscriptions on Sacred Scrolls*, I, p. 508].

ii. Shinran's System of "Two Pairs and Four Levels"

128. Classification-14

Further, the mind aspiring for enlightenment is of two kinds [of orientation]: lengthwise and crosswise.

The lengthwise is further of two kinds: transcending lengthwise and departing lengthwise. These are explained in various teachings—accommodated and real, exoteric and esoteric, Mahayana and Hinayana. They are the mind [with which one attains enlightenment after] going around for many kalpas, the diamond-like mind of self-power, or the great mind of the bodhisattva.

The crosswise is also of two kinds: transcending crosswise and departing crosswise. That characterized by departing crosswise is the mind of enlightenment of right and sundry practices or meditative and non-meditative practices—of self-power within Other Power. That characterized by transcending crosswise is shinjin that is directed to beings through the power of the Vow. It is the mind that aspires to attain Buddhahood. The mind that aspires to attain Buddhahood is the mind aspiring for great enlightenment of crosswise orientation. It is called "the diamond-like mind of crosswise transcendence."

Although the same term is used, the crosswise and the lengthwise minds of aspiration for enlightenment differ in significance; nevertheless, both take entrance into the true as right and essential, both take true mind as their foundation, both reject the wrong and sundry, and both take doubt to be erroneous. . . [*KGSS*, III. I, pp. 107-108, #52].

129. Classification-15

Crosswise means across; *leaping* means "going beyond." This way surpasses all other teachings, and through it one quickly goes beyond the great ocean of birth-and-death and attains supreme enlightenment; therefore the term *leaping* is used. It is made possible by the power of the Vow that embodies the Tathāgata's great compassion [*Notes on "Essentials of Faith Alone,"* I, p. 463].

130. Classification-16

"Crosswise" means laterally or transcendently; "leap" means to go beyond. When we have boarded the ship of the Buddha's karmic power, which has been fulfilled through the great Vow, we go laterally and transcendently beyond the vast ocean of birth-and-death and reach the shore of the true fulfilled land [*Notes on Once-Calling and Many-Calling*, I, p. 476].

131. Classification-17

One cuts off crosswise the five evil courses and the evil courses close naturally (jinen). *Crosswise*: laterally or transcendently. This means that because persons entrust themselves to the power of Tathāgata's Vow—this is the absence of calculation on the part of the practicer—they cut off and abandon the five evil courses and become free of the four modes of birth naturally, by *jinen*; it signifies Other Power. This is the meaning of "crosswise leap." "Crosswise" is used in contrast with lengthwise, "leap" in contrast with going around. "Lengthwise" and "going around" characterize the self-power Path of Sages; the crosswise leap is the fundamental intent of the true teaching of Other Power.

Cuts off means to sever crosswise the bonds of the five evil courses. *The evil courses close naturally*: when a person takes refuge in the power of the Vow, the five courses of birth-and-death are closed off; hence, *close naturally*. That is, drawn by the Primal Vow as the karmic cause, one attains birth in the Pure Land naturally, by *jinen*.

Ascending the way is without limit. Ascending: attaining the supreme nirvana. *Way*: the enlightenment of great nirvana [*Notes on the Inscriptions on Sacred Scrolls*, I, p. 496].

4. Shinran's Respect for Tradition: The Selected Lineage of Seven Pure Land Masters

Note: In all Buddhist traditions, as in perhaps all religious traditions, lineage and tradition is important. Truth is passed down through history from person to person. In Zen Buddhism the truth of Enlightenment is said to be passed from one master's cup to another without losing a drop. In Christianity there is the Apostolic succession, which hands down the understanding of Christ's work and teaching.

Shinran also appreciated that truth was not an individual matter, created by any one person. Rather it is the unfolding of insight, ultimately rooted in Amida Buddha, reality itself. He saw the lineage as the fulfillment of the Seventeenth Vow of Amida, that his name would be praised by all Buddhas, throughout the entire cosmos, including our world system guided by Śākyamuni. We may say Shinran had a "theology" of history as the manifestation of Amida's compassion and wisdom.

As a result of his experience with Hōnen and within the Pure Land tradition, Shinran selected out seven master's whom he considered the beacon lights in the development of the truth of the Primal Vow and the experience of true entrusting. They are Nāgārjuna and Vasubandhu in India, T'an-luan, Tao-ch'o, and Shan-tao in China, and Genshin and Hōnen in Japan. This is a line from India to Japan, the historical course of Buddhism. While Korea is not mentioned, Shinran used texts from Korea. The employment of resources was wider than the list of masters itself.

Shinran's lineage, however, is not strictly historical. There is no direct historical connection between Śākyamuni and Nāgārjuna, nor between Nāgārjuna and Vasubandhu. In China Tao-ch'o visited T'an-luan's grave while Tao-ch'o and Shan-tao did have a student-teacher relationship. Genshin in Japan quoted Shan-tao, which Hōnen read. Hōnen was Shinran's teacher. We may call it more a spiritual lineage as T'an-luan wrote a commentary on Vasubandhu under the influence of Nāgārjuna's Middle Path philosophy. T'an-luan served as a spiritual model for Tao-ch'o and inspired Shan-tao, whose thought became known in Japan and provided insight for Hōnen. Hōnen then guided Shinran whose thought and experience deepened and clarified the intent of the tradition.

132. Tradition-1

How joyous I am, Gutoku Shinran, disciple of Śākyamuni! Rare is it to come upon the sacred scriptures from the westward land of India and the commentaries of the masters of China and Japan, but now I have been able to encounter them. Rare is it to hear them, but already I have been able to hear. Reverently entrusting myself to the teaching, practice, and realization that are the true essence of the Pure Land way, I am especially aware of the profundity of the Tathāgata's benevolence. Here I rejoice in what I have heard and extol what I have attained [*KGSS* I, Preface, I, p. 4; See also *Passages on the Pure Land Way*, I, p. 295].

133. Tradition-2

Thus we know truly from the words of the Great Sage that realization of supreme nirvana is brought about by the directing of virtue through the Vow's power. Benefiting in the aspect of return expresses the true intent of benefiting others. Accordingly, the author of the Treatise, Vasubandhu, proclaims the vast and unhindered mind that is single, thereby universally awakening the multitudes of this passion-defiled world of endurance. Master T'an-luan clarifies Amida's compassionate directing of virtue for our going to the Pure Land and our return to this world; and he widely teaches, with care and concern, the profound significance of being benefited by the Other and of benefiting others. Reverently embrace these words; receive them in deepest homage [*KGSS*, IV. I, p. 174, #18].

a. The Hymn of True Entrusting (*Shōshinge*)

Note: This elegiac poem was composed by Shinran. He placed it at the end of the volume on Practice in the *Kyōgyōshinshō*. It is known as *Shōshin nembutsu ge* in contrast to the version in the *Passages on the Pure Land Way*, which is known as *Nembutsu shōshin ge*. With some differences they have the same intent and general content. We have given both versions here.

This poem is usually referred to by its shorter Japanese name *Shōshinge* and is used in services. It is referred to as a "Sūtra" (*okyō*), a word of the Buddha. The text in 120 verses reviews the teachers selected by Shinran as his Buddhist lineage and contains the leading ideas that are central to Shinran's understanding. It functions as a creed or confession of faith.

The *Shōshinge* became part of the daily ritual for Hongwanji members through the efforts of Zonnyo (1396-1457 C.E.), the seventh Abbot and his son Rennyo (1415-1499 CE.), the eighth Abbot. They produced the text in block print for their members. It is chanted together with six verses from the *Hymns of the Pure Land* (See below under Amida the Savior).

134. Tradition-3

I take refuge in the Tathāgata of Immeasurable Life!
I entrust myself to the Buddha of Inconceivable Light!
Bodhisattva Dharmākara, in his causal stage,
Under the guidance of Lokeśvarāja Buddha,

Searched into the origins of the Buddhas' pure lands,
And the qualities of those lands and their men and devas;
He then established the supreme, incomparable Vow;
He made the great Vow rare and all-encompassing.

In five kalpas of profound thought, he embraced this Vow,
Then resolved again that his Name be heard throughout the
    ten quarters.

Everywhere he casts light immeasurable, boundless,
Unhindered, unequaled, light-lord of all brilliance,

Pure light, joyful light, the light of wisdom,
Light constant, inconceivable, light beyond speaking,
Light excelling sun and moon he sends forth, illumining
    countless worlds;
The multitudes of beings all receive the radiance.

[*The Name embodying the Primal Vow is the act of true settle*
    ment,
The Vow of entrusting with sincere mind is the cause of birth;
We realize the equal of enlightenment and supreme nirvana
Through the fulfillment of the Vow of attaining nirvana without
    fail.

Śākyamuni Tathāgata appeared in this world
Solely to teach the ocean-like Primal Vow of Amida;
We, an ocean of beings in an evil age of five defilements,
Should entrust ourselves to the Tathāgata's words of truth.

When the one thought-moment of joy arises,
Nirvana is attained without severing blind passions;
When ignorant and wise, even grave offenders and slanderers
    of the dharma, all alike turn and enter shinjin,
They are like waters that, on entering the ocean, become one
    in taste with it.

The light of compassion that grasps us illumines and protects
    us always;
The darkness of our ignorance is already broken through;
Still the clouds and mists of greed and desire, anger and
    hatred,
Cover as always the sky of true and real shinjin.

But though light of the sun is veiled by clouds and mists,
Beneath the clouds and mists there is brightness, not dark.
When one realizes shinjin, seeing and revering and attaining
    great joy,
One immediately leaps crosswise, closing off the five evil courses]

[This portion appears also in *Notes on the Inscriptions on Sacred Scrolls*, pp. 517-518.]

All foolish beings, whether good or evil,
When they hear and entrust to Amida's universal Vow,
Are praised by the Buddha as people of vast and excellent
    understanding;
Such a person is called a pure white lotus.

For evil sentient beings of wrong views and arrogance,
The nembutsu that embodies Amida's Primal Vow
Is hard to accept in shinjin;
This most difficult of difficulties, nothing surpasses.

The masters of India in the west, who explained the teaching
    in treatises,
And the eminent monks of China and Japan,
Clarified the Great Sage's true intent in appearing in the
    world,
And revealed that Amida's Primal Vow accords with the
    nature of beings.

Śākyamuni Tathāgata, on Mount Lankā,
Prophesied to the multitudes that in south India
The mahasattva Nāgārjuna would appear in this world
To crush the views of being and non-being;

Proclaiming the unexcelled Mahayana teaching,
He would attain the stage of joy and be born in the land of
    happiness.
Nāgārjuna clarifies the hardship on the overland path of
    difficult practice,
And leads us to entrust to the pleasure on the waterway of
    easy practice.

He teaches that the moment one thinks on Amida's Primal
    Vow,
One is naturally brought to enter the stage of the definitely
    settled;
Solely saying the Tathāgata's Name constantly,

One should respond with gratitude to the universal Vow of
    great compassion.

Bodhisattva Vasubandhu, composing a treatise, declares
That he takes refuge in the Tathāgata of unhindered light,
And that relying on the sutras, he will reveal the true and real
    virtues,
And make widely known the great Vow by which we leap
    crosswise beyond birth-and-death.

He discloses the mind that is single so that all beings be saved
By Amida's directing of virtue through the power of the
    Primal Vow.
When a person turns and enters the great treasure ocean of
    virtue,
Necessarily he joins Amida's assembly;

And when he reaches that lotus-held world,
He immediately realizes the body of suchness or dharma-
    nature.
Then sporting in the forests of blind passions, he manifests
    transcendent powers;
Entering the garden of birth-and-death, he assumes various
    forms to guide others.

Turning toward the dwelling of Master T'an-luan, the
    Emperor of Liang
Always paid homage to him as a bodhisattva.
Bodhiruci, master of the Tripitaka, gave T'an-luan the Pure
    Land teachings,
And T'an-luan, burning his Taoist scriptures, took refuge in
    the land of bliss.

In his commentary on the treatise of Bodhisattva Vasubandhu,
He shows that the cause and attainment of birth in the ful
    filled land lie in the Vow.
Our going and returning, directed to us by Amida, come
    about through Other Power;
The truly decisive cause is shinjin.

When a foolish being of delusion and defilement awakens
    shinjin,
He realizes that birth-and-death is itself nirvana;
Without fail he reaches the land of immeasurable light
And universally guides sentient beings to enlightenment.

Tao-ch'o determined how difficult it is to fulfill the Path of
    Sages,
And reveals that only passage through the Pure Land gate is
    possible for us.
He criticizes self-power endeavor in the myriad good
    practices,
And encourages us solely to say the fulfilled Name embodying
    true virtue.

With kind concern he teaches the three characteristics of
    entrusting and non-entrusting,
Compassionately guiding all identically, whether they live
    when the dharma survives as but form, when in its last
    stage, or when it has become extinct.

Though a person has committed evil all his life, when he
    encounters the Primal Vow,
He will reach the world of peace and realize the perfect fruit
    of enlightenment.
Shan-tao alone in his time clarified the Buddha's true intent;
Sorrowing at the plight of meditative and non-meditative
    practicers and people of grave evil,
He reveals that Amida's light and Name are the causes of
    birth.
When the practicer enters the great ocean of wisdom, the
    Primal Vow,

He receives the diamond-like mind
And accords with the one thought-moment of joy;
    whereupon,
Equally with Vaidehī, he acquires the threefold wisdom
And is immediately brought to attain the eternal bliss of
    dharma-nature.

Genshin, having broadly elucidated the teachings of
    Śākyamuni's lifetime,
Wholeheartedly took refuge in the land of peace and urges all
    to do so;
Ascertaining that minds devoted to single practice are pro
    found, to sundry practice, shallow,
He sets forth truly the difference between the fulfilled land
    and the transformed land.

The person burdened with extreme evil should simply say the
    Name:
Although I too am within Amida's grasp,
Passions obstruct my eyes and I cannot see him;
Nevertheless, great compassion is untiring and illumines me
    always
[See also *Notes on Once-Calling and Many-Calling*, p. 480ff].

Master Genkū, well-versed in the Buddha's teaching,
Turned compassionately to foolish people, both good and evil;
Establishing in this remote land the teaching and realization
    that are the true essence of the Pure Land way,
He transmits the selected Primal Vow to us of the defiled
    world:

Return to this house of transmigration, of birth-and death,
Is decidedly caused by doubt.
Swift entrance into the city of tranquility, the uncreated,
Is necessarily brought about by shinjin.

The mahasattvas and masters who spread the sutras
Save the countless beings of utter defilement and evil.
With the same mind, all people of the present, whether monk
    or lay,
Should rely wholly on the teachings of these venerable
    masters
[*KGSS*, II. I, pp. 69-74].

b. Hymn on the *Nembutsu* and True Entrusting

135. Tradition-4

Honored One in the West, who surpasses all thought!
Bodhisattva Dharmākara, in his causal stage,
Made the Primal Vow, incomparable and all-embracing;
He established his supreme Vow of great compassion.

Five kalpas of profound thought passed in his selection; then,
With the perfect fruit of enlightenment, this Vow was
    fulfilled;
Ten kalpas have passed since its consummation.
The life of Amida is infinite, no measure can be taken;

The compassion deep and far-reaching, like space;
The wisdom replete, a vast ocean.
Pure, wondrous, without bound is Amida's land,
And possessed of great adornments;

The different virtues all reach fulfillment there—
It excels all Buddha-lands of the ten quarters.
Everywhere the Buddha sends light inconceivable and
    unhindered,
Breaking the immense night-dark of ignorance.

Wisdom-light in its brilliance wakens wisdom-eyes,
And the Name is heard throughout the ten quarters.
Only Buddhas can fathom the virtue of Amida Tathāgata;
Śākyamuni gathers Amida's dharma-treasure to bestow on the
    foolish.

Amida Buddha is the sun, illuminating all,
And has already broken through the darkness of our ignorance.
Still the clouds and mists of greed and desire, anger and
    hatred,
Cover as always the sky of pure shinjin.
But even when the sun, moon, and stars in their constellations
Are veiled by smoke, mist, clouds, or fog,
Beneath mist and cloud there is brightness, not dark.
I realize now that Amida's beneficent light surpasses even sun
    and moon.

Necessarily, then: We will reach the dawn of supreme, pure
    shinjin,

Whereupon the clouds of birth-and-death in the three realms
of existence will clear;
Then the pure, unhindered radiance will be luminous,
And the true body of dharma-realm of oneness will become
manifest.

When persons awaken shinjin and utter the Name, Amida's
light embraces and protects them,
And in this life they acquire immeasurable virtue.
This light, boundless and inconceivable, never ceases a
moment,
Nor does it differentiate by time, or place, or any
circumstance.

That the Buddhas protect persons of shinjin is truly beyond
doubt:
In all ten quarters alike they joyfully praise them.
The deluded and defiled and those of grave evil all equally
attain birth;
Those who slander the dharma or who lack seeds of
Buddhahood, when they turn about at heart, all go to the
Pure Land.

In the future, the sutras will all disappear;
The *Larger Sutra* alone is designed to remain a hundred years
thereafter.
How can one vacillate in doubt over the great Vow
[expounded in this sutra]?
Simply entrust yourself to Śākyamuni's true words!

The masters of India in the west, who clarified the teaching in
treatises,
And the eminent monks of China and Japan
Set forth the true intent of the Great Sage, the World-hero,
And revealed that the Tathāgata's Primal Vow accords with
the nature of beings.

Śākyamuni Tathāgata, on Mount Lankā,
Prophesied to the multitudes that in south India
Bodhisattva Nāgārjuna would appear in this world
To crush the views of being and of non-being;

113

Proclaiming the unexcelled Mahayana teaching,
He would attain the stage of joy and be born in the land of
    happiness.
Bodhisattva Nāgārjuna would appear in this world
To crush the one-sided views of being and nonbeing;

Proclaiming the unexcelled Mahayana teaching,
He would attain the stage of joy and be born in the land of
    happiness.
Nāgārjuna wrote the *Commentary on the Ten Bodhisattva
    Stages,*
And particularly sorrowing for those on the steep trails of
    difficult practice,

Therein reveals for all the great way of easy attainment:
With the mind of reverence, one should keep
And say the Name and quickly attain the stage of
    non-retrogression.
When shinjin is pure, one immediately sees the Buddha.

Bodhisattva Vasubandhu declares in a treatise that,
Relying on the sutras, he will reveal the true and real virtues.
Casting light on the universal Primal Vow, by which we leap
    crosswise beyond birth-and-death,
He expounds this Vow that surpasses conception;

He discloses the mind that is single so that we, fettered by
    blind passions,
Be saved by Amida's directing of virtue through the power of
    the Primal Vow.
When persons turn and enter the great treasure-ocean of
    virtue,
Necessarily they join the Tathāgata's great assemblage,

And when they have reached that lotus-held world,
They immediately realize the body of tranquility and equality.
Then sporting in the forests of blind passion, they manifest
    transcendent powers;
Entering the garden of birth-and-death, they assume various
    forms to guide others.

Turning toward the dwelling of the great teacher T'an-luan,
　　the ruler Hsiao of Liang
Always paid homage to him as a bodhisattva.
Bodhiruci, master of the Tripitaka, gave T'an-luan the Pure
　　Land teaching,
And T'an-luan, burning his scriptures on immortality, took
　　refuge in the land of bliss.

In his commentary on the treatise of Bodhisattva Vasubandhu
He reveals the Tathāgata's Vow at work in our saying of the
　　Name;
Our going and returning, directed to us by Amida, is based on
　　the Primal Vow.
When shinjin unfolds in foolish beings possessed of all blind
　　passions,

They immediately attain insight into the non-origination of all
　　existence
And come to realize that birth-and-death is itself nirvana.
Without fail they reach the land of immeasurable light
And universally guide sentient beings to enlightenment.

Tao-ch'o determined how difficult it is to fulfill the Path of
　　Sages
And reveals that only passage through the Pure Land gate is
　　possible for us.
He criticizes endeavor in the myriad good practices,
And encourages us solely to say the fulfilled Name embodying
　　true virtue.
With kind concern he teaches the three characteristics of
　　entrusting and non-entrusting,
Compassionately guiding all identically, whether they live
　　when the dharma survives as but form, when in its last
　　stage, or when it has become extinct.
Though persons have committed evil all their lives, when they
　　encounter the Primal Vow,
They will reach the world of peace and realize the perfect
　　fruit of enlightenment.

Shan-tao alone in his time clarified the Buddha's true intent,
And deeply drawing on the Primal Vow, he established the
　　true teaching.

Sorrowing at the plight of meditative and non-meditative
    practicers, and people of grave evil,
He reveals that Amida's light and Name are the cause of birth.

When one enters this gate leading to nirvana and encounters
    true mind,
Without fail one acquires the insights of confidence, joy, and
    awakening;
And attaining the birth that surpasses comprehension,
One immediately realizes the eternal bliss of suchness.

Genshin, having broadly elucidated the teachings of
    Śākyamuni's lifetime,
Wholeheartedly took refuge in the land of peace and urges all
    to do so;
In accord with the sutras and treatises, he chooses the teaching
    and practice of birth in the Pure Land:
Truly they are eye and limb for us of this defiled world.

Ascertaining the virtue of the single practice and the
    inadequacy of diversified practice,
He leads us to turn and enter the nembutsu-gate, which is
    true and real.
Solely by distinguishing profound and shallow minds of
    devotion,
He sets forth truly the difference between the fulfilled land
    and the transformed land.

Genkū, clearly understanding the sacred scriptures,
Turned compassionately to foolish people, both good and evil;
Establishing in this isolated land the teaching and realization
    that are the true essence of the Pure Land way,
He transmits "the selected Primal Vow" to us of the defiled
    world:

Return to this house of transmigration, of birth-and-death,
Is decidedly caused by doubt.
Swift entrance into the city of tranquility, the non-created,
Is necessarily brought about by shinjin.

Through their treatises and commentaries, these masters, all
    with the same mind,
Save the countless beings of utter defilement and evil.
All people of the present, both monk and lay,
Should rely wholly on the teachings of these venerable
    masters
[*Passages on the Pure Land Way*, I, pp. 304-309].

c. Hymns of the Pure Land Masters (*Kōsō Wasan* selections)

Note: The following hymns-poems (called *wasan* [poems in Japanese]), are selected
from the more extensive collection of verses which set forth in more detail the contributions of the seven teachers in Shinran's lineage.

136. Tradition-5

1. *Bodhisattva Nāgārjuna*

The World-honored one foretold
That a monk named Bodhisattva Nāgārjuna
Would appear in south India and would crush
The wrong views of being and nonbeing
[*Hymns of the Pure Land Masters*, p. 361, #2].

Mahasattva Nāgārjuna appeared in the world
And distinguished the paths of difficult and easy practice;
Thus he leads us, who are wandering in transmigration,
To board the ship of the universal Vow
[*Hymns of the Pure Land Masters*, I, p. 362, #4].

2. *Bodhisattva Vasubandhu*

Vasubandhu, author of the Treatise, took refuge
In the unhindered light with the mind that is single;
He teaches that by entrusting ourselves to the Vow's power,
We will reach the fulfilled land.
To take refuge, with the mind that is single,
In the Buddha of unhindered light filling the ten quarters
Is, in the words of Vasubandhu, author of the Treatise,
The mind that aspires to attain Buddhahood.
The mind that aspires to attain Buddhahood
Is the mind to save all sentient beings;

The mind to save all sentient beings
Is true and real shinjin, which is Amida's benefiting of others.
Shinjin is the mind that is single;
The mind that is single is the diamond-like mind.
The diamond-like mind is the mind aspiring for
    enlightenment;
This mind is itself Other Power
[*Hymns of the Pure Land Masters*, p. 365, #16-19].

3. *Teacher T'an-luan*

Though we had the words of Bodhisattva Vasubandhu,
If Master T'an-luan had not clarified them,
How could we come to know the mind and practice
Of vast, majestic virtues, which are Other Power?
[*Hymns of the Pure Land Masters*, p. 369, #31].

Amida has fulfilled the directing of virtue,
Which has two aspects: that for our going forth and that for
    our return.
Through these aspects of the Buddha's directing of virtue,
We are brought to realize both mind and practice.

The directing of virtue for our going forth is such that
When Amida's active means toward us reaches fulfillment;
We realize the shinjin and practice of the compassionate Vow;
Then birth-and-death is itself nirvana.

The directing of virtue for our return to this world is such
    that
We attain the resultant state of benefiting and guiding others;
Immediately reentering the world of beings,
We engage in the compassionate activity that is the virtue of
    Samantabhadra
[*Hymns of the Pure Land Masters*, p. 370, #34-36].

Through the benefit of the unhindered light,
We realize shinjin of vast, majestic virtues,
And the ice of our blind passions necessarily melts,
Immediately becoming water of enlightenment.

Obstructions of karmic evil turn into virtues;
It is like the relation of ice and water:
The more the ice, the more the water;
The more the obstructions, the more the virtues.
The ocean of the inconceivable Name does not hold
    unchanged
The corpses of the five grave offenses and slander of the
    dharma;
The myriad rivers of evil acts, on entering it,
Become one in taste with the ocean water of virtues
[*Hymns of the Pure Land Masters*, p. 371, #39-41].

Although initially there are nine grades of beings,
Because the birth attained through Amida's pure Primal Vow
Is birth that is no-birth,
The Pure Land is free of such discrimination
[*Hymns of the Pure Land Masters*, I, p. 372, #46].

4. *Teacher Tao-c'ho*

Setting aside the myriad practices of the Path of Sages,
Our teacher, Master Tao-ch'o,
Proclaims the single gate of the Pure Land way
As the only path that affords passage
[*Hymns of the Pure Land Masters*, I, p. 375, #55].

Though we commit evil throughout our lives,
If we say the nembutsu always
With our hearts turned wholly to Amida,
Our obstructions fall away by the [Vow's] spontaneous
    working
[*Hymns of the Pure Land Masters*, I, p. 376, #60].

5. *Teacher Shan-tao*

Manifested from the oceanlike great mind
Was Master Shan-tao;
For the sake of beings of this defiled world in the latter age,
He called on the Buddhas of the ten quarters to bear witness
    to his teaching
[*Hymns of the Pure Land Masters*, I, p. 377, #362].

If women did not entrust themselves to Amida's Name and
    Vow,
They would never become free of the five obstructions,
Even though they passed through myriads of kalpas;
How, then, would their existence as women be transformed?
[*Hymns of the Pure Land Masters*, p. 377, #64].

Performing auxiliary and right practices together is "mixed
    praxis";
Since those who endeavor in this way
Have not attained the mind that is single,
They lack the heart that responds in gratitude to the Buddha's
    benevolence.

Practicers who pray for worldly benefits,
Although they may perform chiefly the saying of the Buddha's
    Name,
Are also termed people of mixed praxis;
In rejecting such practice, it is taught that not one in a
    thousand attains birth
[*Hymns of the Pure Land Masters*, I, p. 378, #66, 67].

Master Shan-tao, calling the Buddhas to bear witness,
Led us to overturn the two minds of meditative and non-
    meditative practices;
Presenting the parable of the two rivers of greed and anger,
He ensured the safeguarding of the shinjin of the universal
    Vow
[(Shan-tao) *Hymns of the Pure Land Masters*, I, p. 379, #69].

The mind and practice of self-power do not bring one
Into the fulfilled land established through the power of the
    Vow;
Hence, sages of the Mahayana and Hinayana
All entrust themselves to Amida's universal Vow
[(Shan-tao) *Hymns of the Pure Land Masters*, I, p. 380, #72].

Śākyamuni and Amida are our father and our mother,
Full of love and compassion for us;
Guiding us through various skillful means,
They bring us to awaken the supreme shinjin

(*Hymns of the Pure Land Masters.* I, p. 380, #74).

Since shinjin arises from the Vow,
We attain Buddhahood through the nembutsu by the [Vow's]
    spontaneous working.
The spontaneous working is itself the fulfilled land;
Our realization of supreme nirvana is beyond doubt
[(Shan-tao) *Hymns of the Pure Land Masters*, I, p. 382, #82].

6. *Teacher Genshin*

Our teacher Genshin earnestly set forth,
From among all the teachings of the Buddha's lifetime,
The single gateway of the nembutsu,
And spread it among the beings of this defiled world in the
    latter age
[*Hymns of the Pure Land Masters*, I, p. 384, # 89].

My eyes being hindered by blind passions,
I cannot perceive the light that grasps me;
Yet the great compassion, without tiring,
Illumines me always
[*Hymns of the Pure Land Masters*, I, p. 385, #95].

7. *Teacher Genkū (Hōnen)*

As our teacher Genkū appeared in the world
And spread the One Vehicle of the universal Vow,
Throughout the entire country of Japan
Favorable conditions for the Pure Land teaching emerged
[*Hymns of the Pure Land Masters*, I, p. 387, # 98].

To encounter a true teacher
Is difficult even among difficult things;
There is no cause for endlessly turning in transmigration
Greater than the hindrance of doubt
[*Hymns of the Pure Land Masters*, I, p. 389, #109].

Amida Tathāgata, manifesting form in this world,
Appeared as our teacher Genkū;

The conditions for teaching having run their course,
He returned to the Pure Land
[*Hymns of the Pure Land Masters*, I, p. 390, #114].

The death of our teacher Genkū
Came in 1212, in early spring;
On the twenty-fifth day of the first month,
He returned to the Pure Land
[*Hymns of the Pure Land Masters*, I, p. 391, #117].

d. The Parable of the White Path by Shan-tao

Note: This famous parable is quoted in full in the chapter on Faith in *KGSS*, III. I, pp. 89-91. We will not quote it here. However, Shinran makes reference to it in his writing and it has become a major parable in Shin Buddhism, illustrating the human condition in this world and the path to salvation. The narrow White Path, four or five inches wide, passes between two rivers, one of water for lust and one of fire for greed and anger. Śākyamuni Buddha calls for the traveler to launch out onto the path, while Amida Buddha calls the person to come across the path to where he is. Through the encouragements of these two Buddhas, the traveler determines to cross the path and reach the Pure Land.

137. Tradition-6

It is great shinjin, rare and unsurpassed. It is the quick path difficult for people to accept. It is the true cause of attaining great nirvana. *It is the white path by which all virtues are fulfilled instantly. It is the ocean of shinjin that is itself suchness or true reality* [*KGSS*, III. I, p. 79, #1].

138. Tradition-7

Truly we know that, in the parable of the two rivers, *the white of the white path four or five inches wide contrasts with black. White* is the white act selected and adopted [in the Vow], the pure act that is the directing of virtue to us for our going forth. *Black* is the black activity of our ignorance and blind passions, the sundry good acts of those of the two vehicles and of human beings and devas. *Path* contrasts with trail. It is the one real, direct path of the Primal Vow, the supreme great way to complete nirvana. "Trail" refers to the bypaths of those of the two or the three vehicles, of the myriad good acts and practices. *Four or five inches wide* refers to the four elements and five aggregates that make up sentient beings. Awakens the pure mind of aspiration means to realize the diamond-like true mind. Since this is the ocean of great shinjin directed to us through the power of the Primal Vow, it cannot be defeated or broken. This is likened to diamond [*KGSS*, III. I, pp. 105-106, #46].

Thus, on reading Master Shan-tao's commentary, we find it written:

Someone on the western bank calls to him, "O traveler, with the mind that is single, with right-mindedness, come at once! I will protect you. Have no fear of plunging to grief in the water or fire."

Further it states:

The white path that spans the river is an image for the awakening of pure aspiration for birth in the midst of greed and anger, of all our blind passions. . . . Reverently embracing Śākyamuni's teaching in his exhortations to advance westward and obeying Amida's call to us with his compassionate heart, the traveler gives no thought to the two rivers of water and fire and entrusts himself to the path of the power of the Vow.

With these words we know that the pure aspiration that one awakens is not the mind of self-power of foolish beings. It is the mind directed to beings out of great compassion. Hence it is called "pure aspiration." Concerning the words, "With the mind that is single, with right-mindedness," then, "right-mindedness" refers to saying the Name. Saying the Name is the nembutsu. "The mind that is single" is deep mind. Deep mind is profound shinjin, which is steadfast. Steadfast, profound shinjin is the true mind. The true mind is the diamond-like mind. The diamond-like mind is the supreme mind. The supreme mind is the mind that is genuine, single, and enduring. The mind that is genuine, single, and enduring is the mind of great joy. When the mind of great joy is realized, this mind negates the three characteristics of non-entrusting; it accords with the three characteristics of entrusting. This mind is the mind of great enlightenment. The mind of great enlightenment is true and real shinjin. True and real shinjin is the aspiration for Buddhahood. The aspiration for Buddhahood is the aspiration to save all beings. The aspiration to save all beings is the mind that grasps sentient beings and brings them to birth in the Pure Land of happiness. This mind is the mind of ultimate equality. It is great compassion. This mind attains Buddhahood. This mind is Buddha. It is "practicing in accord with reality, being in correspondence with the Name." Let this be known [*Passages on the Pure Land Way*, I, pp. 313-314].

139. Tradition-8

Foolish beings: as expressed in the parable of the two rivers of water and fire, we are full of ignorance and blind passion. Our desires are countless, and anger, wrath, jealousy, and envy are overwhelming, arising without pause; to the very last moment of life they do not cease, or disappear, or exhaust themselves. When we, who are so shameful, go a step or two, little by little, along the White Path of the power of the Vow, we are taken in and held by the compassionate heart of the Buddha of unhindered light. It is fundamental that because of this we will unfailingly reach the Pure Land of happiness, whereupon we will be brought to realize the same enlightenment of great nirvana as Amida Tathāgata, being born in the flower of that perfect enlightenment. This is expressed, *Foolish beings, when they become mindful of the Vow, are immediately brought to the attainment of birth; this is made the essential purport.*

In the parable of the two rivers, "going a step or two" signifies the passage of one or two years. The direct teaching for which all Buddhas have appeared in this world—the Tathāgata's fundamental intent in his attainment of the way—has been to make central the bringing of sentient beings to think on Amida's Primal Vow so that they immediately attain birth [*Notes on Once-Calling and Many-Calling*, I, pp. 488-489].

D. Dimensions of Shinran's Interpretation of True Entrusting

1. The Status of Pure Land Teaching

Note: Pure Land teaching has ancient roots in India, though there was never an organized *cultus* there. The origins of Amitābha (Jap. Amida) Buddha are obscure.

It is not found in the Hīnayāna tradition. However certain texts such as the *Larger Pure Land Sūtra* had its origin in India, though like other Mahāyāna Sutras it was probably composed some time in the second or first century B.C.E. together with the emergence of Mahāyāna. There were numerous related texts. Of five Chinese translations of the text of the *Larger Sūtra*, Sanghavarman's version was made in 252 C.E. and is the most widely used. The earliest *Smaller Sūtra* was made in 402 C.E. by Kumarajiva, perhaps the most famous translator. Scholars consider that the *Sūtra of Contemplation* was written in China and a version appeared around 424-453 C.E.

However, by the fifth century the Pure Land teaching emerged as a form of monastic meditation based in visualizations developed by Hui-yuan (334-416 C.E.) and on the popular level with more mass appeal by T'an-luan and his successors. Each Buddha had his own Pure Land with correlated practice. However, Pure Land teaching came to denote the *cultus* of Amitābha, perhaps with Tao-ch'o, who distinguished the Sage Path of difficult practices from the Pure Land gate devoted to Amitābha. Pure Land teaching became a secondary teaching for people unable to engage in the disciplines of Buddhism and aimed at acquiring merit that would eventually give them the capacity to fulfill the practices.

Shan-tao, however, highlighted Amitābha and the practices of monastic meditation, but he also gave an important place to the popular recitation of Amitābha's name as a means to gain birth into the Pure Land. He rewrote the Eighteenth Vow to refer specifically to the practice of recitation. He also systematized the teaching that was later the center of Hōnen's movement and the background for Shinran. His parable of the White Path became very influential as demonstrating the urgency for devoting oneself to Amitābha and Śākyamuni and the character of mind necessary in engaging that teaching. According to the story, the imminent spiritual dangers we face in the world require decisive faith in responding to the urgings to launch out on the path by the Buddhas.

Mirroring this teaching, both Hōnen and Shinran proclaim the Pure Land teaching as the highest and ultimate teaching of Buddhism, aimed at the people of the last age in the decline of the Dharma (*mappō*). Their teachings were designed to demonstrate the superiority of Pure Land teaching because it was based on the Primal Vow of Amitābha Buddha.

In Mahāyāna Buddhism the principle of "One Vehicle" is important in singling out the supreme teaching among the diversity of schools in Buddhism. In the background of Shinran it reflects the Tendai teaching that exalts the *Lotus Sūtra* as the "One Vehicle." Shinran is very clear that Pure Land teaching, as transmitted to him by Hōnen, is the true essence of Buddhism and of the Pure Land tradition. The term is exclusive, since there is one vehicle leading to enlightenment, not two or three.

140. Pure Land-1

In the term "ocean of the One Vehicle," One Vehicle refers to the great vehicle (Mahayana). The great vehicle is the Buddha vehicle. To realize the One Vehicle is to realize the highest perfect enlightenment. The highest perfect enlightenment is none other than the realm of nirvana. The realm of nirvana is the

ultimate dharma-body. To realize the ultimate dharma-body is
to reach the ultimate end of the One Vehicle. There is no other
Tathāgata, there is no other dharma-body. Tathāgata is itself
dharma-body. Reaching the ultimate end of the One Vehicle is
without bound and without cessation. In the great vehicle there
are no "two vehicles" or "three vehicles." The two vehicles
and three vehicles lead one to enter the One Vehicle. The One
Vehicle is the vehicle of highest truth. There is no One Vehicle
other than the One Buddha-Vehicle, the Vow [*KGSS*, II. I, pp.
60-61 #84].

141. Pure Land-2

Respectfully I say to all people who aspire to be born in the
Pure Land: The ocean of the One Vehicle, the universal Vow,
has consummated the highest virtue, which is unhindered,
unbounded, supreme, profound, inexplicable, indescribable,
and inconceivable. How can this be? It is because the Vow
surpasses conceptual understanding. . . . The Vow liberates one
from the castle of the fetters of the three realms of existence
and closes the gateways to the twenty-five forms of existence.
It brings one to attainment of the true and real fulfilled land
and distinguishes the wrong from the right path. It dries up the
ocean of ignorance and causes beings to flow into the ocean
of the Vow. It brings one to ride on the ship of all-knowing
wisdom, so that one sails out into the ocean of beings. It brings
to perfect fulfillment the store of merit and wisdom and opens
the store of provisional means. Truly we should reverently
receive and accept it [*KGSS*, II. I, pp. 66-67, #100].

2. Amida: The Supreme Buddha

Note: The name Amida (Ch. Omito) is a transliteration of the Sanskrit Amitābha or
Amitāyus. Amitābha means Infinite Light, while Amitāyus is Infinite or Eternal Life.
Amita means infinite.

From among a large group of texts relating the career of Amida in Pure Land tradition, three texts attracted major attention, namely, the *Larger Pure Land Sūtra*, the
Contemplation Sūtra, and the *Smaller Pure Land Sūtra* or *Amida Sūtra*. The *Larger
Sūtra* gives Śākyamuni Buddha's account of Bodhisattva Dharmākara's renunciation
of kingship in a far-off country in the cosmos in order to create an ideal world where
people could attain enlightenment without obstruction. Selecting out all the good
points of all Buddha-lands, he achieved his goal by fulfilling with sincere practice

Forty-eight Vows before the Buddha of his time. Through five aeons of virtually infinite time he became Amida Buddha, residing in his perfect Pure Land in the West.

The Vows, which we have given above (59. Vows-1), became the most important in the tradition and the foundation of Shinran's thought.

The *Sūtra of Contemplation* was a major text in the tradition because, with others, it was the basis for the monastic-meditation practices of visualization of the Pure Land. Also, this Sūtra taught the validity of reciting the name of Amida for the most evil incapacitated people at the moment of their death as a means for birth into the Pure Land.

The *Smaller Amida Sūtra* gives a detailed description of the Pure Land and also promotes recitation of the name. It is widely used in funeral services.

Amida Buddha, though prominent, was initially one Buddha among many. With Shan-tao he became the superior Buddha as the focus of the *cultus*. Hōnen and Shinran established Amida as the Supreme Buddha whose virtue, embodied in his name, guarantees birth in the Pure Land when activated in recitation and true entrusting. In Shinran's thought Amida became the Eternal Buddha from whom all Buddhas are manifest. He stresses the aspect of Light which illuminates everything. Light cannot be seen and is formless, yet without it nothing can be seen. He is the Buddha-nature in all things as the expression in form of the inconceivable body of Truth.

Shinran also took up T'an-luan's concept of two bodies of the Buddha. However, he modified T'an-luan's idea by specifying that the Dharma body of suchness manifests itself in the Dharma body as compassion means, which is Amida Buddha as Buddha with form represented in the story of Dharmākara becoming Amida, a Fulfilled or perfected Buddha. In T'an-luan all Buddhas have these dimensions, but here it is singularly Amida who then manifests all Buddhas for the sake of guiding beings. Shinran put Amida in a class by himself as the ultimate or supreme expression of the Dharma body as Suchness, which is formless, inconceivable reality.

Mahāyāna Buddha developed a theory of three bodies of the Buddha to account for the variety of expression concerning Buddha in various sūtras. In the traditional understanding there is added to T'an-luan's concept, the historical dimension, the Transformed body of the Buddha, which is also a manifestation from the Fulfilled body. Hence, as Shinran states, one Buddha is all Buddhas and all Buddhas are one Buddha.

142. Amida-1

> *Take refuge in the Tathāgata of unhindered light filling the ten quarters: Take refuge* translates *Namu.* It means to follow the command of the Tathāgata. *The Tathāgata of unhindered light filling the ten quarters* is Amida Tathāgata. This Tathāgata is light. *Filling the ten quarters:* Filling means going to the ends; completely. The light goes completely to the ends of the worlds throughout the ten quarters. *Unhindered:* unimpeded by the blind passions and karmic evil of sentient beings. *Tathāgata*

of light: Amida Buddha. This Tathāgata is called the Buddha of light surpassing conceptual understanding and is the form of wisdom. Know that Amida pervades the lands countless as particles throughout the ten quarters [*Notes on the Inscriptions on Sacred Scrolls*, I, p. 501].

143. Amida-2

From this treasure ocean of oneness form was manifested, taking the name of Bodhisattva Dharmākara, who, through establishing the unhindered Vow as the cause, became Amida Buddha. For this reason Amida is the "Tathāgata of fulfilled body." Amida has been called "Buddha of unhindered light filling the ten quarters." This Tathāgata is also known as *Namu-fukashigikō-butsu* (Namu-Buddha of inconceivable light) and is the "dharma-body as compassionate means." "Compassionate means" refers to manifesting form, revealing a name, and making itself known to sentient beings. It refers to Amida Buddha. This Tathāgata is light. Light is none other than wisdom; wisdom is the form of light. Wisdom is, in addition, formless; hence this Tathāgata is the Buddha of inconceivable light. This Tathāgata fills the countless worlds in the ten quarters, and so is called "Buddha of boundless light." Further, Bodhisattva Vasubandhu has given the name, "Tathāgata of unhindered light filling the ten quarters" [*Notes on Once-Calling and Many-Calling*, I, pp. 486-487].

144. Amida-3

Since it is with this heart and mind of all sentient beings that they entrust themselves to the Vow of the dharma-body as compassionate means, this shinjin is none other than Buddha-nature. This Buddha-nature is dharma-nature. Dharma-nature is dharma-body. For this reason there are two kinds of dharma-body with regard to the Buddha. The first is called dharma-body as suchness and the second, dharma-body as compassionate means. Dharma-body as suchness has neither color nor form; thus, the mind cannot grasp it nor words describe it. From this oneness was manifested form, called dharma-body as compassionate means.

Taking this form, the Buddha announced the name Bhiksu Dharmākara and established the Forty-eight great Vows that surpass conceptual understanding. Among these Vows are the Primal Vow of immeasurable light and the universal Vow of immeasurable life, and to the form manifesting these two Vows Bodhisattva Vasubandhu gave the title, "Tathāgata of unhindered light filling the ten quarters." This Tathāgata has fulfilled the Vows, which are the cause of that Buddhahood, and thus is called "Tathāgata of the fulfilled body." This is none other than Amida Tathāgata [*Notes on "Essentials of Faith Alone,"* I, p. 461].

145. Amida-4

"Fulfilled" means that the cause for enlightenment has been fulfilled. From the fulfilled body innumerable personified and accommodated bodies are manifested, radiating the unhindered light of wisdom throughout the countless worlds. Thus appearing in the form of light called "Tathāgata of unhindered light filling the ten quarters," it is without color and without form; that is, it is identical with the dharma-body as suchness, dispelling the darkness of ignorance and unobstructed by karmic evil. For this reason it is called "unhindered light." "Unhindered" means that it is not obstructed by the karmic evil and blind passions of beings. Know, therefore, that Amida Buddha is light, and that light is the form taken by wisdom [*Notes on "Essentials of Faith Alone,"* I, pp. 461-462].

146. Amida-5

Unhindered light is great compassion;
This light is the wisdom of all the Buddhas.
In contemplating that world [of the Pure Land], it is
    boundless,
And vast and infinite, like space
[*Hymns of the Two Gateways of Entrance and Emergence,* I, p. 623].

147. Amida-6

Next, concerning "unhindered light," with the light of the sun or moon, when something has come between, the light does not reach us. Amida's light, however, being unobstructed by things, shines on all sentient beings; hence the expression, "Buddha of unhindered light." Amida's light is unhindered by sentient beings' minds of blind passions and karmic evil; hence the expression, "Buddha of unhindered light" [*The Virtue of the Names of Amida Tathāgata*, I, p. 655].

148. Amida-7

Amida Buddha is the light of wisdom. This light is called "Buddha of unhindered light." The reason for the expression "unhindered light" is that it is not obstructed or impeded by the minds of karmic evil and blind passions of all sentient beings of the ten quarters. In order to clarify and to bring us to know that the light of Amida surpasses conceptual understanding, the expression "I take refuge in the Tathāgata of unhindered light filling the ten quarters" is used. When we constantly hold in mind and say the Name of the Buddha of unhindered light, since it embodies the virtues of all the Buddhas of the ten quarters, in saying the Name of Amida, all the virtues and roots of good come to fullness in us [*The Virtue of the Names of Amida Tathāgata*, I, p. 657].

149. Amida-8

Next, concerning "light of joy," it is light attained with roots of good free of anger. Being free of anger means that externally there is no expression of anger or irritation and in the heart and mind there is no feeling of jealousy or envy. It is light attained with such a mind, and has been attained in order to sweep away the karmic evil of sentient beings' anger, wrath, hatred, and envy; hence the expression "light of joy" [*The Virtue of the Names of Amida Tathāgata*, I, p. 656].

150. Amida-9

Reverently contemplating the true Buddha and the true land, I find that the Buddha is the Tathāgata of inconceivable light and that the land also is the land of immeasurable light. Because they have arisen through the fulfillment of Vows of great compassion, they are called true fulfilled Buddha and land. There are relevant Vows that were made: the Vows of light and of life [*KGSS*, V. I, p. 177, #1].

151. Amida-10

Tathāgata is none other than nirvana;
Nirvana is called Buddha-nature.
Beyond our ability to attain it in the state of foolish beings,
We will realize it on reaching the land of peace
[*Hymns of the Pure Land*, I, p. 350, #93].

152. Amida-11

Countless Amida Buddhas reside
In the light of the Buddha of Unhindered Light;
Each one of these transformed Buddhas protects
The person of true and real shinjin
[*Hymns on Benefits in the Present* (*Hymns on the Pure Land*)], I, p. 355, #109].

153. Amida-12

When we take refuge in the Pure Land of Amida,
We take refuge in all the Buddhas.
To praise the one Buddha, Amida, with the mind that is single
Is to praise all the unhindered ones
[*Hymns of the Pure Land*, I, p. 336, #48].

3. Amida: The Eternal Buddha

154. Amida-13

It is taught that ten kalpas have now passed
Since Amida attained Buddhahood,
But he seems a Buddha more ancient
Than kalpas countless as particles
[*Hymns of the Pure Land*, I, p. 340, #55].

Shinran Note: Kalpas countless as particles: Suppose a great thousandfold world is [ground into powder and] made into ink, and with this ink one passes [through a thousand lands], then deposits a dot of it in one land with the tip of a brush, passes through another thousand lands, then deposits another dot of it, until all the ink is used up. If all the lands passed through were ground into dust and counted, the number of particles would be that of the kalpas expressed, "kalpas countless as particles."

Note: The statement by Shinran here is important to indicate how he went beyond the statement of the Sūtra to indicate the inconceivable duration of the Buddha's life. This imagery is based on the *Lotus Sūtra*, chapter sixteen, on the eternity of the Buddha, in that case, Śākyamuni. In effect, Shinran is claiming supreme status for Amida in place of Śākyamuni in the Tendai system which lay in the background of his teaching.

4. Amida: The Savior

155. Amida-14

The Buddha of unhindered light, when in the causal stage,
Awakened this aspiration and established the universal Vow.
The bodhisattva has already attained the mind of wisdom,
Attained the mind of skillful means and the unobstructed
mind,

Fulfilled the wondrous, joyous, excellent, and true mind,
And quickly realized supreme enlightenment.
The virtues of self-benefit and benefiting others have thus
been fulfilled;
Vasubandhu taught this as the gates of entrance and
emergence
[*Hymns of the Two Gateways of Entrance and Emergence*, I, p. 626].

156. Amida-15

Through the fulfillment of the Eighteenth Primal Vow, Bod-hisattva Dharmākara has become Amida Tathāgata, and the benefit that surpasses conceptual understanding has come to transcend all bounds; to express this, Bodhisattva Vasubandhu uses the words, "Tathāgata of unhindered light filling the ten quarters." Truly know, therefore, that without any differen-tiation between people good and bad, and regardless of one's having a heart of blind passions, all beings are certain to attain birth. Describing the manner of entrusting in the nembutsu of the Primal Vow, Genshin, Master of Eshin-in, states in his *Essentials for Attaining Birth*: "It makes no difference whether you are walking, standing still, sitting, or reclining, nor is there a choice to be made among times, places, or other circum-stances." He affirms beyond question that the person who has attained true shinjin has been grasped by the compassionate light. And so, Śākyamuni has taught, at the very moment that we, possessed of ignorance and blind passions, are born into the Pure Land of peace, we attain the supreme fruit of Buddhahood [*Lamp for the Latter Ages*, Letter 2. I, p. 526].

157. Amida-16

No thought of greed, anger, or harmfulness arose in his mind; he cherished no impulse of greed, anger, or harmfulness. He did not cling to objects of perception—color, sound, smell, taste. Abounding in perseverance, he gave no thought to the suffering to be endured. He was content with few desires, and without greed, anger, or folly. Always tranquil in a state of samādhi, he possessed wisdom that knew no impediment. He was free of all thoughts of falsity or deception. Gentle in countenance and loving in speech, he perceived people's thoughts and was attentive to them. He was full of courage and vigor, and being resolute in his acts, knew no fatigue. Seeking solely that which was pure and undefiled, he brought benefit to all beings. He revered the three treasures and served his teachers and elders. He fulfilled all the various kinds of practices, embellishing himself with great adornments, and brought all sentient beings to the attainment of virtues [*Larger Pure Land Sutra*, KGSS, I. I, pp. 95-96, #22].

158. Amida-17

The Buddha's intention is difficult to fathom. Nevertheless, reflecting on this [threefold] mind for myself alone, I find that all beings, an ocean of multitudes, have since the beginningless past down to this day, this very moment, been evil and defiled, completely lacking the mind of purity. They have been false and deceitful, completely lacking the mind of truth and reality. Thus, when the Tathāgata, in profound compassion for the ocean of all sentient beings in pain and affliction, performed bodhisattva practices for inconceivable millions of measureless kalpas, there was not a moment, not an instant, when his practice in the three modes of action was not pure, or lacked this true mind. With this pure, true mind, the Tathāgata brought to fulfillment the perfect, unhindered, inconceivable, indescribable, and inexplicable supreme virtues. The Tathāgata gives this sincere mind to all living beings, an ocean of beings possessed of blind passions, karmic evil, and false wisdom. This mind manifests the true mind of benefiting others. For this reason, it is completely untainted by the hindrance of doubt. This sincere mind takes as its essence the revered Name of supreme virtues [*KGSS*, III. I, p. 94, #21].

159. Amida-18

Concerning beings who are difficult to cure, the Buddha has taught the following. The *Nirvana Sutra* states:

Kasyapa, there are three kinds of people in the world who are hard to cure: those who slander the great vehicle, those who commit the five grave offenses, and those who lack the seed of Buddhahood (icchantika). These three sicknesses are the most severe in the world; they cannot be treated by sravakas, pra-tyekabuddhas, or bodhisattvas. Good sons, suppose a person is stricken with a disease that is certain to be fatal and is without cure, but treatment is given and there is appropriate medicine. Were it not for the treatment or appropriate medicine, in no way would it be possible to cure the illness. Know that the person would be certain beyond any doubt to die. Good sons, these three kinds of people are like this. Following the Buddha and bodhisattvas, they have heard and received the cure—they are able to awaken the mind of aspiration for supreme, perfect enlightenment. But sravakas, pratyekabuddhas, and bodhisat-tvas, whether they preach the dharma or not, cannot bring such people to awaken the mind aspiring for supreme, perfect enlightenment [*KGSS*, III. I, p. 143, #118; See also *Nirvana Sūtra*, *KGSS*, III. I, p. 125, #114].

160. Amida-19

Note: The following six *wasan*-stanzas, based on the *Larger Sūtra*, are used in chanting the *Shōshinge* (Hymn of True Faith).

Amida has passed through ten kalpas now
Since realizing Buddhahood;
Dharma-body's wheel of light is without bound,
Shining on the blind and ignorant of the world.

The light of wisdom exceeds all measure,
And every finite living being
Receives this illumination that is like the dawn,
So take refuge in Amida, the true and real light.

The liberating wheel of light is without bound;
Each person it touches, it is taught,
Is freed from attachments to being and non-being,
So take refuge in Amida, the enlightenment of
    non-discrimination.

The cloud of light is unhindered, like open sky;
There is nothing that impedes it.
Every being is nurtured by this light,
So take refuge in Amida, the one beyond conception.

The light of purity is without compare.
When a person encounters this light,
All bonds of karma fall away;
So take refuge in Amida, the ultimate shelter

The Buddha's light is supreme in radiance;
Thus Amida is called "Buddha, Lord of Blazing Light."
It dispels the darkness of the three courses of affliction,
So take refuge in Amida, the great one worthy of offerings
[*Hymns of the Pure Land*, pp. 325-326, #3-8].

Seeing the sentient beings of the nembutsu
Throughout the worlds, countless as particles, in the ten
    quarters,
The Buddha grasps and never abandons them,
And therefore is named "Amida"
[*Hymns of the Pure Land*, I, p. 347, #82].

161. Amida-20

Amida, who attained Buddhahood in the infinite past,
Full of compassion for foolish beings of the five defilements,
Took the form of Śākyamuni Buddha
And appeared in Gayā
[*Hymns of the Pure Land*, I, p. 349, #88].

162. Amida-21

"When sentient beings think on Amida
Just as a child thinks of its mother,
They indeed see the Tathāgata—who is never distant—
Both in the present and in the future"
[*Hymns of the Pure Land*, I, p. 357, #115].

163. Amida-22

Not discriminating at all between the poor and the rich and
wellborn:
Not discriminating means not choosing, not rejecting. *Poor*
means impoverished and in need. *At all* is for emphasis,
meaning "not at all"; it also means "with" and to lead. *Rich and
wellborn* indicates the wealthy and the people of rank. Thus,
without in the least differentiating among such people, Amida
leads each and every person to the Pure Land.
Not discriminating between the inferior and the highly gifted:
Inferior refers to those whose knowledge is shallow, limited,
and slight. *Highly gifted* indicates those with great ability for
learning. Amida does not choose between the two.
Not choosing the learned and those who uphold pure precepts:
Learned means to hear and believe in numerous and diverse
sacred teachings [*Notes on "Essentials of Faith Alone,"* I, pp. 457-
458].

5. Amida and True Entrusting

Note: The relationship of Amida Buddha and "true entrusting" or *shinjin* is a
hallmark or pivotal principle in Shinran's thought. The reality signified by Amida
Buddha is not a matter for speculation or rational proof. Rather, it is the symbol for
our awakening to our true nature as human beings and to the ground for our spiritual
transformation through encountering and hearing the Dharma which illumines our
life and world.

Hearing, for Shinran, is not the ordinary superficial hearing that we normally
employ in day-to-day relationships, but a hearing that grasps our being; that is, a
"seeing" of ourselves as we really are, as passion-ridden beings who cannot free
ourselves from our egoistic entrapments and addictions of many types. Yet, just
as the brighter the light, the more intense are the shadows, so we realize that this
illumination comes from a more profound source in life itself, which we call Amida
Buddha.

As we have shown above in connection with the Vow Fulfillment passage (62. Vow Completion-1, 63. Vow Completion-2), true entrusting is the manifestation in our human consciousness of Amida Buddha's true mind. For Shinran trust arises within us as the gift of Amida's Vow.

We do not generate entrusting by directing our will as in ordinary believing. Rather, our wills are naturally drawn, or awakened, to this reality as when a light enters a dark room and transforms the darkness, bringing everything to light.

Shinran's personal experience on Mount Hiei and his tutelage under Hōnen came to maturity in exile and his later teaching activity. With the ability of a "philosopher" he formulated a spiritual perspective that transcended the discriminations imposed by society and religious institutions. He opened the doors of salvation to all people, excluding none, and offered a comprehensive understanding of spiritual reality and experience.

164. Entrusting-1

This shinjin is indeed the superlative means of sweeping away doubt and attaining virtues. It is what is truly manifested in the sutra, all virtues being fulfilled instantly in it. It is the wondrous way of attaining longevity and deathlessness. It is the pure shinjin of vast, majestic virtue.

Hence, whether with regard to practice or to shinjin there is nothing whatever that has not been fulfilled through Amida Tathāgata's directing of virtue to beings out of the pure Vow-mind. It is not that there is no cause or that there is some other cause. Let this be known [*Passages on the Pure Land Way*, I, pp. 299-300].

165. Entrusting-2

Next, concerning entrusting, it is the ocean of shinjin, perfect and unhindered, that is the Tathāgata's consummately fulfilled great compassion. Hence, there is no mixture of doubt. It is therefore called "entrusting." The essence of entrusting is the sincere mind of benefiting others and directing virtues. . . .

Why? Because when the Tathāgata was performing bodhisattva practices, there was not a moment—not an instant—when his practice in the three modes of action was tainted by the hindrance of doubt. Because this mind is the Tathāgata's mind of great compassion, it necessarily becomes the truly decisive cause of attaining the fulfilled land. The Tathāgata, turning with compassion toward the ocean of living beings in pain and affliction, has given unhindered and vast pure shinjin to the ocean of sentient beings. This is called the "true and real shinjin that is [Amida's] benefiting of others" [*KGSS*, III. I, pp. 97-98, #28].

166. Entrusting-3

Never at variance with that land, one is drawn there by its spontaneous working (jinen). That land is the Pure Land of peace. *Never at variance* means not upside down, not at variance. Through the karmic power of the great Vow, the person who has realized true and real shinjin naturally is in accord with the cause of birth in the Pure Land and is drawn by the Buddha's karmic power; hence the going is easy, and ascending to and attaining the supreme great nirvana is without limit. Thus the words, *one is drawn there by its spontaneous working (jinen).* One is drawn there naturally by the cause of birth, the entrusting with sincere mind that is Other Power; this is the meaning of *drawn. Jinen* means that there is no calculating on the part of the practicer [*Notes on the Inscriptions on Sacred Scrolls*, I, pp. 496-497].

167. Entrusting-4

In brief, you should take that which is called Buddha of unhindered light as fundamental. You should understand that Buddha of unhindered light is spoken of thus in order to indicate that [this Buddha] seeks to save all beings, unhindered by their being wretched and evil [*A Collection of Letters*, Letter 9. I, p. 571].

168. Entrusting-5

Evil karma is profound: evil people who have committed the ten transgressions or the five grave offenses, people of evil karma who have reviled the teaching or who lack seeds for Buddhahood, those of scant roots of good, those of massive karmic evil, those of shallow inclination to good, those of profound attachment to evil—such wretched men as these, profound in various kinds of evil karma, are described by the word *profound. Profound* means bottomless. Good people, bad people, noble and low, are not differentiated in the Vow of the Buddha of unhindered light, in which the guiding of each person is primary and fundamental. Know that the true essence of the Pure Land teaching (*Jōdo Shinshū*) is that when we realize true and real shinjin, we are born in the true fulfilled land [*Notes on "Essentials of Faith Alone,"* I, p. 458].

But though the light of the sun is veiled by clouds and mists, beneath the clouds and mists there is brightness, not dark: . . . Although the sun and moon may be covered by clouds and mists, the darkness is dispelled and beneath the clouds and mists it is light; know that in the same way, although shinjin is overcast by clouds and mists of greed, desire, anger, and hatred, they form no obstruction to birth in the Pure Land [*Notes on the Inscriptions on Sacred Scrolls,* I, p. 519].

6. The Experience of True Entrusting

Note: True entrusting is an experience. It may not be cataclysmic or highly dramatic. Rather it is a kind of dawning, an awakening that may come about under many circumstances. In contrast with many other religions where a more intellectual assent accompanies belief, Shin Buddhism has "beliefs" but they are not the focal point of the faith. A commonly used image is the finger pointing to the moon. Doctrines and beliefs are the finger that enables a person to see the moon by focusing attention in some part of the night sky. Once the moon is seen, the finger is not needed, but it is retained to help point others toward the moon. It is the experience of the moon which is of major importance.

Shinran in a note describes true entrusting as "diamond-like." He describes it: "*Diamond-like:* never defeated, never decaying, never rent" (*Hymns of the Pure Land,* I, p. 348, note #85).

a. The Nature of True Entrusting

i. The Diamond-like True Mind

169. Entrusting-6

Know that the diamond-like true mind is the ocean of unhindered shinjin [*Gutoku's Notes,* I, p. 592].

170. Entrusting-7

Shinjin is the mind that is single; the mind that is single is the diamond-like mind; the diamond-like mind is the mind aspiring for great enlightenment; and this is Other Power that is true Other Power [*Lamp for the Latter Ages*, Letter 1. I, p. 523].

171. Entrusting-8

Faith is the heart and mind without doubt; it is shinjin, which is true and real. It is the heart and mind free of that which is empty and transitory. "Empty" means vain; "transitory" means provisional. "Empty" means not real, not sincere; "transitory" means not true. To be free of self-power, having entrusted oneself to the Other Power of the Primal Vow—this is *faith alone* [*Notes on "Essentials of Faith Alone,"* I, p. 451].

172. Entrusting-9

Shinjin is the source of enlightenment, the mother of virtues;
It nurtures all forms of goodness.
It cuts away the net of doubt and breaks free from the
    currents of desire;
It unfolds the supreme enlightenment of nirvana.
Shinjin harbors no defiled thoughts, it is pure,
Eradicating all arrogance; it is the root of reverence
And the foremost treasure of the dharma-store.
It is the hand of purity, holding all practices within itself.
Shinjin gives freely and ungrudgingly;
Shinjin rejoices and enters the Buddha-dharma;
Shinjin makes wisdom and virtues increase;
Shinjin unfailingly reaches the stage of Tathāgata.
Shinjin purifies the faculties, makes them clear and sharp;
Its power is firm and steadfast, nothing can destroy it.
Shinjin sunders forever the root of blind passions;
Shinjin leads one to seek the virtues of Buddha alone.
Shinjin knows no attachment to objects;
It separates one from the adversities, so that one attains the
    realm free of them.
Shinjin transcends the domain of maras
And manifests the path of unexcelled emancipation.
Shinjin keeps the seeds of virtues from destruction;
Shinjin nurtures the tree of enlightenment.
Shinjin makes supreme wisdom grow.
Shinjin makes all the Buddhas manifest
[*Garland Sutra, KGSS*, III. I, pp. 100-101, # 36].

Note: This poem is not itself a word of Shinran, but quoted by him it becomes part of his thought. It is taken from the *Garland Sūtra* or *Avatamsaka Sūtra*, which is a fundamental Mahāyāna text. It is an eloquent statement of how true entrusting expresses itself in our lives.

ii. True Entrusting and Buddha-Nature

173. Entrusting-10

The Nirvana Sutra states:

Good sons! Great love and great compassion are called Buddha-nature. Why? Because great love and great compassion always accompany the bodhisattva, just as shadows accompany things. All sentient beings will without fail ultimately realize great love and great compassion. Therefore it is taught, "All sentient beings are possessed of Buddha-nature." Great love and great compassion are Buddha-nature. Buddha-nature is Tathāgata.

Great joy and great even-mindedness are called Buddha-nature. Why? Because if a bodhisattva-mahasattva were incapable of the twenty-five forms of existence, he could not attain the supreme, perfect enlightenment. All sentient beings will ultimately attain great joy and great even-mindedness. Therefore it is taught, "All sentient beings are possessed of Buddha-nature." Great joy and great even-mindedness are none other than Buddha-nature. Buddha-nature is Tathāgata.

Buddha-nature is great shinjin. Why? Because through shinjin the bodhisattva-mahasattva has acquired all the paramitas from charity to wisdom. All sentient beings will without fail ultimately realize great shinjin. Therefore it is taught, "All sentient beings are possessed of Buddha-nature." Great shinjin is none other than Buddha-nature. Buddha-nature is Tathāgata.

Buddha-nature is called "the state of regarding each being as one's only child." Why? Because through the conditions of the state of regarding each being as one's only child, the bodhisattva has realized the mind of equality concerning all sentient beings. All sentient beings will without fail ultimately attain the state of regarding each being as one's only child. Therefore it is taught, "All sentient beings are possessed of Buddha-nature." The state of regarding each being as one's only child is none other than Buddha-nature. Buddha-nature is Tathāgata [*Nirvana Sutra, KGSS*, III. I, p. 99, #31].

Note: In this passage from the Mahāyāna *Nirvana Sūtra*, Shinran links true entrusting and Buddha-nature, a basic concept of general Mahāyāna. It is important because Hōnen had been accused by his critics of rejecting the concept of Buddha-nature and therefore not being truly Buddhist. Shinran restored that connection. In Shinran's view the experience and reality of true entrusting is the reality of Buddha-nature as the coming to consciousness of Amida's true-mind. Love and compassion are the qualities of a Buddha and their emergence in the devotee is the mark of Buddha-nature-true entrusting. It must be understood that in the transformation of mind that comes about through true entrusting we do not become Buddha itself, an ineffable state, but our nature as foolish being is illuminated and awareness of love and compassion awakened.

174. Entrusting-11

This mind attains Buddhahood. This mind is itself Buddha. There is no Buddha apart from this mind [Shan-tao, *KGSS*, III. I, p. 113, # 69].

iii. The Ultimacy of True Entrusting

175. Entrusting-12

Reverently contemplating Amida's directing of virtue for our going forth, I find there is great shinjin. Great shinjin is the superlative means for attaining longevity and deathlessness. It is the wondrous way to awaken aspiration for the pure and rejection of the defiled. It is the straightforward mind directed to us through the selected Vow. It is shinjin that actualizes Amida's profound and vast benefiting of others. It is true mind that is diamond-like and indestructible. It is pure shinjin by which a person easily reaches the Pure Land where no one goes. It is the mind that is single, realized by the person who is grasped and protected by the compassionate light. It is great shinjin, rare and unsurpassed. It is the quick path difficult for people to accept. It is the true cause of attaining great nirvana. It is the white path by which all virtues are fulfilled instantly. It is the ocean of shinjin that is itself suchness or true reality [*KGSS*, III. I, p, 79, #1].

iv. Two Types of Deep Entrusting

176. Entrusting-13

[It is stated:]

The second is deep mind. Deep mind is the deeply entrusting mind. There are two aspects. The first is to believe deeply and decidedly that you are in actuality a foolish being of karmic evil caught in birth-and-death, ever sinking and ever wandering in transmigration from innumerable kalpas in the past, with never a condition that would lead to emancipation. The second is to believe deeply and decidedly that Amida Buddha's Forty-eight Vows grasp sentient beings, and that allowing yourself to be carried by the power of the Vow without any doubt or apprehension, you will attain birth [Shan-tao, *KGSS*, III. I, p. 85, #13].

177. Entrusting-14

The deeply entrusting mind expounded above is the diamond-like mind that is the consummation of Other Power, the ocean of true and real shinjin that is the supreme One Vehicle.

Reflecting on the meaning of this passage, we find that in deeply entrusting mind there are seven forms of deep entrusting and six forms of decidedness.

The seven forms of deep entrusting are:

1. Deep entrusting is "to believe deeply and decidedly that you [are a foolish being of karmic evil caught in birth-and-death] . . ." This is, in other words, shinjin that is self-benefiting.

2. Deep entrusting is "to believe deeply and decidedly . . . being carried by the power of the Vow . . . [they will attain birth]." This is, in other words, the ocean of shinjin that is [Amida's] benefiting of others.

3. To believe deeply and decidedly in the *Contemplation Sutra*.

4. To believe deeply and decidedly in the *Amida Sutra*.

5. To entrust oneself to the Buddha's words alone and rely decidedly on the practice [of the nembutsu].

6. In accord with the [*Contemplation*] *Sutra*, to entrust oneself deeply [to the practice of the nembutsu].

7. Further, the deep trust that is deep mind is to decidedly settle one's own mind [*Gutoku's Notes*, I, pp. 604-605].

b. Reception of True Entrusting

Note: The following entries, 178. Entrusting-15-184. Entrusting-21, express Shin Buddhism as a teaching of transformation. It is not merely changing behavior externally, but an inner condition of the mind. One's way of understanding and thinking about oneself is changed. The egocentric self is given a broader and deeper context for seeing the self in relation to reality and other selves. The personality is not. "Turning of the mind" is a word used for conversion and we may view it as a redirection of the energy of the self. As an example, we may note Shinran himself. He laments that he poses as a teacher as a result of his passion, but at the same time that energy is placed at the service of humanity. The drive to serve the self becomes a means of serving and sharing with others.

178. Entrusting-15

My fervent wish is this: Whether monk or layperson, when on board the ship of the great compassionate Vow, let pure shinjin be the favorable wind, and in the dark night of ignorance, let the jewel of virtue be a great torch. Those whose minds are dark and whose understanding deficient, endeavor in this way with reverence! Those whose evils are heavy and whose karmic obstructions manifold, deeply revere this shinjin! Ah, hard to encounter, even in many lifetimes, is the decisive cause of birth, Amida's universal Vow; and hard to realize, even in myriads of kalpas, is pure shinjin that is true and real. If you should come to realize shinjin, rejoice at the conditions from the distant past that have brought it about. But if in this lifetime still you are entangled in a net of doubt, then unavoidably you must pass once more in the stream of birth-and-death through myriads of kalpas and countless lives. Hear and reflect on the truth that one is grasped, never to be abandoned—the teaching of attaining birth in the Pure Land with transcendent quickness and ease; and let there be no wavering or apprehension [*Passages on the Pure Land Way*, I, p. 303; See also *KGSS*, Preface, I, p. 4].

179. Entrusting-16

"To abandon the mind of self-power" admonishes the various and diverse kinds of people—master of Hinayana or Mahayana, ignorant beings good or evil—to abandon the conviction that one is good, to cease relying on the self; to stop reflecting knowingly on one's evil heart, and further to abandon the judging of people as good and bad. When such shackled foolish beings—the lowly who are hunters and peddlers—thus wholly entrust themselves to the Name embodying great wisdom, the inconceivable Vow of the Buddha of unhindered light, then while burdened as they are with blind passion, they all attain supreme nirvana. "Shackled" describes us, who are bound by all our various blind passions. Blind passions refers to pains which torment the body and afflictions which distress the heart and mind. The hunter is one who slaughters many kinds of living things; this is the huntsman. The peddler is one who buys and sells things; this is the trader. They are called "low." Such peddlers, hunters, and others are none other than we, who are like stones and tiles and pebbles.

I can make bits of rubble change into gold

This is a metaphor. When we entrust ourselves to the Tathāgata's Primal Vow, we, who are like bits of tile and pebbles, are turned into gold. Peddlers and hunters, who are like stones and tiles and pebbles, are grasped and never abandoned by the Tathāgata's light. Know that this comes about solely through true shinjin. We speak of the light that grasps because we are taken into the heart of the Buddha of unhindered light; thus, shinjin is said to be diamond-like [*Notes on "Essentials of Faith Alone,"* I, pp. 459-460].

180. Entrusting-17

The Larger Amida Sutra states:

One will be able to abandon this world, transcending and parting from it. When one is born in that land of Amida Buddha, one cuts off crosswise the five evil courses, and they close naturally. Ascending the way is without limit; to go is easy and yet no one is born there. Never at variance with that land, one is drawn there by its spontaneous working.

Concerning the term *cut off*: because we have awakened the mind that is single, which is directed to us for our going forth,

there is no further state of existence into which we must be
born, no further realm into which we must pass. Already the
causes leading to the six courses and the four modes of birth
have died away and their results become null. Therefore we
immediately and swiftly cut off birth-and-death in the three
realms of existence. Hence, *cut off.* The *four currents* are the four
turbulent currents. They also refer to birth, aging, sickness, and
death [*KGSS*, III. I, p. 115, #77-78].

Note: The Larger Amida Sūtra is an older version, perhaps from the second century
C.E., of the Larger Pure Land Sūtra which became the central text of the Pure Land
tradition. It was translated by Chih-ch'ien (late second-early third centuries C.E.)
    The "six courses" refer to the various levels and conditions of existence in trans-
migration or the stream of birth and death: hells, hungry spirits, animals, human
beings, fearsome (sometimes evil) spirits, gods. They are common to all sects. The
three realms of existence are the worlds of desire, form, and formless, in Buddhist
cosmology. The four modes of birth, such as womb-birth, birth from eggs, birth
from moisture, and transformation-births from heaven, hell, or states in-between,
lives as a result of karma.
    We may also note that the term "immediately" expresses the idea of sudden
enlightenment or fulfillment which is a criterion of the highest level of Mahāyāna
teaching in Mahāyāna systems of critical classification of doctrine. It contrasts with
gradual attainment.

181. Entrusting-18

Contemplating true and real shinjin, I find there is the one
thought-moment. One thought-moment expresses the ultimate
brevity of the instant of realization of shinjin and manifests the
vast inconceivable mind of joyfulness [*KGSS*, II. I, pp. 110-111,
#60; See statement by Wang Juh-hsiu, *KGSS*, III. I, p. 122 , #99; *Notes
on Once-Calling and Many-Calling*, I, p. 474].

182. Entrusting-19

They then attain birth: then (*soku*) means immediately, without
any time elapsing, without a day passing [*Notes on Once-Calling
and Many-Calling*, I, p. 474].

183. Entrusting-20

When one realizes true and real shinjin, one is immediately grasped and held within the heart of the Buddha of unhindered light, never to be abandoned.

"To grasp" (*sesshu*) means to take in (*setsu*) and to receive and hold (*shu*). When we are grasped by Amida, immediately—without a moment or a day elapsing—we ascend to and become established in the stage of the truly settled; this is the meaning of *attain birth* [*Notes on Once-Calling and Many-Calling*, I, p. 475].

Note: The stage of the truly settled or assured means that one's birth in the Pure Land is completely determined because it is the working of Amida's Vow power. The distinctive feature of Shinran's thought on this point is that it becomes a reality in this life. He compares the certainty of Enlightenment for those with *shinjin* to Maitreya, who is designated as the next Buddha. Though he is really a bodhisattva still, he is called a Buddha because of his certain attainment of Buddhahood. See entry 210. Status-2.

In traditional Pure Land teaching, the attainment of this state came with birth in the Pure Land where the conditions enabling Enlightenment were present. It is also known as the state of non-retrogression, because there is nothing to obstruct the sure progress to Enlightenment. Shinran makes this all a matter of the present. In effect, our birth in the Pure Land has already occurred at the moment of true entrusting. This is because its reality is not our doing, but the reality of Amida's Vow working in us.

184. Entrusting-21

To respond to your question concerning the cause of birth, at the moment we realize true and real shinjin, we receive [the benefit of] Amida's grasping, never to abandon us; hence, we unfailingly come to dwell in the Tathāgata's Vow. We find this in the compassionate Vow, which states: "If, when I attain Buddhahood, the human beings and devas in my land do not dwell among the settled and necessarily attain nirvana, may I not attain the supreme enlightenment." If it is understood that the person of shinjin dwells in the stage of the truly settled, there is no calculation on the part of the practicer; hence, we speak of Other Power, in which no working is true working. Since practicers have become free of calculation as to whether they are good or evil, pure or defiled, it is said that no working is true working [*A Collection of Letters*, Letter #7. I, pp. 573-574].

185. Entrusting-22

Solely making beings turn about instructs us, single-heartedly make your heart turn about!
Turn about means to overturn and discard the mind of self-power. Since those people who are to be born in the true fulfilled land are without fail taken into the heart of the Buddha of unhindered light, they realize diamond-like shinjin. Thus, they "abundantly say the Name" [*Notes on "Essentials of Faith Alone,"* I, p. 459].

Note: The principle of absolute Other-Power means that there is no contribution from the human side in effecting salvation. Nevertheless, on the level of ordinary human experience, the challenge of the teaching must be presented and appeals for trust proclaimed that awaken us to the reality of Amida's Vow. This is a paradox of religious faith which is similarly found in other traditions of Other-Power such as Islam and Calvinism in Christianity.

186. Entrusting-23

Those who attain true and real shinjin
Immediately join the truly settled;
Thus having entered the stage of non-retrogression,
They necessarily attain nirvana
[*Hymns of the Pure Land*, I, p. 341, #59].

187. Entrusting-24

Through the benefit of the unhindered light,
We realize shinjin of vast, majestic virtues,
And the ice of our blind passions necessarily melts,
Immediately becoming water of enlightenment.
Obstructions of karmic evil turn into virtues;
It is like the relation of ice and water:
The more the ice, the more the water;
The more the obstructions, the more the virtues.

The ocean of the inconceivable Name does not hold
    unchanged
The corpses of the five grave offenses and slander of the
    dharma;

The myriad rivers of evil acts, on entering it,
Become one in taste with the ocean water of virtues.

Rivers of blind passions, on entering the ocean—
The great, compassionate Vow
Of unhindered light filling the ten quarters—
Become one in taste with that sea of wisdom
[*Hymns of the Pure Land Masters* (T'an-luan), I, p. 371, #39-42].

188. Entrusting-25

When the waters of the mind entrusting to Other Power enter
The ocean waters of Amida's Vow of wisdom,
Then in accord with the nature of the true and real fulfilled
    land,
Blind passions and enlightenment come to be of one taste
[*Hymns of the Dharma-Ages*, I, p. 404, #23].

189. Entrusting-26

When the waters—the minds, good and evil, of foolish beings
Have entered the vast ocean
Of Amida's Vow of wisdom, they are immediately
Transformed into the mind of great compassion
[*Hymns of the Dharma-Ages*, I, pp. 408-409, #40].

190. Entrusting-27

This is a metaphor stating that when lesser sages, foolish beings,
those committing the five grave offenses, those reviling the
dharma, those keeping no precepts, those devoid of seeds for
Buddhahood—when any such people have experienced a turnabout and entered the ocean of true and real shinjin, they are
like river waters becoming one in taste with the ocean upon
entering it [*Notes on the Inscriptions on Sacred Scrolls*, I, p. 519].

c. The Mind of True Entrusting

191. Entrusting-28

The term *practicing the saying of the Name* alone that occurs in Master [Shan-tao] is single practice; *wholehearted thought* is single-heartedness. Thus, the term *one thought-moment* in the passage teaching the fulfillment of the Vow is wholehearted thought. Wholehearted thought is deep mind. Deep mind is deep entrusting. Deep entrusting is deep entrusting that is steadfast and firm. Deep entrusting that is steadfast and firm is decisive mind. Decisive mind is supreme mind. Supreme mind is true mind. True mind is enduring mind. Enduring mind is genuine mind. Genuine mind is mindfulness. Mindfulness is the true and real mind that is single. The true and real mind that is single is the mind of great joy. The mind of great joy is true and real shinjin. True and real shinjin is the diamond-like mind. The diamond-like mind is the mind that aspires for Buddhahood. The mind that aspires for Buddhahood is the mind to save sentient beings. The mind to save sentient beings is the mind to grasp sentient beings and bring them to birth in the Pure Land of peace. This mind is the mind aspiring for great enlightenment. This mind is the mind of great compassion. For this mind arises from the wisdom of immeasurable light. The ocean of the Vow is characterized by sameness; therefore, the aspiration awakened is the same. Since the aspiration awakened is the same, the path is the same. Since the path is the same, the great compassion is the same. For great compassion is the right cause of realizing the enlightenment of Buddha [*KGSS*, III. I, pp. 112-113, #66].

Note: We should take note that the mind of true entrusting involves a deep conviction and commitment. As Shinran depicts the quality of true entrusting, he concludes that its mark is great compassion, which like the compassion of Amida, aspires for the welfare of all beings. It is not only an awareness to be enjoyed solitarily in the self, but aspires to reach out to the world as the Buddha has done in his Vows.

192. Entrusting-29

As to the matter you raise, although the one moment of shinjin and the one moment of nembutsu are two, there is no nembutsu separate from shinjin, nor is the one moment of shinjin separate from the one moment of nembutsu. The reason is that the practice of nembutsu is to say it perhaps once, perhaps ten times, on hearing and realizing that birth into the Pure Land

is attained by saying the Name fulfilled in the Primal Vow. To
hear this Vow and be completely without doubt is the one
moment of shinjin. Thus, although shinjin and nembutsu are
two, since shinjin is to hear and not doubt that you are saved by
only a single pronouncing, which is the fulfillment of practice,
there is no shinjin separate from nembutsu; this is the teaching
I have received. You should know further that there can be no
nembutsu separate from shinjin. Both should be understood to
be Amida's Vow. Nembutsu and shinjin on our part are themselves the manifestation of the Vow [*Lamp for the Latter Ages*,
Letter 11. I, p. 538].

Note: In the background of Shinran's statement of the inseparability of true entrusting
and the recitation of the name, or *nembutsu*, is the use in general Buddhism of the
recitation of the name as a *mantra*, a specially charged word. People believe in the
power of such words and recite it for benefits and protection, as well as to gain merit
for birth in the Pure Land. For Shinran the fundamental issue is the turnabout, the
transformation of the mind through the arising of true entrusting in Amida's Vow.
The exclamation *Namu amida butsu* spontaneously arises from this inner movement
of the heart-mind. The first evocation indicates that one has been grasped never to
be abandoned by the Buddha. All other evocations are responses of gratitude to this
wondrous experience. Therefore, they are inseparable, both entrusting and recitation
being expressions of the Vow and not a contrivance of the devotee.

193. Entrusting-30

With sincere mind entrusting themselves: Sincere means true and
real. "True and real"; this is what *sincere mind* means. From the
very beginning sentient beings, who are filled with blind passions, lack a mind true and real, a heart of purity, for they are
possessed of defilements, evil, and wrong views. *Entrusting* is
to be free of doubt, believing deeply and without any double-
mindedness that the Tathāgata's Primal Vow is true and real.
This *entrusting with sincere mind*, then, is that arising from the
Vow in which Amida urges every being throughout the ten
quarters, "Entrust yourself to my Vow, which is true and real";
it does not arise from the hearts and minds of foolish beings of
self-power [*Notes on the Inscription on Sacred Scrolls*, I, p. 493].

Note: Shinran was very astute in attributing the sincerity required in religious faith to
Amida and not the devotee. He indicates in his confessions his own insincerity as a
foolish being. We are always being told that we must be sincere in doing something.
However, it is impossible to know one's own sincerity, because on reflection, we

see our hidden agendas and ulterior motives that complicate our feelings. Sincerity is a value that becomes visible to others through consistent action. It is not something we can claim as our virtue.

194. Entrusting-31

To take refuge, with the mind that is single,
In the Buddha of unhindered light filling the ten quarters
Is, in the words of Vasubandhu, author of the Treatise,
The mind that aspires to attain Buddhahood.

The mind that aspires to attain Buddhahood
Is the mind to save all sentient beings;
The mind to save all sentient beings
Is true and real shinjin, which is Amida's benefiting of others
[*Hymns of the Pure Land Masters*, p. 365, #17-18].

Shinjin is the mind that is single;
The mind that is single is the diamond-like mind.
The diamond-like mind is the mind aspiring for
    enlightenment;
This mind is itself Other Power
[*Hymns of the Pure Land Masters* (Vasubandhu), I, p. 365, #17-19].

195. Entrusting-32

Concerning the aspiration for supreme enlightenment in the
    Pure Land path,
We are urged to realize the mind that seeks to attain
    Buddhahood;
The mind that seeks to attain Buddhahood
Is itself the mind that seeks to save all sentient beings
[*Hymns of the Dharma-Ages*, I, p. 403, #20].

196. Entrusting-33

Hence *with singleness* furthermore means "Be of one-mind!" Be wholly of single practice and of one mind! Moreover, *singleness* means "one." *Wholly* implies, "Do not be of two minds!" Thus, not wavering in any way is one mind. Amida grasps, never to abandon, such a person of this single practice and one mind, and therefore is called Amida. . . [*Notes on "Essentials of Faith Alone,"* I, p. 463].

Note: Following the teaching of Vasubandhu in his treatise on the Pure Land, Shinran focuses on the term *single-minded* as a central characteristic of true entrusting. It is consonant with his emphasis on the inner awareness of Amida's compassion and wisdom, which moves the heart-mind to devote itself to Amida and Amida alone. This feature reflects itself even in later tradition where Shin people were known as the *Ikkō-shu*, single-minded followers who totally relied on Amida.

d. Three Minds of the Eighteenth Vow

Note: Shinran, by elevating the *Larger Pure Land Sūtra* to the supreme teaching of the Pure Land school, shifted the emphasis of the teaching from the principle of striving for enlightenment through meritorious practices, including reciting the *nembutsu*, to the inward arising of trust and reliance upon the fact that we are saved through Amida's Vow. This trust, though viewed by Shinran as a single movement of the heart-mind, originating with the transfer of Amida's true mind, had three aspects indicated by the Eighteenth Vow: sincerity, joyful trust, and aspiration for birth in the Pure Land. Shinran's focus on the Eighteenth Vow freed the principle of the three minds from the disciplinary connotation that is associated with the three minds in the *Contemplation Sūtra*, which had been central to the Pure Land teaching. In his style of interpretation, the two sets of three minds are distinct on the surface level, as observed in the texts, though they are united as expressions of Amida's mind on the deeper spiritual level of Amida's intention to save all beings. See Section III, C-2 above, pp. 84-85.

197. Entrusting-34

Looking into the literal meanings of the three minds, I find that the three should be taken as one. Why? In "sincere mind" (*shishin*), *shi* means truth, reality, sincerity; *shin* means seed, kernel. In "entrusting" (*shingyō*), *shin* means truth, reality, sincerity, fullness, ultimacy, accomplishment, reliance, reverence, discernment, distinctness, clarity, faithfulness; *gyō* means aspiration, wish, desire, exultation, delight, joy, gladness, happiness. In "aspiration for birth" (*yokushō*), *yoku* means wish, desire, awakening, awareness; *shō* means accomplishment, fulfillment, performance, establishment [*KGSS*, III. I, p. 94, #20].

198. Entrusting-35

Further, to consider the three minds, the first is sincere mind. This is the true and real mind that perfectly embodies and fully possesses the Tathāgata's consummate virtues. Amida Tathāgata gives to all these true and real virtues [of sincere mind]; this is the significance of the Name being the essence of sincere mind. By contrast, the sentient beings of the ten quarters are utterly evil and defiled and completely lack a mind of purity. Being false and poisoned, they lack a true and real mind. Thus, for the Tathāgata, when performing practices as a bodhisattva in the stage leading to Buddhahood, there was not a single moment—not an instant—in his endeavor in the three modes of action when his heart was not pure, true, and real. The Tathāgata directs this pure, true mind to all sentient beings [*Passages on the Pure Land Way*, I, pp. 310-311].

199. Entrusting-36

We see clearly that sincere mind is the mind that is the seed of truth, reality, and sincerity; hence, it is completely untainted by the hindrance of doubt. Entrusting is the mind full of truth, reality, and sincerity; the mind of ultimacy, accomplishment, reliance, and reverence; the mind of discernment, distinctness, clarity, and faithfulness; the mind of aspiration, wish, desire, and exultation; the mind of delight, joy, gladness, and happiness; hence, it is completely untainted by the hindrance of doubt. Aspiration for birth is the mind of wish, desire, awakening, and awareness; the mind of accomplishment, fulfillment, performance, and establishment. It is the mind of great compassion directing itself to beings; hence, it is completely untainted by the hindrance of doubt.

Here, in considering the literal meanings of the terms for them, we find that the three minds are the mind of truth and reality, free of any taint of falsity; they are the mind right and straightforward, free of any taint of wrong and deceit. Truly we know, then, that this is called shinjin because it is untainted by the hindrance of doubt. Shinjin is the mind that is single. The mind that is single is shinjin that is true and real. Therefore, the author of the Treatise states, at the outset, "With the mind that is single." Reflect on this [*KGSS*, III. I, p. 94, #20].

200. Entrusting-37

Reflecting within myself on the birth through the three minds taught in the *Contemplation Sūtra*, I see that this refers to the three minds of self-power that are individually different for each practicer. They are taught in order to bring each practicer to take refuge in the threefold shinjin of the *Larger Sūtra*, and to enter into the threefold shinjin [*Gutoku's Notes*, I, p. 619].

e. The Unity of the Three Minds

201. Entrusting-38

Truly we know that although the terms "sincere mind," "entrusting," and "aspiration for birth" differ, their significance is the same. Why? Because these three minds are already completely untainted by the hindrance of doubt. They are therefore the true and real mind that is single. This is called the diamond-like true mind. The diamond-like true mind is true and real shinjin. True and real shinjin is unfailingly accompanied by [saying] the Name. [Saying] the Name, however, is not necessarily accompanied by shinjin that is the power of the Vow. Thus, the author of the Treatise opens with the words, "I, with the mind that is single." Further he states, "One wishes to be in correspondence with [the Name] by practicing in accord with reality" [*KGSS*, III. I, p. 107, #50].

Note: We should observe here Shinran's important statement that true entrusting inspires the recitation of the Name or *nembutsu*. *Nembutsu* is not a means to gain salvation but a reflection of it. Shinran acknowledges there is *nembutsu* without true entrusting because he lived in an environment where *nembutsu* was recited for benefits and merit. By itself it cannot produce true entrusting. Nevertheless, they are inseparable as *nembutsu* spontaneously results from the awareness of Amida's embrace and all *nembutsu* following that is for the sake of gratitude as we are constantly aware of the Buddha's compassion and wisdom.

202. Entrusting-39

Sincere mind, then, is the mind that is the seed of sincerity, the kernel of truth. It is therefore altogether free of doubt.

Entrusting is the mind full of truth, reality, and sincerity, the mind of ultimacy, accomplishment, reliance, and reverence; the mind of aspiration, desire, discernment, and distinctness; the mind of happiness, joy, and gladness. It is therefore altogether free of doubt. Aspiration for birth is the mind of desire and wish, the mind of awakening, knowing, completion, and establishment. Thus, these three minds are all true and real and completely free of doubt. Because they are free of doubt, they are the mind that is single [*Passages on the Pure Land Way*, I, p. 310].

Note: See below j. True Entrusting and Doubt, p. 168.

203. Entrusting-40

Since these three minds are all directed to beings by the mind of great compassion they are pure, true, and real, and completely free of doubt. Hence they are the mind that is single [*Passages on the Pure Land Way*, I, p. 313].

204. Entrusting-41

With these words we know that the pure aspiration that one awakens is not the mind of self-power of foolish beings. It is the mind directed to beings out of great compassion. Hence it is called "pure aspiration." Concerning the words, "With the mind that is single, with right-mindedness," then, "right-mindedness" refers to saying the Name. Saying the Name is the *nembutsu*. "The mind that is single" is deep mind. Deep mind is profound shinjin, which is steadfast. Steadfast, profound shinjin is the true mind. The true mind is the diamond-like mind. The diamond-like mind is the supreme mind. The supreme mind is the mind that is genuine, single, and enduring. The mind that is genuine, single, and enduring is the mind of great joy. When the mind of great joy is realized, this mind negates the three characteristics of non-entrusting; it accords with the three characteristics of entrusting. This mind is the mind of great enlightenment. The mind of great enlightenment is true and real shinjin. True and real shinjin is the aspiration for Buddhahood. The aspiration for Buddhahood is the aspiration to save all beings. The aspiration to save all beings is the mind that grasps sentient beings and brings them to birth in the Pure Land of happiness. This mind is the mind of ultimate equality. It is great compassion. This mind attains Buddhahood. This mind is Buddha. It is "practicing in accord with reality, being in correspondence with the Name." Let this be known. Here ends the explanation that the three minds are the mind that is single [*Passages on the Pure Land Way*, I, pp. 313-314].

205. Entrusting-42

Bodhisattva Vasubandhu declares that this true and real shinjin is none other than the aspiration to become a Buddha. This is the great thought of enlightenment of the Pure Land. This aspiration for Buddhahood is none other than the wish to save all beings. The wish to save all beings is the wish to carry all beings across the great ocean of birth-and-death. This shinjin is the aspiration to bring all beings to the attainment of supreme nirvana; it is the heart of great love and great compassion. This shinjin is Buddha-nature and Buddha-nature is Tathāgata. To realize this shinjin is *to rejoice and be glad.* People who rejoice and are glad are called "people equal to the Buddhas" [*Notes on "Essentials of Faith Alone,"* I, p. 463].

206. Entrusting-43

This is shinjin, which is called "the mind that is single."
Foolish beings possessed of blind passions
Attain nirvana without severing blind passions;
This is the virtue of the land of happiness, which is the
    spontaneous working [of the Vow]
[*Hymns of the Two Gateways of Entrance and Emergence*, I, p. 627].

207. Entrusting-44

Hence, the Buddhas all encourage us to follow the Pure Land
    path.
Though we may commit evil all our lives,
Shinjin of three aspects in correspondence [with the Name] is
    the mind that is single;
The mind that is single is the genuine mind and is in accord
    with reality

[*Hymns of the Two Gateways of Entrance and Emergence*, I, p. 628].

f. Aspiration for Birth

208. Entrusting-45

Finally, "aspire for birth" is the command of the Tathāgata calling to and summoning the multitudes of all beings. That is, true and real entrusting is the essence of aspiration for birth. Truly, [aspiration for birth] is not the directing of merit through the self-power of meditative and non-meditative practices, whether performed by ordinary people or sages of the Mahayana or the Hinayana. Therefore it is called "not-directing" [*KGSS*, III. I, p.103, # 39].

Note: The aspiration for birth in the Pure Land is viewed as one of the aspects of the three minds, but also as an expression of the single-minded entrusting in which the desire to be reborn in the Pure Land embodies all aspects. Its manifestation in religious consciousness is also seen as the call of Amida to come to the Pure Land, as indicated in the parable of the White path. It is expressed in our religious conscious-ness as the desire to transcend the world in spiritual growth and hope.

The aspiration is also to become Buddha, which is the ultimate outcome of birth in the Pure Land. Becoming Buddha expresses the embracing, inclusive perspective of Mahāyāna Buddhism and Pure Land teaching, which wants to share this compas-sion with all beings. According to Shinran, those who are engaged in entrusting with the aspiration for birth in the Pure Land and becoming a Buddha to save all beings, are "equal to the Tathāgata or Buddha." They are not in fact Buddhas with all the qualities of a Buddha; they are still foolish being. However, in their minds and hearts their aspiration is that of a Buddha wishing to share with all others.

g. Status of Persons of True Entrusting

Note: According to Shinran, persons of true entrusting are really disciples of Śākyamuni Buddha. Even today in Shin ordination, ordinands are called Shaku so-and-so, indicating Śākyamuni's disciple. See Inagaki, *The Three Pure Land Sutras*, "The Larger Sutra," pp. 288-289, for Maitreya's confession that Śākyamuni's "com-passionate revelation of the Great Way has opened our eyes and ears, awakening us to emancipation." In the *Contemplation Sūtra*, it is stated that "all who are mindful of that Buddha are like white lotus-flowers among humankind; the Bodhisattvas Avalokiteśvara and Mahāsthāmaprāpta become their good friends" (Inagaki, *The Three Pure Land Sutras*, p. 350). This praise has been expanded in Shan-tao's *Sanz-engi* (*Shinshū Shōgyō Zensho*, I, p. 558) and appropriated by Shinran in the passage below (210. Status-2) to describe those who truly entrust.

209. Status-1

In the term *true disciple of Buddha, true* contrasts with false and provisional. *Disciple* indicates a disciple of Śākyamuni and the other Buddhas. This expression refers to the practicer who has realized the diamond-like heart and mind. Through this shinjin and practice, one will without fail transcend and realize great nirvana; hence, one is called *true disciple of Buddha* [KGSS, III. I, p. 117, #84].

210. Status-2

Yet, it is very rare that people of this corrupt world of the five defilements embrace the teaching of the one Buddha, Śākyamuni, alone, and for this reason all the Buddhas throughout the ten quarters, countless as the sands of the Ganges, have become witnesses to the attainment of birth through the nembutsu that embodies Amida's Primal Vow; this Master Shan-tao has written in his commentary. He explains that Śākyamuni, Amida, and the Buddhas of the ten quarters, all with the same mind, are no more apart from sentient beings of the nembutsu than shadows from things. Hence it is that Śākyamuni rejoices in persons of shinjin, saying, "They are my true companions." Persons of shinjin are the true disciples of the Buddha; they are the ones who abide in right-mindedness. Since they have been grasped never to be abandoned, they are said to have attained the diamond-like mind. They are called "the best among the best," "excellent persons," "wondrous, excellent persons," "the very finest persons," "rare persons." Such people have become established in the stage of the truly settled and are declared, therefore, to be the equal of Maitreya Buddha. This means that since they have realized true shinjin, they will necessarily be born in the true and real fulfilled land. You should know that this shinjin is bestowed through the compassionate means of Śākyamuni, Amida, and all the Buddhas in the quarters. Therefore you should not disparage the teachings of other Buddhas or the people who perform good acts other than nembutsu. Neither should you despise those who scorn and slander people of nembutsu; rather, you should have compassion and care for them. This was Hōnen's teaching [*Lamp for the Latter Ages*, Letter

2, pp. 526-527; See also *Notes on Once-Calling and Many-Calling*, I, p. 478].

211. Status-3

The foolish being possessed of blind passions,
Through the power of the Buddha's Vow, comes to be
    grasped.
Such a person does not belong to the group of ordinary beings;
Such a person is a white lotus among people;

This person of shinjin is the finest and most rare among
    human beings;
This person is wondrous, excellent, the best among the best.
On reaching the land of happiness, necessarily, by the
    spontaneous working [of the Vow],
Such a person immediately attains the eternal bliss of
    dharma-nature
[*Hymns of the Two Gateways of Entrance and Emergence*, I, p. 629].

212. Status-4

The person who attains shinjin and joy
Is taught to be equal to the Tathāgatas.
Great shinjin is itself Buddha-nature;
Buddha-nature is none other than Tathāgata
[*Hymns of the Pure Land*, I, p. 351, #94].

213. Status-5

Since it is with this heart and mind of all sentient beings that they entrust themselves to the Vow of the dharma-body as compassionate means, this shinjin is none other than Buddha-nature [*Notes on "Essentials of Faith Alone,"* I, p. 461].

h. Benefits of True Entrusting

Note: In the context of Japanese religion, Shinran could not avoid speaking of the benefits that result from true entrusting. Benefits in Japanese religion relate to salvation, spiritual protection in life, and matters of health, wealth, and success.

Shinran was unequivocal that true entrusting, rooted in Amida's true mind, brought assurance of birth into the Pure Land, regardless of accidental circumstances of life. Spiritual protection is also promised since Amida's embrace is supreme over all other spiritual powers. Therefore one need not fear spirits or demons, delusive powers called *maras*. True entrusting releases people from spiritual oppression, intimidation, and exploitation. We may note that the ten benefits of entrusting concern our positive relationship to spiritual reality.

Shinran never promised physical healing, acquisition of wealth, or personal success as a result of true entrusting or prayers. Over its history, Shin Buddhism did not attempt to lure members with such appeals. The practice of petitionary prayer for benefits was not encouraged and spiritual protection was the natural outcome of true entrusting. Shinran, however, teaches the recitation of the *nembutsu* for the welfare of others, if our own entrusting is firm (see 287. Peace-1). Shinran clearly avoided egocentric, self-seeking religion.

214. Benefit-1

> The word *hear* in the passage from the [*Larger*] *Sutra* means that sentient beings, having heard how the Buddha's Vow arose—its origin and fulfillment—are altogether free of doubt. This is to hear. *Shinjin* is shinjin that is directed to beings through the power of the Primal Vow. *Joy* expresses gladness in body and mind. *Even* includes both many and few. *One thought-moment*: because shinjin is free of double-mindedness, one thought-moment is used. It is the mind that is single. The mind that is single is the true cause of [birth in] the pure fulfilled land. When we realize the diamond-like true mind, we transcend crosswise the paths of the five courses and eight hindered existences and unfailingly gain ten benefits in the present life. What are these ten?
>
> 1. The benefit of being protected and sustained by unseen powers.
> 2. The benefit of being possessed of supreme virtues.
> 3. The benefit of our karmic evil being transformed into good.
> 4. The benefit of being protected and cared for by all the Buddhas.
> 5. The benefit of being praised by all the Buddhas.
> 6. The benefit of being constantly protected by the light of the Buddha's heart.
> 7. The benefit of having great joy in our hearts.
> 8. The benefit of being aware of Amida's benevolence and of responding in gratitude to his virtue.
> 9. The benefit of constantly practicing great compassion.

10. The benefit of entering the stage of the truly settled
    [*KGSS*, III. I, p.112, #65].

215. Benefit-2

When we say "Namu-amida-butsu,"
Which surpasses all virtues,
Our heavy obstructions of evil—past, present, and future—
Are all unfailingly transformed, becoming light.

When we say "Namu-amida-butsu,"
The benefits we gain in the present are boundless;
The karmic evil of our transmigration in birth-and-death
    disappears,
And determinate karma and untimely death are eliminated.

When we say "Namu-amida-butsu,"
Brahma and Indra venerate us;
All the benevolent gods of the heavens
Protect us constantly, day and night.

When we say "Namu-amida-butsu,"
The four great deva-kings together
Protect us constantly, day and night,
And let no evil spirits come near.

* * *

When we say "Namu-amida-butsu,"
Yama, the king of the dead, reveres us,
And the officers who judge the beings of the five courses of
    existence
All protect us constantly, day and night.

When we say "Namu-amida-butsu,"
We are protected by the great king of maras
Residing in the sixth heaven;
This he vowed to do in the presence of Śākyamuni Buddha.

The gods of the heavens and earth
Are all to be called good,

For together they protect
The person of the nembutsu.

Shinjin that is the inconceivable working of the power of the
Vow
Is none other than the mind aspiring for great enlightenment;
The evil spirits that abound in heaven and earth
All hold in awe the person who has attained it
[*Hymns on Benefits in the Present* (*Hymns of the Pure Land*), I, pp.
352-354, #98-107].

216. Benefit-3

Protected means that the Buddha protects the person of shinjin
without pause—in all places, at all times, and without discrimination among people. "Protected" means that one cannot
be deterred by those who have taken up other teachings and
beliefs, nor obstructed by those of different understandings and
practices; one is not threatened by the heavenly demon Pāpīyas,
nor troubled by evil gods and demons [*Notes on Once-Calling and
Many-Calling*, I, p. 479].

217. Benefit-4

Constantly illumines me: Unhindered light constantly illumines
the person of shinjin. *Constantly illumines* means constantly
protects. *Me*: Realize that great love and compassion tirelessly
and constantly protects this self. This is the blessing of being
grasped, never to be abandoned. Know that this passage sets
forth the meaning of the words, "Sentient beings of the nembutsu are grasped, never to be abandoned" [*Notes on the Inscriptions on Sacred Scrolls*, I, p. 510].

218. Benefit-5

The clouds of doubt clear forever. The heart that doubts the
power of the Vow is likened to clouds. *Clear forever.* When the
clouds of the doubting heart have been swept away forever,
one is born without fail in the Pure Land of peace. The person
who has realized shinjin is constantly illumined and protected
by the compassionate light that grasps, never to abandon, of the
Buddha of unhindered light; hence, *the Buddha's light encircles*

the head. These words praise Genkū, stating that the Buddha's compassion constantly and brightly shines upon the head of the person of shinjin. Know that this is because one has been grasped by Amida [*Notes on the Inscriptions on Sacred Scrolls*, I, p. 511].

219. Benefit-6

The compassionate light of the Buddha of unhindered light always illumines and protects the person who has realized shinjin; hence the darkness of ignorance has already cleared, and the long night of birth-and-death is already dispelled and become dawn. Let this be known. . . . Know that when one realizes shinjin, it is as though dawn has broken [*Notes on the Inscriptions on Sacred Scrolls*, I, p. 519].

220. Benefit-7

The nembutsu is the single path free of hindrances. Why is this? To practicers who have realized shinjin, the gods of the heavens and earth bow in homage, and maras and non-buddhists present no obstruction. No evil act can bring about karmic results, nor can any good act equal the nembutsu [*A Record in Lament of Divergences*, I, p. 665, #7; See KGSS, III, #16, I, pp. 92-93].

i. The Paradox of True Entrusting

Note: The Pure Land teaching has always emphasized that it belongs to the "easy path" tradition stemming from Nāgārjuna, who introduced that terminology and compared the easy path with riding a ship in comparison to traveling overland. Nevertheless, in many passages Shinran speaks of the great difficulty of the path of true entrusting. Depending on our karmic heritage, it is difficult to meet teachers who guide us into the path, but it is also difficult to accept such teaching. The *Larger Sūtra* also states that it is easy to go but no one goes (see CWS, I, p. 79).

The difficulty lies in the fact that it appears too good to be true. In business when something is too good to be true, it usually is. So the buyer must be wary. This attitude carries over into spiritual issues. It goes against reason, which places a premium on virtue and achievement. See *A Record in Lament of Divergences* (99. Other Power-2) where he states: "Though it is so, people commonly say, 'Even an evil person attains birth, so it goes without saying that a good person will.' This statement may seem well founded at first, but it runs counter to the intent of the Primal Vow, which is Other Power."

However, it is easy because it is the fruit of Amida's Vow and his power in awakening true entrusting. It is difficult when approached from the perspective of self power as a means to attain salvation. One cannot easily generate true entrusting through one's own determination. When the truth of Amida's compassion and Vow grasp one, the paradox is transcended.

221. Paradox-1

It is difficult to meet true teachers
And difficult for them to instruct.
It is difficult to hear the teaching well,
And more difficult still to accept it
[*Hymns of the Pure Land*, p. 344, #69].

222. Paradox-2

For the foolish and ignorant who are ever sinking in birth-and-death, the multitudes turning in transmigration, it is not attainment of the unexcelled, incomparable fruit of enlightenment that is difficult; the genuine difficulty is realizing true and real shinjin. Why? Because this realization takes place through the Tathāgata's supportive power; because it comes about wholly through the power of great compassion and all-embracing wisdom. If pure shinjin should be realized, that mind will not be inverted; that mind will not be vain or false. Thereupon that sentient being of extreme evil, profound and immense, will realize the mind of great joy and receive the veneration and love of all the sacred honored ones [*KGSS*, III. I, pp. 79-80, #1].

223. Paradox-3

Truly we know that those who perform single praxis with a combined mind do not attain great joy. Hence, the master [Shan-tao] states:

Such people do not realize the Buddha's benevolence and do not respond in gratitude to it; though they perform practices, they give rise to contempt and arrogance in their hearts. For they act always for the sake of fame and profit; they have been enveloped in self-attachment unawares, and do not approach fellow practicers and true teachers; preferring to involve themselves in worldly affairs, they obstruct themselves and block others from the right practice for birth.

How grievous it is that, since the beginningless past, foolish, ignorant human beings possessed of defilements and hindrances have mixed the auxiliary and right and combined the minds of the meditative and non-meditative practices, so that they have had no chance of attaining emancipation. Reflecting on our transmigration in birth-and-death, we realize how hard it is to take refuge in the power of the Buddha's Vow, how hard it is to enter the ocean of great shinjin, even in the passage of countless kalpas. Truly we must sorrow at this; we must deeply lament.

Sages of the Mahayana and Hinayana and all good people make the auspicious Name of the Primal Vow their own root of good; hence, they cannot give rise to shinjin and do not apprehend the Buddha's wisdom. Because they cannot comprehend [the Buddha's intent in] establishing the cause [of birth], they do not enter the fulfilled land [*KGSS*, VI. I, pp. 239-240, #67].

224. Paradox-4

More difficult even than trust in the teachings of Śākyamuni's
  lifetime
Is the true entrusting of the universal Vow,
The sutra teaches that it is "the most difficult of all
  difficulties,"
That "nothing surpasses this difficulty"
[*Hymns of the Pure Land*, I, p. 344, #70].

225. Paradox-5

Realization of true and real shinjin
Is rare in the defiled world of the last dharma-age;
The witness of Buddhas countless as the sands of the Ganges
Reveals how difficult it is to attain
[*Hymns of the Dharma-Ages*, I, p. 410, #4].

226. Paradox-6

Entrusting ourselves to the inconceivable Buddha-wisdom
Is taught to be the cause of birth in the fulfilled land.
Realization of shinjin, which is the true cause
[*Hymns of the Dharma-Ages*, I, p. 410, # 48].

227. Paradox-7

It is the consummate teaching among consummate teachings,
The sudden teaching among sudden teachings.
It is hard to encounter the true essence of the Pure Land way,
    hard to realize shinjin.
This is the most difficult of difficulties; nothing surpasses it
[*Hymns of the Two Gateways of Entrance and Emergence*, I, p. 629].

228. Paradox-8

The difficulty of realizing this shinjin is taught in the *Larger Sutra*: "The most difficult of all difficulties is to hear this sutra and accept it in shinjin; nothing surpasses this difficulty"; and in the *Smaller Sutra* we find, "It is the dharma that is most difficult to accept." But Śākyamuni Tathāgata, appearing in this evil world of five defilements, put this dharma that is difficult to accept into practice and attained the supreme nirvana. He then gave this Name embodying wisdom to the sentient beings living in defilement. The witness of the Buddhas throughout the ten quarters and the protection of the Tathāgatas as numberless as the sands of the Ganges are solely for the sake of people of true and real shinjin. Know that Śākyamuni, our loving father, and Amida, our compassionate mother, guide us to shinjin as our own parents [*Notes on "Essentials of Faith Alone,"* I, p. 464; See also *Passages on the Pure Land Way*, I, pp. 316-317].

229. Paradox-9

To go is easy and yet no one is born there. To go is easy: When persons allow themselves to be carried by the power of the Primal Vow, they are certain to be born in the land that has been fulfilled through it; hence, it is easy going there. *No one is born there:* Because people of true and real shinjin are extremely rare, those born in the true fulfilled land are few [*Notes on the Inscriptions on Sacred Scrolls*, p. 496; See also *KGSS*, III. I, p. 115, #76, 77].

j. True Entrusting and Doubt

Note: We may note in Shinran's writings that he refers frequently to the absence of doubt as a mark of true entrusting. Religious leaders often urge their followers not to doubt or otherwise question their beliefs. If one questions, one's salvation is in doubt. It is the opinion of this author that that is not the doubt that Shinran is referring to. He entertained many questions from his disciples and never tried to suppress them.

It is a deeper form of doubt that the focus is on here, the doubt concerning the possibility of such a salvation. It is doubt about the principle of salvation, not merely certain so-called "facts" relating to its history. It is doubt concerning the truth of one's own life and the awareness of being embraced by the Buddha's compassion. It is doubt of one's own perception that calls into question one's very being itself. For those who experience true entrusting, the reality symbolized by Amida Buddha becomes self-evident; one identifies his/her life with that world and reality. To doubt that is to doubt one's own experience.

Therefore Shinran indicates that pursuing salvation through self power is an expression of doubt, because the devotee does not trust the Vow, the ground of the *nembutsu*, as sufficient in itself to save people.

The positive side of this experience is described by Shinran as the diamond-like trust. See the section the Diamond-like True Mind: 169. Entrusting-6-170. Entrusting-7. The diamond has a hardness, a firmness that external conditions cannot damage. Nevertheless, diamond-like faith is not rigid or brittle as a dry branch broken by the wind, but supple like the bamboo or grass that maintains its position while buffeted by winds.

Based in Buddhist tradition, the rarity of birth in this life makes one's encounter with the teaching of crucial importance. If one is deterred by doubt, the opportunity will not come about for aeons in the process of births and deaths. Therefore, despite the fact that salvation is Amida's work, it is a matter of great urgency to respond with trust in his embrace. Subject to karmic retribution, one may be reborn in a hell or the border land of the Pure Land termed transformed land, embryonic birth, or land of sloth and pride. Those regions are for those lacking a resolute mind or who recite the *nembutsu* in self power.

230. Doubt-1

Ah, hard to encounter, even in many lifetimes, is the decisive cause of birth, Amida's universal Vow! Hard to realize, even in myriads of kalpas, is pure shinjin that is true and real! If you should come to realize this practice and shinjin, rejoice at the conditions from the distant past that have brought it about. But if in this lifetime still you are entangled in a net of doubt, then unavoidably you must pass once more in the stream of birth-and-death through myriads of kalpas. Wholly sincere, indeed, are the words of truth that one is grasped, never to be abandoned, the right dharma all-surpassing and wondrous! Hear and reflect, and let there be no wavering or apprehension [*KGSS*, Preface. I, p. 4].

231. Doubt-2

Pure shinjin is shinjin that actualizes Amida's profound and vast benefiting of others. It arises from the Vow of birth through the nembutsu, also known as "the Vow of sincere mind and entrusting." It may further be called "the Vow of shinjin, which is Amida's directing of virtue for our going forth." However, for the shallowest of foolish beings—we multitudes of the basest level—it is impossible to realize pure shinjin, impossible to attain the highest end. This is because we do not depend on Amida's directing of virtue for our going forth and because we are entangled in a net of doubt. It is through the Tathāgata's supportive power, and through the vast power of great compassion and all-embracing wisdom, that a person realizes pure, true, and real shinjin. Therefore, that mind will not be inverted; that mind will not be vain or false. Truly we know that the supreme, perfect fruit of enlightenment is not difficult to attain; it is pure shinjin, true and real, that is indeed difficult to realize [*Passages on the Pure Land Way*, I, p. 299].

232. Doubt-3

Entrusting ourselves to the inconceivable Buddha-wisdom
Is taught to be the cause of birth in the fulfilled land.
Realization of shinjin, which is the true cause,
Is among all difficulties even more difficult
[*Hymns of the Dharma-Ages*, I, p. 410, #48].

233. Doubt-4

Sentient beings who, with hindered understandings,
Doubt the Buddha's unhindered wisdom,
Will sink for many kalpas in various forms of pain
In the hells of Saṃvara and Piṇḍala.

Shinran Note: Hindered: obstructed by various things.
Saṃvara and Piṇḍala: The beings therein see those in Avici hell and think it pleasant for them compared with their own state. Those who slander the Buddha-dharma fall into these hells and remain there for eighty thousand kalpas, where they undergo immense pain.
[*Hymns of the Pure Land*, I, p. 351, #95]

234. Doubt-5

Doubting the inconceivable Buddha-wisdom,
People devote themselves to saying the nembutsu in
    self-power;
Hence they remain in the borderland or the realm of
    indolence and pride,
Without responding in gratitude to the Buddha's benevolence
[*Hymns of the Dharma-Ages*, I, p. 413, #61].

235. Doubt-6

Those who practice the root of good
While believing deeply in the recompense of good and evil
Are good people whose minds are possessed of doubt;
Hence, they remain in the provisional, transformed lands
[*Hymns of the Dharma-Ages*, I, p. 415, #74].

236. Doubt-7

It further states, *Know that because of doubt one remains in the
house of birth-and-death*: When one doubts the inconceivable
karmic power of the great Vow, one remains in the six courses,
the four manners of arising, the twenty-five forms of existence,
and the twelve kinds of arising. We are to realize that up to now
we have been wandering for aeons in such a realm of illusion
[*Notes on the Inscriptions on Sacred Scrolls*, I, p. 513].

237. Doubt-8

Concerning the nature of shinjin, I have learned from the Master
of Kuang-ming temple that after true shinjin has become settled
in us, even if Buddhas like Amida or Śākyamuni should fill
the skies and proclaim that Śākyamuni's teaching and Amida's
Primal Vow are false, we will not have even one moment of
doubt [*Letters of the Tradition*, Letter 2, I, p. 575].

7. True Entrusting and *Nembutsu* Practice

Note: As Shinran notes in his writings, the name *Namu-amida-butsu* or *nembutsu* is
the fruit of the Bodhisattva Dharmākara's Enlightenment, providing a way of salvation for all beings. This name, praised by all Buddhas, according to the Seventeenth

Vow, embodies Amida's compassion-wisdom. It is "incarnation" in a name, that is, the Buddha is fully present in his name.

The name gains its significance among all names because Shinran taught that in true entrusting the name embodies the essence of Amida. When it is recited with trust, one's ultimate enlightenment becomes assured. In a sense, as Christians believe that Jesus was an incarnation of God, Shinran taught that through the fulfillment of his Vows, Amida Buddha became embodied, or "incarnated" (a metaphor), that is, spiritually present, in the name. Thereby he is continually available to us. When Amida is represented in art the name is written placed on a lotus blossom, signifying that it is a Buddha. It is highly symbolic. Rennyo, the 8th Abbot, declared that a picture of Amida is better than an image, and the written name is better than a picture.

As he states, this name is not simply a name like any other name. We may understand this in comparison to other names of people and things. Other names are designations and signs, distinguishing one thing from another, like a label or street sign. In the case of Amida, the name is popularly used in the manner of a label of one Buddha among many, misleading people to consider it a theism.

However, the name stands for reality itself, the Infinite, not as one thing among many, but as that which is totally inclusive. Properly understanding the name of Amida, we do not think of a specific being, but inconceivable reality. Thus Shinran emphasized the aspect of light. Amida is the form of light, the form of no-form. However, because of the limits of human understanding, he manifests as form and the direct expression of the Dharma body of suchness.

In the *Namu-amida-butsu* the *Namu* (in some forms *Kimyō*) refers to the trusting person and means "to take refuge (in Amida Buddha)," while *Amida* embraces the person never to abandon. Amida Buddha is not a god standing outside, apart from us, but is our inner aspiration and inspiration as the reality revealed through the experience of entrusting. The Infinite embraces the finite, enabling spiritual transformation. Through hearing and reciting the name, we encounter reality itself which frees and transforms the reality of our own being.

a. The Name

238. Name-1

The Name of the Tathāgata of unhindered light
And the light that is the embodiment of wisdom
Dispel the darkness of the long night of ignorance
And fulfill the aspirations of sentient beings
[*Hymns of the Pure Land Masters*, I, p. 373, #47].

239. Name-2

Although I am without shame and self-reproach
And lack a mind of truth and sincerity,

Because the Name is directed by Amida,
Its virtues fill the ten quarters
[*Hymns of the Dharma Ages*, I, p. 421, #97].

240. Name-3

Name (*go*) indicates the name of a Buddha after the attainment
of Buddhahood; another term (*myo*) indicates the name before
this attainment. The sacred Name of the Tathāgata surpasses
measure, description, and conceptual understanding; it is the
Name of the Vow embodying great love and great compassion, which brings all sentient beings into the supreme nirvana.
The Name of this Buddha surpasses the names of all the other
Tathāgatas, for it is based on the Vow to save all beings [*Notes
on "Essentials of Faith Alone,"* I, p. 452].

241. Name-4

We know, therefore, that the auspicious Name embodying the
perfectly fulfilled supreme virtues is true wisdom that transforms our evil into virtue, and that the diamond-like shinjin so
difficult to accept is true reality that sweeps away doubt and
brings us to attainment of enlightenment [*KGSS*, Preface. I, p. 3].

242. Name-5

These passages reveal that saying the Name breaks through all
the ignorance of sentient beings and fulfills their aspirations.
Saying the Name is the right act, supreme, true, and excellent.
The right act is the nembutsu. The nembutsu is Namu-amida-
butsu. Namu-amida-butsu is right-mindedness. Let this be
known [*KGSS*, II. I, pp. 17-18, #12].

243. Name-6

Namu-amida-butsu is the Name embodying wisdom; hence,
when persons accept and entrust themselves to this Name of
the Buddha of inconceivable wisdom-light, holding it in mindfulness, Avalokiteśvara and Mahāsthāmaprāpta accompany
them constantly, as shadows do things. The Buddha of unhindered light appears as Avalokiteśvara, and becomes manifest

as Mahāsthāmaprāpta [*Notes on "Essentials of Faith Alone,"* I, p. 453].

Note: Avalokiteśvara (Kannon) is the Bodhisattva of Compassion and Mahāsthāmaprāpta (Great Power) is the Bodhisattva of Wisdom. They are pictured in Buddhist iconography as companions of Amitābha/Amida Buddha and are understood as personalizations of his attributes of compassion and wisdom.

244. Name-7

The Name spreads universally throughout the worlds in the ten quarters, countless as minute particles, and guides all to the practice of the Buddha's teaching. This means that, since there is no one—whether among the wise of the Mahayana or the Hinayana, or the ignorant, good or evil—who can attain supreme nirvana through his or her own self-cultivated wisdom, we are encouraged to enter the ocean of the wisdom-Vow of the Buddha of unhindered light, for the Buddha's form is the light of wisdom. This form comprehends the wisdom of all the Buddhas. It should be understood that light is none other than wisdom [*Notes on "Essentials of Faith Alone,"* I, p. 452].

245. Name-8

The radiant light, unhindered and inconceivable, eradicates suffering and brings realization of joy; the excellent Name, perfectly embodying all practices, eliminates obstacles and dispels doubt. This is the teaching and practice for our latter age; devote yourself solely to it. It is eye and limb in this defiled world; do not fail to endeavor in it. Accepting and living the supreme, universal Vow, then, abandon the defiled and aspire for the pure. Reverently embracing the Tathāgata's teaching, respond in gratitude to his benevolence and be thankful for his compassion [*Passages on the Pure Land Way*, Preface, I, p. 295].

246. Name-9

The practice of the Pure Land way is the great practice that embodies Amida's perfect benefiting of others. It is revealed in the Vow that all the Buddhas praise the Name, also known as "the Vow that all the Buddhas say the Name." It may further be called "the Vow of the right act, which is Amida's directing of virtue for our going forth."

Amida's directing of virtue to beings through the power of the Primal Vow has two aspects: the aspect for our going forth to the Pure Land and the aspect for our return to this world. Regarding the aspect for going forth, there is great practice, there is pure shinjin [*Passages on the Pure Land Way*, I, p. 296].

247. Name-10

With these passages from the sacred words of the Buddha and from the treatises, we know in particular that the great practice is not a foolish being's practice of directing his or her own merit toward attainment of birth. It is the fulfilled practice that Amida directs to beings out of great compassion, and therefore is called "not-directing virtue [on the part of beings]." This practice indeed embodies the Primal Vow, in which the nembutsu is selected and adopted. It is the supreme, all-surpassing universal Vow. It is the true and wondrous right dharma that is the One Vehicle. It is the unexcelled practice that perfectly embodies all good acts [*Passages on the Pure Land Way*, I, p. 298].

248. Name-11

Clearly we know, then, that the nembutsu is not a self-power practice performed by foolish beings or sages; it is therefore called the practice of "not-directing virtue [on the part of beings]." Masters of the Mahayana and Hinayana and people burdened with karmic evil, whether heavy or light, should all in the same way take refuge in the great treasure ocean of the selected Vow and attain Buddhahood through the nembutsu [*KGSS*, II. I, I, p. 53, #69].

249. Name-12

Truly we know that without the virtuous Name, our compassionate father, we would lack the direct cause for birth. Without the light, our compassionate mother, we would stand apart from the indirect cause of birth. Although direct and indirect causes may come together, if the karmic-consciousness of shinjin is lacking, one will not reach the land of light. The karmic-consciousness of true and real shinjin is the inner cause. The Name and light—our father and mother—are the outer cause. When the inner and outer causes merge, one realizes the true body in the fulfilled land [*KGSS*, II. I, p. 54, #72].

250. Name-13

The *Sutra of the Treasure Name* states: "The nembutsu of Amida's Primal Vow is not our practice, it is not our good; it is simply keeping the Name of the Buddha." It is the Name that is good, the Name that is the practice. When we speak of practice, we mean doing good. The Primal Vow is clearly the Buddha's promise. When we have understood this, we see that the Vow is not our good, nor is it our practice. Hence we speak of Other Power.

The Name fulfilled in the Primal Vow is the direct cause of our birth; in other words, it is our father. The radiant light of great compassion is the indirect cause of our birth; it is our mother [*Lamp for the Latter Ages*, Letter 22, I, p. 555].

b. The *Nembutsu* as Great Practice

Note: In the *Kyōgyōshinshō* ("Teaching, Practice, Faith, and Realization") Shinran quotes numerous passages concerning practice which suggest the practitioner's practice. However, this section of the text is devoted to the point that the *nembutsu*, though recited by the devotee, is really the practice established by Amida Buddha and that the practice of all Buddhas carries the name through the universe in accord with the Seventeenth Vow. The problem is when practitioners take the recitation as their own root of good as a means by which they gain birth in the Pure Land.

In traditional Buddhism the order of terms in the process of salvation would be Faith (believing), Understanding, Practice, Realization. One believes in the teaching, understands its requirements, practices and realizes it's truth. In the case of Shinran, the Teaching is the *Larger Sūtra*, which is the expression of the Seventeenth Vow in our world system; Practice is the practice of the Buddhas and bodhisattvas of the universe, proclaiming Amida's name; Trust is that which is inspired in the person through hearing of Amida and his work; and Realization combines birth in the Pure Land with return to the world of finitude to work for the salvation of others and finally Buddhahood.

In this process, the *nembutsu* is not the mere recitation of words to attain birth, but it is also the call of Amida to inspire trust. We may interpret the call of Amida broadly to mean any activity or event in which a person comes to know of the meaning and reality of Amida Buddha.

251. Nembutsu-1

These passages are clear testimony revealing the true and real practice. We know indeed that this practice embodies the Primal Vow, in which the nembutsu was selected and adopted. It is the supreme practice, rare and all-surpassing. It is the true and wondrous right dharma in which all virtues are perfectly fulfilled. It is the great practice, ultimate and unhindered. Let this be known [*KGSS*, II. I, p. 57, # 80].

252. Nembutsu-2

The great practice is to say the Name of the Tathāgata of unhindered light. This practice, embodying all good acts and possessing all roots of virtue, is perfect and most rapid in bringing about birth. It is the treasure ocean of virtues that is suchness or true reality. For this reason, it is called great practice. This practice arises from the Vow of great compassion, which is known as "the Vow that all Buddhas extol the Name," "the Vow that all Buddhas say the Name," and "the Vow that all Buddhas praise the Name" [*KGSS*, II. I, p. 13, #1].

253. Nembutsu-3

Concerning the nembutsu, no working is true working. For it is beyond description, explanation, and conceptual understanding [*A Record in Lament of Divergences*, I, p. 666, #10].

c. *Nembutsu* as Amida's Call

254. Nembutsu-4

From these passages we see that the word *Namu* means to take refuge. In the term to take refuge (*kimyō*), *ki* means to arrive at. Further, it is used in compounds to mean to yield joyfully to (*kietsu*) and to take shelter in (*kisai*). *Myō* means to act, to invite, to command, to teach, path, message, to devise, to summon. Thus, *kimyō* is the command of the Primal Vow calling to and summoning us.

Aspiring for birth and directing virtue indicates the mind of the Tathāgata who, having already established the Vow, gives sentient beings the practice necessary for their birth. The practice is the selected Primal Vow.

One necessarily attains birth elucidates the attainment of the stage of non-retrogression. Concerning this, the [*Larger*] *Sutra* states, "Immediately attains," and [Nāgārjuna's] commentary, "definitely settled." "Immediately" reveals the ultimate brevity of the instant in which the true cause of one's birth in the fulfilled land becomes definitely settled through one's hearing the power of the Vow. "Definitely" characterizes the realization of the diamond-like mind [*KGSS*, II. I, p. 38, #34].

255. *Nembutsu-5*

Finally, "aspire for birth" is the command of the Tathāgata calling to and summoning the multitudes of all beings. That is, true and real entrusting is the essence of aspiration for birth. Truly, [aspiration for birth] is not the directing of merit through the self-power of meditative and non-meditative practices, whether performed by ordinary people or sages of the Mahayana or the Hinayana. Therefore it is called "not-directing" [*KGSS*, III. I, p. 103, #39].

256. *Nembutsu-6*

Take refuge in the Tathāgata of unhindered light filling the ten quarters: *Take refuge* translates *Namu*. It means to follow the command of the Tathāgata. *The Tathāgata of unhindered light filling the ten quarters* is Amida Tathāgata. This Tathāgata is light. *Filling the ten quarters*: Filling means going to the ends; completely. The light goes completely to the ends of the worlds throughout the ten quarters. *Unhindered*: unimpeded by the blind passions and karmic evil of sentient beings. *Tathāgata of light*: Amida Buddha. This Tathāgata is called the Buddha of light surpassing conceptual understanding and is the form of wisdom. Know that Amida pervades the lands countless as particles throughout the ten quarters [*Notes on the Inscriptions on Sacred Scrolls*, p. 501].

257. *Nembutsu*-7

Namu means "to take refuge." "To take refuge" is to respond to the command and follow the call of the two honored ones, Śākyamuni and Amida. Thus Shan-tao explains, *Namu* means to take refuge. It further signifies aspiring for birth [*Notes on the Inscriptions on Sacred Scrolls*, I, pp. 504-505].

258. *Nembutsu*-8

With these sacred words we know clearly that this third mind arises as the call by which the great compassion of the Tathāgata summons all sentient beings. The aspiration for birth that is great compassion—this is true directing of virtue [*Passages on the Pure Land Way*, I, p. 313].

d. *Nembutsu* Recitation

259. *Nembutsu*-9

Though we commit evil throughout our lives,
If we say the nembutsu always
With our hearts turned wholly to Amida,
Our obstructions fall away by the [Vow's] spontaneous
    working
[*Hymns of the Pure Land Masters* (T'an-luan), I, p. 376, #60].

260. *Nembutsu*-10

For all people—men and women, of high station and low—
Saying the Name of Amida is such
That whether one is walking, standing, sitting, or reclining is
    of no concern
And time, place, and condition are not restricted
[*Hymns of the Pure Land Masters* (Genshin), I, p. 385, #94].

261. *Nembutsu*-11

We who aspire for Amida's fulfilled land,
Though we differ in outward condition and conduct,

Should truly receive the Name of the Primal Vow
And never forget it, whether waking or sleeping
[*Hymns of the Pure Land Masters* (Genshin), I, p. 386, #96].

262. *Nembutsu-12*

It is taught, concerning Namu-amida-butsu,
That its virtue is like the vast waters of the ocean;
Having myself received that pure good,
I direct it equally to all sentient beings
[*Hymns of the Pure Land Masters* (Genkū), I, p. 393, #119].

263. *Nembutsu-13*

Those who deeply entrust themselves
To Amida's Vow of great compassion
Should all say Namu-amida-butsu constantly,
Whether they are waking or sleeping
[*Hymns of the Dharma-Ages*, I, p. 411, #54].

264. *Nembutsu-14*

Know from the words *ten times* that appear from the beginning
in the Vow itself that saying the Name is not limited to one
utterance. And the word *perhaps even* makes it clearer still that
there is no set number of times one should say the Name. This
Vow shows the way that is easy to traverse and easy to practice;
it reveals the boundlessness of great love and great compassion
[*Notes on Once-Calling and Many-Calling*, I, p. 482].

265. *Nembutsu-15*

Solely saying Amida's Name is wholehearted single practice.
"Wholehearted" means not shifting to other good acts, not
turning one's thoughts to other Buddhas; "single practice" is
solely to practice the Name that embodies the Primal Vow,
free of all doubt. "Practice" means to amend and rectify the
unsettledness of the heart and say the nembutsu. "Single"
means sole, one. "Sole" means having no thought of shifting
to other good acts or other Buddhas [*Notes on Once-Calling and
Many-Calling*, I, p. 483].

266. *Nembutsu*-16

Whether walking, standing, sitting, or reclining—without regard to the length of time, and without abandoning it from moment to moment: for *time* (*jisetsu*), *ji* is time in terms of the twelve hours of the day; *setsu* indicates time as the twelve months and four seasons. That times are not distinguished means that there is no need to avoid impure occasions. Because there is no discrimination among various activities, the word *without regard* is used [*Notes on Once-Calling and Many-Calling*, I, p. 483].

267. *Nembutsu*-17

Saying (*shō*) means to utter the Name. *Shō* also means to weigh, to determine the measure of something. This means that when a person says the Name even ten times or but once, hearing it and being without even the slightest doubt, he or she will be born in the true fulfilled land [*Notes on Once-Calling and Many-Calling*, I, p. 489].

268. *Nembutsu*-18

Saying my Name perhaps even ten times: In encouraging us to say the Name that embodies the Vow, the Tathāgata added *perhaps even* to the words *ten times* to show that there is no set number of times the Name must be said and to teach sentient beings that there is no determined hour or occasion for saying it. Since we have been given this Vow by the Tathāgata, we can take any occasion in daily life for saying the Name and need not wait to recite it at the very end of life; we should simply give ourselves up totally to the entrusting with sincere mind of the Tathāgata. When persons realize this true and real shinjin, they enter completely into the compassionate light that grasps, never to abandon, and hence become established in the stage of the truly settled. Thus it is written [*Notes on the Inscriptions on Sacred Scrolls*, I, p. 494].

269. *Nembutsu*-19

If sentient beings are mindful of Amida Buddha and say the Name: if a sentient being keeps the Buddha in mind and says the

Name. *Without fail they will see the Buddha in the present and in the future. The Buddha will never be far from them. Without depending on any expedient means they will naturally attain awakening in their hearts.* Both in this life and in the future they will see the Buddha without fail. The Buddha will never be apart from them. Without depending on expedient means, they will attain enlightenment naturally, by *jinen* [*Notes on the Inscriptions on Sacred Scrolls*, I, p. 498].

270. *Nembutsu*-20

In answer to your question about the Nembutsu: it is completely mistaken to look down upon people who believe in birth through the Nembutsu, saying that they are destined for birth in the borderland. For Amida vowed to take into the land of bliss those who say the Name, and thus to entrust oneself deeply and say the Name is to be in perfect accord with the Primal Vow. Though a person may have shinjin, if he or she does not say the Name it is of no avail. And conversely, even though a person fervently say the Name, if that person's shinjin is shallow he cannot attain birth. Thus, it is the person who both deeply entrusts himself to birth through the Nembutsu and undertakes to say the Name who is certain to be born in the true fulfilled land [*Lamp for the Latter Ages*, Letter 12. I, p. 539].

271. *Nembutsu*-21

It is the greatest of errors to say that one must not say *mugekō butsu* [Buddha of unhindered light] in addition to *Namu-amida-butsu*. *Kimyō* corresponds to *Namu*. *Mugekō butsu* is light; it is wisdom. This wisdom is itself Amida Buddha. Since people do not know the form of Amida Buddha, Bodhisattva Vasubandhu, exhausting all his resources, created this expression in order that we might know Amida's form with perfect certainty [*Lamp for the Latter Ages*, Letter 14, I, p. 543].

272. *Nembutsu*-22

That the nembutsu said beyond one utterance should be directed to the sentient beings of the ten quarters is also correct.

Since one is directing the nembutsu to the sentient beings of the ten quarters, it is an error to think that saying it twice or three times is bad for one's attainment of birth. I have been taught that, since it is the Primal Vow of birth through the nembutsu, whether one says the nembutsu many times or whether one says it only once, one will be born [*A Collection of Letters*, Letter 3, I, p. 561].

e. The *Nembutsu* and Spiritual Transformation

273. *Nembutsu-23*

Obstructions of karmic evil turn into virtues;
It is like the relation of ice and water:
The more the ice, the more the water;
The more the obstructions, the more the virtues
[*Hymns of the Pure Land Masters*, I, p. 371, #40].

f. *Nembutsu* and Gratitude

274. *Nembutsu-24*

I praise Amida's wisdom and virtue
So that beings with mature conditions throughout the ten
    quarters may hear.
Let those who have already realized shinjin
Constantly respond in gratitude to the Buddha's benevolence.

Amida's wisdom and virtue: great love and compassion and virtue [*Hymns of the Pure Land*, I, p. 337, #50].

275. *Nembutsu-25*

The Buddhas' protection and witness
Arise from the fulfillment of the Vow of compassion;
So let those who attain the diamond-like mind
Respond in gratitude to Amida's great benevolence [*Hymns of the Pure Land*, I, p. 348, #85].

276. *Nembutsu-26*

Persons who truly realize shinjin
As they utter Amida's Name,
Being mindful of the Buddha always,
Wish to respond in gratitude to the great benevolence
[*Hymns of the Dharma-Ages*, I, p. 406, #30].

277. Nembutsu-27

Through the compassion of Śākyamuni and Amida,
We have been brought to realize the mind that seeks to attain
    Buddhahood.
It is by entering the wisdom of shinjin
That we become persons who respond in gratitude to the
    Buddhas' benevolence
[*Hymns of the Dharma-Ages*, I, p. 407, #34].

E. Shinran and the Nembutsu *Way of Life: True Entrusting in the World*

Note: Contemplation of the *nembutsu* opens our spiritual eyes to all-embracing reality which surrounds, permeates, and is one with our limited fragment of passionate life. While we ourselves as foolish beings cannot say that we have the qualities of a Buddha, true entrusting awakens us to our true self and our potentiality to contribute positively to the world and society as bearers of compassion and wisdom, which are the essence of Buddhahood.

In the following sections we have assembled Shinran's words concerning various issues of his time. He cannot answer all our contemporary questions, but his words suggest an orientation in society that can help us assess the various issues that mark our time.

On the background of the ethnocentrism that has been a feature of transplanted immigrant Buddhism in the West, we can note Shinran's universalism, which is in line with the character of Buddhism throughout its history. The principle of karma, as well as the infinite embrace of Amida Buddha, whose Vows are aimed at all sentient beings, demonstrate the universality of the teaching. On the crucial issue of filial piety, Shinran respected his parents, but recognized the breadth and scope of the teaching.

1. The Universal Dharma

278. Nembutsu-28

In that land of happiness, every single being is born transformed from the pure lotus of Amida Tathāgata's perfect enlightenment, for they are the same in practicing the nembutsu and follow no other way. This extends even to this world, so that all nembutsu practicers within the four seas are brothers and sisters. The fellow beings are innumerable. How can this be conceived? [*KGSS*, IV. I, p. 155, #7].

279. *Nembutsu-29*

As for me, Shinran, I have never said the nembutsu even once for the repose of my departed father and mother. For all sentient beings, without exception, have been our parents and brothers and sisters in the course of countless lives in the many states of existence. On attaining Buddhahood after this present life, we can save every one of them.

Were saying the nembutsu indeed a good act in which I strove through my own powers, then I might direct the merit thus gained towards saving my father and mother. But this is not the case.

If, however, simply abandoning self-power, we quickly attain enlightenment in the Pure Land, we will be able to save, by means of transcendent powers, first those with whom we have close karmic relations, whatever karmic suffering they may have sunk to in the six realms through the four modes of birth [*A Record of Lament at Divergences*, I, p. 664, #5].

2. Shinran's Non-discriminating Dharma: Equal Companions on the Way

Note: Based on the Mahāyāna Buddhist principles that all beings have Buddha-nature, all sentient beings are essentially equal in principle and to be treated with respect, despite the differences and limitations resulting from karma. Shinran gave concrete expression to this understanding by regarding his disciples as equal companions in the Dharma and not assuming superiority as a teacher. He declared that everyone received their trust equally from Amida, and that he did not have even one disciple. His effort was to communicate with the lowliest person, though many might consider it futile.

In the passage below on the Great Sea of Entrusting we peer directly into Shinran's mind, which sought to remove all barriers between people and saw everyone in Amida's embrace, no matter what their status. This passage is perhaps one of the most radical in declaring that the trust endowed by Amida can come to even the most desperate, as well as the most righteous. No socially imposed distinction that people may use to function in society or judge another offers any basis to claim one's own spiritual superiority. In the section on Shōtoku we see that Shinran was aware of the problem of justice in society.

280. Non-Discrimination-1

That people of the countryside, who do not know the meanings of written characters and who are painfully and hopelessly ignorant, may easily understand, I have repeated the same things over and over. The educated will probably find this writing peculiar and may ridicule it. But paying no heed to such criticisms, I write only that ignorant people may easily grasp the meaning [*Notes on "Essentials of Faith Alone,"* I, p. 468; See also *Notes on Once-Calling and Many-Calling*, I, p. 490].

281. Non-discrimination-2

In reflecting on the great ocean of shinjin, I realize that there is no discrimination between noble and humble or black-robed monks and white-clothed laity, no differentiation between man and woman, old and young. The amount of evil one has committed is not considered; the duration of any performance of religious practices is of no concern. It is a matter of neither practice nor good acts, neither sudden attainment nor gradual attainment, neither meditative practice nor non-meditative practice, neither right contemplation nor wrong contemplation, neither thought nor no-thought, neither daily life nor the moment of death, neither many-calling nor once-calling. It is simply shinjin that is inconceivable, inexplicable, and indescribable. It is like the medicine that eradicates all poisons. The medicine of the Tathāgata's Vow destroys the poisons of our wisdom and foolishness [*KGGS*, III. I, p. 107].

282. Non-discrimination-3

Not discriminating at all between the poor and the rich and wellborn:

Not discriminating means not choosing, not rejecting. *Poor* means impoverished and in need. *At all* is for emphasis, meaning "not at all"; it also means "with" and "to lead." *Rich and wellborn* indicates the wealthy and the people of rank. Thus, without in the least differentiating among such people, Amida leads each and every person to the Pure Land.

Not discriminating between the inferior and the highly gifted:

Inferior refers to those whose knowledge is shallow, limited, and slight. *Highly gifted* indicates those with great ability for learning. Amida does not choose between the two.

Not choosing the learned and those who uphold pure precepts:

Learned means to hear and believe in numerous and diverse sacred teachings [*Notes on "Essentials of Faith Alone,"* I, pp. 457-458].

3. Shinran and Women (Thirty-Fifth Vow)

Note: The issue of the status of women in Buddhism has long been a topic of discussion among scholars in the light of the modern women's movement. It has generally been true that women have been discriminated against in all patriarchal societies, something that is imbedded in their religions. In the case of Buddhism, from early times, a Buddha possessed 32 major marks and 80 minor marks of a great man. One of these was the male organ. Consequently, women lacking these marks could not become a Buddha. Through the process of transmigration she would eventually be born a male and capable of pursuing such enlightenment. However in the Mahāyāna tradition, which adhered to the imagery of the great man, women had to undergo a transformation at the point of death in order to be born into the Pure Land and to be able to attain Buddhahood. While modern people object to this discrimination, from the ancient teachers' viewpoint such passages as the thirty-fifth Vow of Amida seemed a great boon because a woman, through her faith, could attain the transformation immediately and enter the Pure Land, resulting in her Buddhahood. The *Lotus Sūtra* dramatically portrays this situation in the transformation of the Naga king's daughter because of her faith (Chapter 12).

Shinran held that the Vow of Amida Buddha did not discriminate between men and women and in the passage above on the Great Sea of True Entrusting (above 281. Non-discrimination-2), man and woman are not distinguished. Nevertheless, Shinran extolled the thirty-fifth Vow and adopted the view of Shan-tao and Genshin regarding the issue of transformation.

283. Women-1

So profound is Amida's great compassion
That, manifesting inconceivable Buddha-wisdom,
The Buddha established the Vow of transformation into men,
Thereby vowing to enable women to attain Buddhahood
[*Hymns of the Pure Land*, I, p. 341, #60].

284. Women-2

Women, the disabled, and those of the two vehicles
Are never born in the Pure Land of happiness as they are;
The sages of the Tathāgata's pure lotus
Are born transformed from Dharmākara's lotus of perfect
    enlightenment.

Although there are initially nine grades among practicers,
Now [in the Pure Land] there are no distinctions whatever;
For all are the same in saying the nembutsu, following no other way.
It is like the rivers Tzu and Sheng becoming one taste on
entering the sea [*Hymns of the Two Gateways of Entrance and Emer-
gence*, I, p. 624].

285. Women-3

If women did not entrust themselves to Amida's Name and
    Vow,
They would never become free of the five obstructions,
Even though they passed through myriads of kalpas;
How, then, would their existence as women be transformed?
[*Hymns of the Pure Land Masters* [*Shan-tao*], I, p. 377, #64].

286. Women-4

Directing the merit of meditative and non-meditative
    practices, enter the precious land;
These are the Tathāgata's distinct provisional means.
Vaidehī being a woman, her condition was that
Of a foolish being filled with greed and anger
[Genshin, *KGSS*, VI. I, p. 220, #29].

4. *Nembutsu* and Peace

Note: All the great religions reject violence in pursuit of spiritual goals. Shinran also urged his followers to seek peace in their human relations and the world, even praying for those who persecuted them. He believed the teaching could only spread in a peaceful environment.

287. Peace-1

Nevertheless, since the prohibition of the nembutsu [in the past] led to the arising of disturbances in society, on this occasion I hope that everyone will, deeply entrusting themselves to the nembutsu and firmly embracing prayers [for peace in the world] in their hearts, together say the nembutsu. . . .

Your general defense, as you have written of it in your letter, has been well thought out. I am very pleased. In the final analysis, it would be splendid if all people who say the nembutsu, not just yourself, do so not with thoughts of themselves, but for the sake of the imperial court and for the sake of the people of the country. Those who feel uncertain of birth should say the nembutsu aspiring first for their own birth. Those who feel that their own birth is completely settled should, mindful of the Buddha's benevolence, hold the nembutsu in their hearts and say it to respond in gratitude to that benevolence, with the wish, "May there be peace in the world, and may the Buddha's teaching spread!" Please consider this carefully. I do not think you need to deliberate about any matters beyond this [*A Collection of Letters*, Letter 2. I, p. 560].

288. Peace-2

Those people, described here as such, perform deeds that will bring about the suppression of the nembutsu and act out of malice toward people of the nembutsu. In this regard, without bearing any ill will toward such persons, you should keep in mind the thought that, saying the nembutsu, you are to help them [*A Collection of Letters*, Letter 5. I, p. 566].

289. Peace-3

While holding the nembutsu in your heart and saying it always, please pray for the present life and also the next life of those who slander it. With the understanding of the people there, what more is necessary now regarding the nembutsu? But if you simply pray for the people in society who are in error and desire to lead them into Amida's Vow, it will be a response out of gratitude for the Buddha's benevolence [*A Collection of Letters*, Letter 8. I, p. 570].

5. Shinran and Prince Shōtoku

Note: Prince Shōtoku (574-622 C.E.) is referred to by Shinran as the founder of Japanese Buddhism, though it had been introduced at a much earlier time (officially 552

C.E.) The high regard Shinran extended to Shōtoku stems from the cult of Shōtoku promoted by the Tendai sect. The Prince was revered as an incarnation of Kannon in Japan, as well as Queen Śrimala in India, and the eminent monk, Hui-ssu (514-577 C.E.), a patriarch of the Tendai sect in China. For more detail on Shinran's view see his *Hymns in Praise of Prince Shōtoku*, I, pp. 433-447.

Further, Shōtoku was the prototype in Japan of the ideal Buddhist layperson who supports Buddhism, advocating it in his 17 point "Constitution," and studying Buddhist Sūtras. The constitution, though not a formal theory of government, provides a guideline for humane and just government, which certainly attracted Shinran to the passage he quoted.

Shōtoku is also credited with commentaries on the *Lotus Sūtra*, the *Vimalakīrti*, and *Queen Śrimala Sūtras*. These texts highlight lay people in contrast to the monks. Shōtoku is also noted for establishing the major festivals of Hanamatsuri, commemorating Buddha's birth, and Obon, an ancestral festival, as well as constructing numerous temples and images. As the regent for Empress Seiko (reigned 593-628 C.E.), he contributed to reorganizing the government and unifying the nation.

290. Shōtoku-1

Take refuge in Prince Shōtoku of the country of Japan!
Our indebtedness to his propagation of the Buddhist teaching
    is profound.
His compassionate activity to save sentient beings is far-
    reaching;
Do not be lax in reverent praise of him!
[*Hymns in Praise of Prince Shōtoku*, I, p. 433, #1].

291. Shōtoku-2

Great Bodhisattva Avalokiteśvara, the world-savior,
Who appeared as Prince Shōtoku,
Is like a father, never leaving us,
And like a mother, always watching over us
[*Hymns of the Dharma-Ages: Praise of Prince Shōtoku*, I, p. 418, #84].

292. Shōtoku-3

Prince Shōtoku, the world savior of great love,
Stays close to us, like a father;
Avalokiteśvara, the world savior of great compassion,
Stays close to us, like a mother
[*Hymns of the Dharma-Ages: Praise of Prince Shōtoku*, I, p. 419, #88].

293. Shōtoku-4

Out of deep care for the beings of Japan,
Prince Shōtoku, appearing from his original state,
Widely proclaimed the Tathāgata's compassionate Vow;
Let us rejoice and reverently praise him!
[*Hymns of the Dharma-Ages: Praise of Prince Shōtoku*, I, p. 419, #91].

294. Shōtoku-5

He composed the seventeen-article constitution
As the standard for the imperial law.
It is the rule for the peace and stability of the state,
The treasure that makes the country prosperous
[*Hymns in Praise of Prince Shōtoku*, I, p. 443, #58].

295. Shōtoku-6

What age, and what people, will not take refuge?
If they do not rely on the Three Treasures,
How can the people of this world
Make straight what is twisted and bent?
[*Hymns in Praise of Prince Shōtoku*, p. 446, #74].

296. Shōtoku-7

The petitions of the wealthy
Are like putting stones into water;
The claims of the poor
Are like putting water into stone
[*Hymns in Praise of Prince Shōtoku*, I, p. 446, #75].

6. Sharing the Dharma: Propagation

Note: During Shinran's lifetime scholars suggest that his community grew to several thousand, though we can only estimate from indication in the writings that leaders such as Chūtarō of Ōbu had some 90 members in his *sangha* (*A Collection of Letters*, #6, p. 567). Shinran did not designate successors nor create an ongoing organization.

One thing he did stipulate was that the followers were not to depend on secular power or outsiders to propagate the teaching. Undoubtedly he had observed the problems that arose from the Buddhist Order being supported by political power in his own contemporary age. He excoriated the priests and monks for their secular reliance (See: *Hymns of the Dharma-Ages*, I, p. 423, #100, 108).

Shinran propagated through his writings, which he shared with his followers. He made copies of his anthology, the *Kyōgyōshinshō*, which he translated to Japanese from the Chinese-style writing; wrote collections of poems-*wasan*s; disseminated copies of texts by Pure Land teachers; composed commentaries to those texts; and sent numerous letters to his disciples. Some of these materials were specifically designed to make the teaching more accessible for ordinary people. Often he would request that the letters be read to the followers in general. He declared that he wrote for the unlettered. Shinran was not a teacher with a closed fist, meaning a secret teaching. From the lowest to the highest, the teaching was available. Placing his teaching in writing secured it for the future and enabled propagation activities

Shinran believed that it was the Buddha's intention to embrace all beings with his compassion and wisdom. In this he was quite in line with Mahāyāna Buddhist tradition. Mahāyāna Buddhism is perhaps one of the major world missionary religions. Propagation, or sharing the Dharma, is its essential nature. As illustrated in the story of Dharmākara Bodhisattva in the Pure Land tradition, his Vows represent the essential Mahāyāna perspective that the person striving to become Buddha does not accept Enlightenment unless he can bring all others with him. There is a spiritual solidarity in Mahāyāna Buddhism that seeks the welfare of all beings. Initially the person intent on becoming Buddha begins the discipline to secure his/her own Enlightenment, but as they ascend the stages, they discover the indivisibility of Enlightenment and begin to work on behalf of others. They refuse final Enlightenment to return to the world to guide others to the goal.

The phrase taken from Shan-tao that the way to repay the benevolence of the Buddha is to "teach people the faith that one has received oneself" (*jishin kyōninshin*). It is widely used in Shin Buddhism to encourage more involvement of the members in the process of sharing the Dharma.

297. Propagation-1

True and real shinjin is the diamond-like mind. The diamond-like mind is the mind that aspires for Buddhahood. The mind that aspires for Buddhahood is the mind to save sentient beings. The mind to save sentient beings is the mind to grasp sentient beings and bring them to birth in the Pure Land of peace. This mind is the mind aspiring for great enlightenment. This mind is the mind of great compassion [*KGSS*, III. I, p. 113, #66].

298. Propagation-2

The mind that aspires to attain Buddhahood
Is the mind to save all sentient beings;
The mind to save all sentient beings
Is true and real shinjin, which is Amida's benefiting of others

[*Hymns of the Pure Land Masters*, I, p. 365, #18].

299. Propagation-3

Extremely difficult is it to encounter an age in which the
    Buddha appears,
And difficult indeed for a person to realize the wisdom of
    shinjin.
To come to hear the dharma rarely met with
Is again among all things most difficult.
To realize shinjin oneself and to guide others to shinjin
Is among difficult things yet even more difficult.
To awaken beings everywhere to great compassion
Is truly to respond in gratitude to the Buddha's benevolence
[Shan-tao, *KGSS*, III. I, p. 120, #94].

300. Propagation-4

You must not in any way design to spread the nembutsu by
utilizing outside people for support. The spread of the nembutsu in that area must come about through the working of the
revered Buddha [*A Collection of Letters*, Letter 7, p. 568].

301. Propagation-5

What is "great compassion"? Those who continue solely in
the nembutsu without any interruption will thereby be born
without fail in the land of happiness at the end of life. If these
people encourage each other and bring others to say the Name,
they are all called "people who practice great compassion" [*The
Sūtra of Great Compassion, KGSS*, III. I, p. 119, # 992].

302. Propagation-6

Through quoting from the various Mahayana scriptures, the
method and model for teaching and for listening will be clarified. The Great Assembly states:

The person who teaches the dharma should think of himself
as king among physicians and of his work as the elimination of

pain. He should think of the dharma that he teaches as sweet nectar (*amṛta*) or milk of the finest taste (**maṇḍa**).

The person who listens to the dharma should think that excellent understanding thereby increases and grows and that his sickness is being cured.

Such a teacher and listener together can make the Buddha-dharma flourish. They dwell always in the presence of the Buddhas [Tao-ch'o, *Passages on the Land of Happiness; KGSS*, III. I, p. 118, #92].

7. True Entrusting, the World of the Gods, and Popular Religion: Rejecting Magic and Superstition

Note: Shinran was very clear that people with true entrusting were to respect the gods and buddhas but not rely on them. According to him, Amida Buddha and also the spiritual beings in the universe support the person of true entrusting. Shinran's idea is rooted in Buddhist teaching that the gods themselves are in need of salvation in that their status, though elevated, is the product of karma. Eventually it will exhaust itself. In the meantime they serve the Buddha, dealing with the earthly needs of people. The buddhas as manifestations of Amida also assist people in the process of salvation. As a consequence of this belief, for Shinran there is no need to pray to the deities or buddhas for special needs as they are already engaged in protecting those who trust in Amida's Vow and recite *nembutsu*. All devotion is to be directed to Amida and respect is to be paid to gods and buddhas by not slandering them or ridiculing them. Trust in Amida's compassion and wisdom was a liberating experience from the anxieties, fears, and oppression of folk religion.

303. Gods-1

Those who have realized the threefold shinjin of Other Power must never disparage the other good practices or malign the other Buddhas and bodhisattvas [*Notes on "Essentials of Faith Alone,"* p. 464; See also: *Lamp for the Latter Ages*, Letter 2. I, pp. 526-527].

304. Gods-2

It is those who argue over once-calling and many-calling who are termed people of *other teachings* and *different understandings*. *Other teachings* applies to those who incline toward the Path of Sages or non-buddhist ways, endeavor in other practices, think on other Buddhas, observe lucky days and auspicious occasions, and depend on fortune-telling and ritual purification. Such people belong to non-buddhist ways, disparage the teachings of other Buddhas, or the people who perform good acts other than nembutsu. Neither should you despise those who scorn and slander people of nembutsu; rather, you should have compassion and care for them. This was Honen's teaching [*Lamp for the Latter Ages*, Letter 2. I, p. 527].

305. Gods-3

To begin with, it should never happen under any circumstances that the Buddhas and bodhisattvas be thought of lightly or that the gods and deities be despised and neglected. In the course of countless lives in many states of existence, through the benefit of innumerable, incalculable Buddhas and bodhisattvas, we have practiced all the various good acts, but we were unable to gain freedom from birth-and-death through such self-power practice. Accordingly, through the encouragement of the Buddhas and bodhisattvas for countless kalpas and innumerable lives, we now encounter Amida's Vow, which is difficult to encounter. To speak slightingly of the Buddhas and bodhisattvas out of ignorance of our indebtedness to them is to be totally lacking in gratitude for their profound benevolence.

Those who deeply entrust themselves to the Buddha's teaching are protected by all the gods of the heavens and earth, who accompany them just as shadows do things; hence, people who have entrusted themselves to the nembutsu should never think of neglecting the gods of the heavens and the earth. Even the gods and deities do not abandon us; hence, as for the Buddhas and bodhisattvas, how could we speak disparagingly or think slightingly of them? If one speaks slightingly of the Buddhas, then one is surely a person who does not entrust oneself to the nembutsu and who does not say Amida's Name [*A Collection of Letters*, Letter 4. I, p. 563].

306. Gods-4

Nirvana Sutra states: If one has taken refuge in the Buddha, one must not further take refuge in various gods [*Nirvana Sutra*; KGSS, VI. I, p. 255, #82].

307. Gods-5

Those among laywomen who hear of this samadhi and seek to learn it: . . . Take refuge in the Buddha yourself, take refuge in the dharma, take refuge in the sangha. Do not serve other teachings, do not worship devas, do not enshrine spirits, do not heed days considered lucky [*The Sūtra of the Samadhi of All Buddhas' Presence;* KGSS, VI. I, p. 255, #83].

308. Gods-6

One must give up divination, study right views, and believe deeply and decidedly in the causation of evil and merit [*Garland Sūtra;* KGSS, VI. I, p. 272, #94].

309. Gods-7

The rule of the person who renounces worldly life is not to pay homage to the king, not to pay homage to one's parents, not to serve the six kinds of blood-relatives, and not to worship spirits [*Sūtra of the Bodhisattva Precepts;* KGSS, VI. I, p. 274, #102].

Note: This passage has been very controversial in modern Shin Buddhism. Some have argued that it was directed to monks whose life transcended the secular world. Hui-yuan (334-416 C.E.), a famous monk in ancient China, had written a treatise that "Monks do not Bow before Kings." They serve a higher principle, being engaged in gaining Enlightenment. Therefore the Order is independent of the secular realm.

However, Shinran quoted this text apparently in the context of the Shin community, perhaps transferring the admonition in the passage to his community, not to involve themselves in the political conflict that disturbed the society of that time or to rely on secular power to promote the teaching. The passage also indicates that the Buddhist religious life transcends the ancestor cult, as well as the worship of spirits.

8. Ethics and Licensed Evil

Note: Licensed evil or antinomianism occurs in religions which proclaim that salvation depends completely on the divine. St. Paul in the New Testament confronted it, as did Luther in the Reformation. Shinran also had to contend with it. Essentially it declares that doing evil is no problem because it is the nature of Amida's Vow to embrace and never abandon foolish beings. Shinran's answer was that we do not take poison simply because there is an antidote.

For the good of the movement and in response to Buddha's embrace, ethics become an expression of entrusting. Nevertheless, Shinran recognizes that our passion-ridden human nature sometimes causes us to do evil. That evil is embraced by the Buddha and through entrusting, our minds may be transformed. His issue is with the conscious or intentional evil done in the belief that Amida will save us in any case.

310. Evil-1

If a person, justifying himself by saying he is a foolish being, can do anything he wants, then is he also to steal or to murder? Even that person who has been inclined to steal will naturally undergo a change of heart if he comes to say the nembutsu aspiring for the land of bliss. Yet people who show no such sign are being told that it is permissible to do wrong; this should never occur under any circumstances.

Maddened beyond control by blind passions, we do things we should not and say things we should not and think things we should not. But if a person is deceitful in his relations with others, doing what he should not and saying what he should not because he thinks it will not hinder his birth, then it is not an instance of being maddened by passion. Since he purposely does these things, they are simply misdeeds that should never have been done. . . .

It is deplorable that you have told people to abandon themselves to their hearts' desires and to do anything they want. One must seek to cast off the evil of this world and to cease doing wretched deeds; this is what it means to reject the world and to live the nembutsu. When people who may have said the nembutsu for many years abuse others in word or deed, there is no indication of rejecting this world. Thus Shan-tao teaches in the passage on sincere mind that we should be careful to keep our distance from those people who are given to evil. When has it ever been said that one should act in accordance with one's mind and heart, which are evil? You, who are totally ignorant of the sutras and commentaries and ignorant of the Tathāgata's words, must never instruct others in this way [*Lamp for the Latter Ages*, Letter 16. I, pp. 547-548].

311. Evil-2

You must not do what should not be done, think what should not be thought, or say what should not be said, thinking that you can be born in the Pure Land regardless of it. Human beings are such that, maddened by the passions of greed, we desire to possess; maddened by the passions of anger, we hate that which should not be hated, seeking to go against the law of cause and effect; led astray by the passions of ignorance, we do what should not even be thought. But the person who purposely thinks and does what he or she should not, saying that it is permissible because of the Buddha's wondrous Vow to save the foolish being, does not truly desire to reject the world, nor does such a one consciously feel himself a being of karmic evil. Hence such people have no aspiration for the nembutsu nor for the Buddha's Vow; thus, however they engage in nembutsu with such an attitude, it is difficult for them to attain birth in the next life [*Lamp for the Latter Ages*, Letter 18. I, pp. 550-551].

312. Evil-3

Signs of long years of saying the nembutsu and aspiring for birth can be seen in the change in the heart that had been bad and in the deep warmth for friends and fellow-practicers; this is the sign of rejecting the world. You should understand this fully [*Lamp for the Latter Ages*, Letter 18. I, p. 551].

313. Evil-4

There was a time for each of you when you knew nothing of Amida's Vow and did not say the Name of Amida Buddha, but now, guided by the compassionate means of Śākyamuni and Amida, you have begun to hear the Vow. Formerly you were drunk with the wine of ignorance and had a liking only for the three poisons of greed, anger, and folly, but since you have begun to hear the Buddha's Vow you have gradually awakened from the drunkenness of ignorance, gradually rejected the three poisons, and come to prefer at all times the medicine of Amida Buddha [*Lamp for the Latter Ages*, Letter 20, I, p. 553].

314. Evil-5

It is indeed sorrowful to give way to impulses with the excuse that one is by nature possessed of blind passions—excusing acts that should not be committed, words that should not be said, and thoughts that should not be harbored—and to say that one may follow one's desires in any way whatever. It is like offering more wine before the person has become sober or urging him to take even more poison before the poison has abated. "Here's some medicine, so drink all the poison you like"—words like these should never be said.

In people who have long heard the Buddha's Name and said the nembutsu, surely there are signs of rejecting the evil of this world and signs of their desire to cast off the evil in themselves. When people first begin to hear the Buddha's Vow, they wonder, having become thoroughly aware of the karmic evil in their hearts and minds, how they will ever attain birth as they are. To such people we teach that since we are possessed of blind passions, the Buddha receives us without judging whether our hearts are good or bad.

When, upon hearing this, a person's trust in the Buddha has grown deep, he or she comes to abhor such a self and to lament continued existence in birth-and-death; and such a person then joyfully says the Name of Amida Buddha deeply entrusting himself to the Vow. That people seek to stop doing wrong as the heart moves them, although earlier they gave thought to such things and committed them as their minds dictated, is surely a sign of having rejected this world. . . .

Moreover, since shinjin that aspires for attainment of birth arises through the encouragement of Śākyamuni and Amida, once the true and real mind is made to arise in us, how can we remain as we were, possessed of blind passions? . . .

. . . Moreover, in explaining the sincere mind it teaches that one should keep a respectful distance and not become familiar with those who give themselves to such wrongdoing. It teaches us rather to draw close to and become companions of our teachers and fellow-practicers. As for becoming friends with those who are given to wrongdoing, it is only after we go to the Pure Land and return to benefit sentient beings that we can become close to and friendly with them. That, however, is not our own design; only by being saved by Amida's Vow can we act as we want. But at this moment, as we are, what can we possibly do? Please consider this very carefully. Since the diamond-like mind that aspires for birth is awakened through the Buddha's working, persons who realize the diamond-like mind will surely not slander their master or be contemptuous of their true teachers [*Lamp for the Latter Ages*, Letter 20, I, pp. 553-554].

315. Evil-6

You should understand that, while your existence is one possessed of blind passions and it is difficult for you to still your mind, you will unfailingly attain birth; it is this that, in general, the masters and true teachers have taught. It is not at all taught that you should perform acts that become hindrances to people of the nembutsu and bring censure on the masters and true teachers, intentionally preferring wrong because the self is so evil. Having encountered Amida's Vow, which is rare to encounter, one should seek to respond in gratitude to the Buddha's benevolence [*A Collection of Letters*, Letter 4, I, p. 564].

9. Polemics and Disputations

Note: Shinran's understanding of true entrusting involved him in a dispute with other disciples of Hōnen and gave rise to differences among his own disciples. He was also critical of the Buddhist world in general. The *Kyōgyōshinshō* is essentially a polemical text in which Shinran documents his distinctive interpretation of Pure Land teaching and backs up his claim that he correctly represented Hōnen. Shinran employed the term *Jōdo Shinshū* (The True Essence of the Pure Land Teaching) to focus this issue.

In the Postscript of the *Record in Lament of Divergences* (I, p. 678) there is an account of an incident in which Shinran challenged the other disciples of Hōnen with the assertion that his faith was the same as Hōnen's. Doubting his claim, they inquired of Hōnen who agreed with Shinran. Also in Shinran's letters (10. Variant views-1, 11. Variant Views-2) he comments on his differences with some of Hōnen's successors and how they have changed his teaching. It is not with Hōnen but his later interpreters with whom Shinran differs. Nevertheless, he affirms Seikaku (1166-1235 C.E.) and Ryūkan (1148-1227 C.E.), whose work *Clarification of Once-calling and Many-calling* Shinran disseminated to his followers with his own commentary.

With respect to Shinran's own disciples, it appears that there were a variety of misunderstandings. Shinran was at pains in his letters to clarify these disputes and explain the correct understanding. The *Record in Lament of Divergences* also addresses problems of doctrine and practice. On the background of the Buddhism of his day Shinran's understanding of absolute Other-Power and true entrusting proved subtle and open to misinterpretation.

316. Polemics-1

As I reflect, I find that our attainment of shinjin arises from the heart and mind with which Amida Tathāgata selected the Vow, and that the clarification of true mind has been taught for us through the skillful works of compassion of the Great Sage,

Śākyamuni. But the monks and laity of this latter age and the religious teachers of these times are floundering in concepts of "self-nature" and "mind-only," and they disparage the true realization of enlightenment in the Pure Land Way. Or lost in the self-power attitude of meditative and non-meditative practices, they are ignorant of true shinjin, which is diamond-like.

Here I, Gutoku Shinran, disciple of Śākyamuni, reverently embrace the true teaching of the Buddhas and Tathāgatas and look to the essential meaning of the treatises and commentaries of the masters. Fully guided by the beneficent light of the three sutras, I seek in particular to clarify the luminous passage on the "mind that is single." I will pose questions concerning it and then present clear testimony in which explanation is found.

Mindful solely of the depth and vastness of the Buddha's benevolence, I am unconcerned about being personally abused. Let companions who aspire for the Pure Land and all who abhor this defiled world accept or discard what they will of this work, but let them not ridicule the teaching [*KGSS*, III, Preface, I, p. 77].

317. Polemics-2

That the Tathāgata's Primal Vow is spreading is indeed splendid and gladdening above all else. In this, however, there must never be any arguing, person with person in each locality, while adhering to one's own view. In the capital also there seems to be much arguing over such matters as "once-calling" and "many-calling"; this should never take place at all.

Ultimately, you should read carefully and constantly such writings as *Essentials of Faith Alone, On the Afterlife,* and *Self-power and Other Power,* and not diverge from their message. Please tell this to all people, wherever they may be. Further, if there are matters that are unclear, since I am still alive today, please take the trouble of coming to see me. Or you may ask someone to deliver a message. Please be sure to relate all of this to the people of Kashima, Namekata, and the neighboring areas also. In such disputation over once-calling and many-calling, merely futile and argumentative words are voiced. You should by all means avoid it.

Respectfully.

People who do not understand these matters discuss things of little significance. You should avoid such arguments by all means.

Second month, 3rd day

Shinran
[*A Collection of Letters*, Letter 1, I, p. 539].

10. The Teaching Encounters Opposition

Note: Pure Land teaching was a part of all East Asian Buddhist traditions as a means of giving hope to the masses. It was regarded as an *upāya* or compassionate teaching of the Buddha for people who could not undertake the rigorous practices for Enlightenment in the monastic system. Consequently there was no opposition to the teaching itself on the part of the establishment.

However, with Hōnen and his followers the situation changed. He proclaimed that in the last age in the decline of the Dharma, Amida Buddha, through his Vow, had designated the *nembutsu*, the recitation of his name, as the sole means for birth into the Pure Land (for Shinran see 251. *Nembutsu*-1). Hōnen eloquently defended this in his major work treatise on the *Nembutsu of the Select Primal Vow*. Here *nembutsu* practice was sufficient in itself to bring birth in the Pure Land and hence, became a threat to the monopoly of the established Orders, becoming the primary teaching rather than a secondary teaching. Shinran criticized some followers of Hōnen because they compromised with the traditional Buddhism, using the sundry-diverse practices as supplements to the *nembutsu*.

The great temples of Nara and Mount Hiei reacted by claiming Hōnen's Pure Land teaching was a heretical teaching and subversive to society, as well as immoral.

Sole devotion to Amida and liberation from superstition often led followers to ignore and ridicule the folk religious tradition, which disturbed the leaders whose social authority was based in traditional religion. Persecution ensued. Eventually Hōnen and his leading disciples were exiled and banished from Kyoto at the insistence of the religious establishment. Hōnen went to Tosa in Shikoku, while Shinran went to Echigo, angry with the unjust punishment.

Later, Shinran's community also faced opposition and persecution. The antagonism of the political authorities was aroused because of the anti-social activities generally termed "licensed evil," probably the breaking of conventions in various ways, ridiculing gods and buddhas, and breaking taboos. To stem rising conflict with the authorities, Shinran sent his eldest son Zenran to resolve the problem. However, Zenran may have acted too severely and assumed authority which Shinran and the leading disciples did not accept. His actions misrepresented Shinran and were contradictory to his teaching of Other-Power and equality. The disciple Shōshin and others had to go to Kamakura to defend the teaching, in a suit, apparently brought about by Zenran. Shōshin was successful. Shinran painfully disowned Zenran in order to restore the confidence of the disciples in his leadership and sincerity.

In his later letters Shinran counsels the disciples on persecution and admonishes them not to give the authorities any reason to repress the teaching. True entrusting works a transformation in thinking and acting in the devotee which would inspire proper behavior in society.

318. Opposition-1

Teachers of the past have stated that practicers of the nem-butsu should act with compassion for those who commit such obstruction, feel pity for them, and earnestly say the nembutsu, thereby helping those who seek to hinder them. You should carefully ponder this [*A Collection of Letters*, Letter 4, I, p. 564].

319. Opposition-2

The right teaching must not be lost sight of just because those people are speaking falsehoods. This is also the case with worldly matters. Even though manor lords, bailiffs, and landowners are involved in wrongdoing, people should not be confused. No one can destroy the Buddhist teaching. As a metaphor for those affiliated with the Buddhist teaching who act to destroy it, it is said [in a sūtra] that they are like the worms within the body of the lion that injure the lion. Thus, there are people affiliated with the Buddhist teaching who attack and obstruct people of the nembutsu. You should have a clear understanding of this [*A Collection of Letters*, Letter 5, I, p. 566; See the entirety of the letter quoted in the entry 317. Polemics-2].

F. Life Fulfillment

1. The Pure Land

Note: All major world religions have to account for human fulfillment and the after-life. One of the first questions teachers of religion encounter is: "What happens to me when I die?" The loss of loved ones and close friends and the prospect of one's own demise, as we advance in age and the end of life draws near, prompts this question. In our contemporary age end of life issues also raise the question of human fulfillment in this world and beyond.

The concept of the Pure Land is often compared with the concept of Heaven or Paradise in other religions, such as Christianity and Islam. Because of oppression and despotism in society, the Pure Land, like a heaven, often appears as an alternative to suffering in this world. It is depicted as "Otherworldly." In popular Pure Land teaching emphasis was placed on the aspect of "going to" the Pure Land so many millions of miles to the West, reinforcing its otherworldly character.

While there are afterlife dimensions, the Pure Land, in some interpretations, is also an aspect of this world. When the Buddhist concept is fully presented, there are considerable differences from the concept of Heaven in other faiths.

We may note, first of all, that in the early tradition, now known as Theravāda, there is no conception of the Pure Land. When the Buddha completed his course in this world, he achieved *Nirvāna* without residue in contrast to *Nirvāna* with residue, which he attained with his enlightenment. Gautama Buddha had chosen, according to Theravāda Buddhist understanding, to remain in this world to share the Dharma, even though he had done everything required to enter *Nirvāna*. *Nirvāna* was an ineffable, inconceivable state where karma was exhausted and the conditions that create new life forms were dissolved. When the Buddha left this world, his state was indescribable. Consequently, early representations of the Buddha show him as an empty seat. He was the trackless one.

However, as Buddhist thought continued to evolve, it eventually gave rise to the Mahāyāna teaching. In Mahāyāna thought each Buddha purified a land where he taught the beings who were born there. Basing itself on an idealized understanding of Gautama Buddha, people during his time gained enlightenment through the influence of his presence. Therefore, people could attain Buddhahood in a Buddha land that was absolutely pure, because a Buddha was present in that land. As Mahāyāna mythology unfolded, innumerable Buddha lands are depicted in every sector of the universe, termed the ten directions (four cardinal points, four intermediate directions, the nadir, and zenith). They are the great universe of three thousand great chiliocosms. Initially the Western Pure Land of Amida was one of these lands. In the course of history the cult of Amida grew, becoming the supreme goal of fulfillment within the Pure Land movement, which reached its peak with Shinran and other successors of Hōnen in Japan.

For some people the Pure Land of Amida became an object of meditation and visualization promoted by the dissemination of the *Samādhi of Direct Encounter with the Buddhas of the Present Sūtra* (*Pratyutpanna Samādhi Sūtra* [abbreviated name]) and the *Contemplation Sūtra*. Gradually the recitation of the name of Amida also became a means for entering the *samādhi*-trace state aimed at visualizing Amida and the Pure Land. Through such "mystical" or spiritual experiences, a practitioner gained union with Amida Buddha and an assurance of birth in that land.

The recitation of the name gradually became an independent practice and source of merit toward birth into the Pure Land for ordinary people who could not engage in the rigorous monastic discipline. This development reached its culmination in Hōnen, who made it the sole practice whereby monks and lay people could attain birth in the Pure Land during the Last Age. The Pure Land, from one perspective, is a symbolic expression for *Nirvāna*. The bliss, joy, and freedom of that land embody the conditions that attend the realization of *Nirvāna* itself. However, it is given mythic, symbolic expression as the object of meditation. Visualization of the Pure Land brings union with Amida.

On the popular level, the ordinary person viewed the Pure Land as liberation from the bondage to life and its sufferings in this world. In this aspect, it would appear as a heaven. Shinran, in some of his letters, affirms the belief of his followers that they will meet in the Pure Land and there will be reunion there with those we lose by separation in this world. This is the natural yearning of the heart in the face of great loss. It is also a response to the human desire for continuity and survival. However, it is to be noted that the Pure Land is a world of non-ego and not a sphere for the satisfaction of personal desire. Therefore, T'an-luan, an early Chinese teacher declared: "A person who, without awakening the mind aspiring for supreme enlightenment, simply hears that bliss is enjoyed in that land without interruption and desires to be born there for the sake of the bliss; such a person will not be able to attain birth. Thus it is said, They do not seek the sustained bliss for their own sake, but think only of freeing all sentient beings from pain" (*KGSS*, III. I, pp. 108-109).

The popular belief also supports the belief in the existence of the Pure Land beyond this world. However, in line with Mahāyāna teaching, the existence of the Pure Land cannot be substantial or objective. Substantiality (the belief that things have independent, self-standing existence) and objectivity (the belief that things exist outside or apart from our minds and consciousness) are considered delusions of the unenlightened mind. While at a certain level of spiritual development the disciple may entertain such beliefs, through their spiritual growth they come to know the true status of such beliefs. They are *upāya* or compassionate means taught to encourage hope and commitment while educating the disciple to the deeper understanding.

The Pure Land Sūtras, supporting the popular tradition, depict the Pure Land dualistically as a world at great distance from this world. However, traditions which stress forms of meditation striving for non-dual experience, such as Zen, teach that through spiritual discipline and spiritual purification, one may see that this world is already the Pure Land. However, Shinran appears to dispute the idea that the Pure Land is only a matter of one's condition of mind, which he associates with self power practice (See 316. Polemics-1).

A major point concerning the Pure Land in Mahāyāna tradition is that the devotee does not remain in the Pure Land enjoying the paradisiacal existence for itself. Rather, the Mahāyāna Bodhisattva teaching follows the example of Gautama: After achieving *Nirvāna* by his Enlightenment, the Buddha remained in the world to teach others and open the door to Enlightenment for all. Likewise the devotee, on birth into the Pure Land, achieves Enlightenment under optimum conditions and as a Bodhisattva, devotes himself to bringing others to Enlightenment before entering *Nirvāna*. The principle of returning from the Pure Land, based on the twenty-second Vow (See 59. Vows-1), is the other side of seeking to go to the Pure Land and has not received as much emphasis in the popular view. Amida's Vows indicate that the Bodhisattva will not accept final Enlightenment until all can attain it with him.

The principle of the solidarity of Enlightenment, putting the Enlightenment of others before one's own, is an expression of the self-giving aspect of Mahāyāna teaching and contrasts with the belief that entry into heaven is an individual, personal salvation from this world, unrelated to the salvation of others left behind.

Shinran distinguishes the True Buddha Land and the Transformed Buddha Land. In the fifth volume of the *Kyōgyōshinshō*, he presents the True Buddha Land which is *Nirvāna*, where the devotee immediately becomes Buddha with no elapse of time. It is the realm realized by true entrusting. The Transformed Buddha Land, taken up in the sixth volume is the traditional Pure Land where one goes as a result of meritorious practice and karma. It represents the fulfillment of self-power practice. Shinran employed the symbolism derived from the Sūtras, such as birth in the Border Land which is also called Embryonic birth, Land of Sloth and Pride, or Transformed Land, where they spend time before entering the True Pure Land.

A point of concern for Shinran and Pure Land teachers who proclaimed the unconditional compassion of Amida Buddha was the exclusionary clause of the Eighteenth Vow. The Vow declared that those people who committed the five grave offenses or slandered the Dharma could not enter the Pure Land. Shan-tao interpreted the clause as a cautionary statement to prevent people from committing those deeds. Shinran followed him in that view and simply quoted his text. Ultimately, all people, despite their evil, will be born in the Pure Land, undergoing a transformation through true entrusting.

320. Pure Land-1

Casting off long kalpas of painful existence in this world of
   Sahā,
We live in expectation of the Pure Land, the uncreated;
This is the power of our teacher, Śākyamuni;
Let us respond always in gratitude for his compassion and
   benevolence
[*Hymns of the Pure Land Masters* (Shan-tao), I, p. 383, #87].

321. Pure Land-2

Reverently contemplating the true Buddha and the true land, I find that the Buddha is the Tathāgata of inconceivable light and that the land also is the land of immeasurable light. Because they have arisen through the fulfillment of Vows of great compassion, they are called true fulfilled Buddha and land. There are relevant Vows that were made: the Vows of light and of life [*KGSS*, V. I, p. 177, #1].

322. Pure Land-3

Contemplating the features of that world, I see that it transcends the three realms: He sees that world of happiness to be boundless, like empty space; its breadth and vastness are likened to empty space [*Notes on the Inscription on Sacred Scrolls*, I, p. 502].

323. Pure Land-4

In the pure fulfilled land of the Great Vow, grade and level are irrelevant; in the space of an instant, one swiftly transcends and realizes the supreme, perfect, true enlightenment. Hence, transcending crosswise [*KGSS*, III. I, p. 114, #73].

324. Pure Land-5

In the land of happiness, sravakas, bodhisattvas,
Human beings, and devas all possess luminous wisdom,
And their bodily features and adornments are all the same;
Different terms are used for them only in accord with the forms of existence in other worlds.
[*Hymns of the Pure Land*, I, p. 330, #22]

325. Pure Land-6

Although initially there are nine grades of beings,
Because the birth attained through Amida's pure Primal Vow
Is birth that is no-birth,
The Pure Land is free of such discrimination.

Shinran Note: Birth that is no-birth: birth that is apart from birth in the six courses. Persons of true and real shinjin are not born in the six courses or four forms of birth; hence, "no-birth."

Nine grades of beings: Although originally there are nine grades of sentient beings, once they have been born in the fulfilled land, not a single one is differentiated [*Hymns of the Pure Land Masters*, T'an-luan, I, pp. 372-373, #46].

326. Pure Land-7

Come also means to return. To return is to attain the supreme nirvana without fail because one has already entered the ocean of the Vow; this is called "returning to the city of dharma-nature." The city of dharma-nature is none other than the enlightenment of Tathāgata, called dharma-body, unfolded naturally. When persons become enlightened, we say they "return to the city of dharma-nature." It is also called realizing true reality or suchness, realizing the uncreated or dharma-body, attaining emancipation, realizing the eternal bliss of dharma-nature, and attaining the supreme enlightenment. When persons attain this enlightenment, with great love and great compassion immediately reaching their fullness in them, they return to the ocean of birth-and-death to save all sentient beings; this is known as attaining the virtue of Bodhisattva Samantabhadra. To attain this benefit is *come*; that is, "to return to the city of dharma-nature" [*Notes on "Essentials of Faith Alone,"* I, p. 454].

Note: Interpreting the term Tathāgata, "Thus come, Thus go," Shinran indicates two "returnings" whereby through true entrusting we return to the city of dharma-nature, the Pure Land, which is Enlightenment. On the other hand, the second returning is to return to this world in order to save all beings.

327. Pure Land-8

Concerning the true land, the *Larger Sutra* states, "Land of immeasurable light" and "Land of all-knowing wisdom."

The *Treatise* states, "It is infinite, like space, vast and boundless."

Concerning birth, the *Larger Sutra* states, "All receive the body of naturalness (*jinen*) or of emptiness, the body of boundlessness."

The *Treatise* states, "The beings of the Tathāgata's pure lotus are born transformed from the lotus of perfect enlightenment." Further, "For they are the same in practicing the nembutsu and follow no other way."

Further, the words, "Birth that is inconceivable," refer to this.

Provisional Buddhas and lands are discussed below.

We have noted already that both true and provisional were fulfilled from the ocean-like Vow of great compassion; we know, therefore, that both are fulfilled Buddha and land. Since there are thousands of differences in the causes of birth in the provisional Buddha-lands, there are thousands of differences in the lands. They are termed "transformed bodies of skillful means" and "transformed lands of skillful means." Being ignorant of the distinction between true and provisional, people misunderstand and lose sight of the Tathāgata's vast benevolence [*KGSS*, V. I, p. 203].

328. Pure Land-9

The Pure Land is free forever from slander and dislike; all are equal, with no anxieties or afflictions. Whether human or deva, good or evil, all can reach the Pure Land. On attaining it, their distinctions vanish; all equally enter the stage of non-retrogression. Why is it thus? It comes about because Amida, in his causal stage, under the guidance of Lokeśvararāja Buddha, abandoned his throne and left his home, and awakening the mind of compassion and wisdom, widely proclaimed his Forty-eight Vows. Through the power of the Buddha's Vows, the karmic evil of the five grave offenses and the ten transgressions is eradicated and all are brought to attainment of birth. When those who slander the dharma or abandon the seed of Buddhahood turn about at heart, they all reach the Pure Land [Shan-tao, *KGSS*, III. I, p. 149, #122].

Note: This passage from Shan-tao is quoted as a word of Shinran here because he simply accepts Shan-tao's explanation of the exclusionary clause in the Eighteenth Vow. Popular Pure Land teaching held to the universality of salvation of even the most wicked person and therefore it was necessary to explain away the clear exclusion stated in the Vow. Excluding anyone from final salvation seemed contradictory to the constant and consistent expression of Amida's compassion and wisdom throughout the Sūtras.

329. Pure Land-10

To reveal, with reverence, the transformed Buddha-bodies and lands: The Buddha is as taught in the *Sutra of Contemplation on the Buddha of Immeasurable Life*; the Buddha in the "contemplation of the true body" is such a Buddha-body. The land refers to the Pure Land as described in the *Contemplation Sutra* and is also as taught in such sutras as the *Sutra of the Bodhisattvas' Dwelling in the Womb*; the "realm of indolence and pride" is such a land. Or again, it is as taught in the *Larger Sutra of Immeasurable Life*; the "city of doubt" and "womb-palace" are such [*KGSS*, VI. I, p. 207 #1].

330. Pure Land-11

All the good acts and myriad practices,
Because they are performed with a sincere mind and

aspiration,
Become, without exception, provisional good
That will lead to birth in the Pure Land
[*Hymns of the Pure Land*, I, p. 342, #63].

331. Pure Land-12

Those who say the Name in self-power, whether meditative
   or non-meditative—
Having indeed taken refuge in the Vow that beings ultimately
   attain birth
Will spontaneously, even without being taught,
Turn about and enter the gate of suchness.

Shinran Note: Ultimately attain: Amida vowed that those who
say the Name with a mind of self-power will ultimately attain
birth.

   Turn about and enter the gate of suchness: to turn, changing
into one who will attain the enlightenment of dharma-body
[*Hymns of the Pure Land*, I, p. 343, #66].

332. Pure Land-13

The depth of the Buddha's benevolence is such that even with
birth in the realm of indolence and pride, the borderland, the
city of doubt, or the womb-palace, which is brought about
only through the compassion revealed in Amida's Nineteenth
and Twentieth Vows, we meet with a happiness that surpasses
understanding. Thus the depth of the Buddha's benevolence
is without bound. But how much more should we realize the
benevolence of the Buddha with birth into the true and real fulfilled land and attainment of the enlightenment of the supreme
nirvana. This is not a matter that Shōshin-bō or I have decided
ourselves. Not in any way at all.

Kenchō 7 [1255], Tenth month, 3rd day

Gutoku Shinran
Written at age 83
[*Lamp for the Latter Ages*, Letter 2, I, p. 527].

333. Pure Land-14

The Master of Kuang-ming temple states:

Question: According to the Forty-eight Vows, only those who commit the five grave offenses and those who slander the right dharma are excluded and cannot attain birth. Here, according to the passage on the lowest grade of the lowest rank in the *Contemplation Sutra*, those who slander the dharma are set apart and those who commit the five grave offenses are grasped. What does this mean?

Answer: The intent may be understood as a teaching to make us desist from evil. . . . When sentient beings commit them, they plunge directly into Avici hell, where they undergo long kalpas of terror and panic without any means of emerging. The Tathāgata, fearing that we would commit these two kinds of faults, seeks to stop us through compassionate means by declaring that we will then not be able to attain birth. This does not mean that we will not be grasped.

It is taught, concerning the lowest grade of the lowest rank, that those who commit the five grave offenses are taken up but those who slander the dharma are excluded; this is because beings [of the lowest grade] have already committed the five grave offenses, but must not be abandoned to endless trans-migration. Thus Amida, awakening great compassion, grasps them and brings them to birth. Since, however, they have yet to commit the karmic evil of slandering the dharma, in order to prevent them from doing so it is stated that if one slanders the dharma one will not attain birth. This is to be understood as relevant to those who have not committed this evil. Even if one has committed it, one will nevertheless be grasped and brought to attainment of birth. Although one attains birth in the Pure Land, however, one must pass many kalpas enclosed in a lotus bud. . . . But apart from these obstructions, they do not undergo any form of pain [*KGSS*, III. I, p. 148].

334. Pure Land-15

In reflecting on the *Sutra of Immeasurable Life* taught at Rajagrha, it is clear that although among the three levels of practicers some are superior in practice and some inferior, not one has failed to awaken the mind aspiring for supreme enlightenment. This mind aspiring for supreme enlightenment is the mind that aspires to attain Buddhahood. The mind that aspires to attain Buddhahood is the mind to save all sentient beings. The mind to save all sentient beings is the mind to grasp sentient beings and brings them to birth in the land where the Buddha is. Thus, the person who aspires to be born in the Pure Land of happiness must unfailingly awaken the mind aspiring for supreme enlightenment. Suppose there is a person who, without awakening the mind aspiring for supreme enlightenment, simply hears that bliss is enjoyed in that land without interruption and desires to be born there for the sake of the bliss; such a person will not be able to attain birth. Thus it is said, They do not seek the sustained bliss for their own sake, but think only of freeing all sentient beings from pain. Sustained bliss means that the Pure Land of happiness is sustained by the power of Amida Tathāgata's Primal Vow, and that the enjoyment of bliss is without interruption [T'an-luan, *KGSS*, IV. I, pp. 167-168, #17].

2. Assurance of Fulfillment

Note: Shinran assured his followers that in the moment of reception of true entrusting, our birth becomes determined and secure. This could be because true entrusting was grounded in Buddha's Vow of the embrace that never abandons and not on the vagaries of individual believing. In the experience of true entrusting, the person experiences the conviction of the truth of the Vow as something given, not something generated by one's own will. In the interplay between the awareness of one's passion-ridden condition and hearing about Amida's Vow, true entrusting emerges that this is the truth of one's life. It is not a fact for intellectual assent, but a self-evident truth in one's consciousness.

On the background of Japanese Buddhist tradition, it was a major shift in religious orientation. Till Shinran, the focus of religion was on practice, meditation, morality, etc. It was cumulative and meritorious. In Pure Land tradition there was emphasis on counting the number of *nembutsu*. But the question was always: "Am I pure enough?", "Have I done enough?" From the human side of the equation there is always anxiety, present in the belief in the potency of the last thought at the moment of death and requiring the deathbed rites picturing the belief in the descent of the Buddha to welcome the devotee to the Pure Land.

From the standpoint of Buddhist teaching in Shinran's background, the devotee would attain the status of non-retrogression in the Pure Land. In translation it is called the Rightly Established State, Stage of the Truly Settled, or Company of the Truly Assured. According to the Eleventh Vow, it is in the Pure Land where this status is attained (See 59. Vows-1). There one received assurance of final enlighten-ment. Shinran shifted the time from the future in the Pure Land to the present life, here and now. There is an emphasis on immediacy. The moment of the turning of the mind and reception of true entrusting is the moment, in effect, when one is born into the Pure Land. One's actual death is to become Buddha immediately without elapse of time as in the traditional Pure Land teaching.

335. Assurance-1

Persons who truly realize shinjin,
Which is directed to them through Amida's Vow of wisdom,
Receive the benefit of being grasped, never to be abandoned;
Hence they attain the stage equal to perfect enlightenment
[*Hymns of the Dharma-Ages*, I, p. 405, #25].

336. Assurance-2

The person who attains the stage equal to perfect
    enlightenment
By the working of the Vow of birth through the nembutsu,
Being the same as Maitreya,
Will realize great, complete nirvana
[*Hymns of the Dharma-Ages*, I, p. 405, #27].

When we entrust ourselves to the inconceivable Buddha-
    wisdom,
We dwell in the stage of the truly settled
Those who are born transformed [in the Pure Land] are of
    superior wisdom,
And they realize the supreme enlightenment
[*Hymns of the Dharma-Ages*, I, p. 410, #47].

337. Assurance-3

The *Larger Sutra of the Buddha of Immeasurable Life* states:
    All sentient beings aspire to be born in that land; they then attain birth and dwell in the stage of non-retrogression.
    Aspire to be born in that land is a command: All beings should aspire to be born in that land!
    They then attain birth means that when a person realizes shinjin, he or she is born immediately. "To be born immedi-ately" is to dwell in the stage of non-retrogression. To dwell in

the stage of non-retrogression is to become established in the stage of the truly settled. This is also called the attainment of the equal of perfect enlightenment. Such is the meaning of *they then attain birth.*

Then means immediately; "immediately" means without any passage of time and without any passage of days [*Notes on "Essentials of Faith Alone,"* I, p. 455].

338. Assurance-4

You should understand that the moment of settling of those who entrust themselves to Tathāgata's Vow is none other than the settling into the stage of non-retrogression, because they receive the benefit of being grasped, never to be abandoned. Whether we speak of the settling of true shinjin or the settling of the diamond-like shinjin, both come about through being grasped, never to be abandoned. Thus is awakened the heart and mind that will attain the supreme enlightenment. This is called the stage of non-retrogression, the stage of the truly settled, and the stage equal to the perfect enlightenment.

The Buddhas in the ten quarters rejoice in the settling of this mind and praise it as being equal to the hearts and minds of all Buddhas. Thus, the person of true shinjin is said to be equal to Buddhas. He is also regarded as being the same as Maitreya, who is in [the rank of] succession to Buddhahood [*Lamp for the Latter Ages*, Letter 7, I, p. 532].

339. Assurance-5

Further, concerning being equal to Tathāgata: illuminated by the light of the Buddha, foolish beings possessed of blind passions attain shinjin and rejoice. Because they attain shinjin and rejoice, they abide in the stage of the truly settled. Shinjin is wisdom. This wisdom is the wisdom attained because we are grasped by the light of Other Power. The Buddha's light is also wisdom. Thus we can say that the person of shinjin and the Tathāgata are the same. "Same" means that, in shinjin, they are equals. The stage of joy signifies the stage in which people rejoice in shinjin. Since a person rejoices in shinjin, he or she is said to be the same as the Tathāgata [*Lamp for the Latter Ages*, Letter 14, I, p. 544].

340. Assurance-6

In this compassionate Vow it has been vowed that the person who has realized true and real shinjin is decidedly brought to attain the equal of perfect enlightenment. The equal of perfect enlightenment is the stage of the truly settled. With regard to the equal of perfect enlightenment, it is vowed that one is brought to be the same as Bodhisattva Maitreya, who is in the rank of succession to Buddhahood. These selected Primal Vows are Bodhisattva Dharmākara's universal Vows that surpass conceptual understanding. Thus, in the *Larger Sutra*, the nembutsu practicer of true and real shinjin is said to be "next [to enlightenment], like Maitreya." It is taught that these are the great Vows of directing of virtue in the aspect for our going forth to the Pure Land [*Passages on the Two Aspects of Tathāgata's Directing of Virtue*, I, p. 634].

341. Assurance-7

At the moment persons encounter Amida's Vow—which is Other Power giving itself to us—and the heart that receives true shinjin and rejoices becomes settled in them, they are grasped, never to be abandoned. Hence, the moment they realize the diamond-like mind, they are said to abide in the stage of the truly settled and to attain the same stage as Bodhisattva Maitreya. . . .

Since persons of true and real shinjin are of the same stage as Maitreya, they are equal to Buddhas. Moreover, all Buddhas feel great joy when such a person rejoices in the realization of true shinjin, and they proclaim, "This person is our equal."

Śākyamuni's words of rejoicing are found in the *Larger Sutra*: "The one who sees, reveres, and attains [the dharma] and greatly rejoices—that person is my excellent, close companion"; thus he teaches that the person who has attained shinjin is equal to Buddhas.

Further, since Maitreya has already become one who is certain to attain Buddhahood, he is called Maitreya *Buddha*. By this we know that the person who has already realized shinjin that is Other Power can be said to be equal to Buddhas. You should have no doubts about this [*Lamp for the Latter Ages*, Letter 18, I, p. 549].

342. Assurance-8

Any assertion that we will not be born is clearly baseless.
We necessarily attain birth in the land of happiness,
And thereupon realize that birth-and-death is itself great
nirvana.
This is the path of easy practice; it is termed Other Power
[*Hymns of the Two Gateways of Entrance and Emergence*, I, p. 628].

3. The Presentness of Salvation

Note: It is one of Shinran's contributions to the development of Pure Land Buddhism that he made it a matter of this life, what he calls "ordinary times" (See below 349. Equality-7), and not merely the future in the afterlife. In traditional teaching one carried out the practice with the expectation of future fulfillment. However, Shinran highlighted the experience of true entrusting and its accompaniments of joy and confidence in the embrace of the Buddha. Shinran distinguished between the joy of what has been attained and the joy of what will be attained. The joy that is attained is the assurance that one's birth in the Pure Land is determined and no longer a matter of concern, while we are also joyful that eventually we shall be born into the Pure Land and attain Buddhahood.

Shinran's interpretation offered liberation from religious fears concerning this life and the hereafter. Shinran did not reject the afterlife, but it no longer held the terrors of transmigration and passing through hells. Death was immediate attainment of Buddhahood, the crosswise transcending which distinguishes Shin Buddhism from other traditions in Shinran's classification of doctrines (See above pp. 103-105). For this reason Shinran could declare that he never said *nembutsu* even once out of filial piety (See 278. *Nembutsu*-29; *A Record in Lament of Divergences*, Chapter 5. I, p. 664). While he cared for his relatives and all sentient beings, salvation was given through the power of the Vow and not self-power actions in the transfer of merit by recitation of the Name.

a. Equality with the Buddha

Note: Another aspect of the assurance a person receives through true entrusting is the attainment of equality with the Tathāgata (Buddha), Maitreya, Vaidehī, etc. The basis for Shinran's view is that the causes for Buddhahood are all established through Amida's embrace and our resultant trust in the Vow. Shinran likens it to a Crown Prince who will ascend the throne, but is not elevated yet. It is possible that Shinran came to this idea as a counterbalance to the basic principle of the Esoteric Buddhist effort (Tendai and Shingon) to become Buddha in this very body through ritual and meditative discipline.

It is important to note that Shinran is not saying that we actually become Buddhas but that the causes are established for our becoming Buddha upon our death. Shinran is very clear that in this life we remain foolish beings and are not fully realized Buddhas with all the spiritual perfection and infallibility that implies. Shinran's purpose was to give confidence to those who felt they were undeserving, and not to build egos.

343. Equality-1

Truly we know that because Mahasattva Maitreya has perfectly realized the diamond-like mind of the stage equal to enlightenment, he will without fail attain the stage of supreme enlightenment beneath a dragon-flower tree at the dawn of the three assemblies. Because sentient beings of the nembutsu have perfectly realized the diamond-like mind of crosswise transcendence, they transcend and realize great, complete nirvana on the eve of the moment of death. Hence the words, *As such,* the same.

Moreover, the people who have realized the diamond-like mind are the equals of Vaidehī and have been able to realize the insights of joy, awakening, and confidence. This is because they have thoroughly attained the true mind directed to them for their going forth, and because this accords with [the working of] the Primal Vow, which surpasses conceptual understanding [*KGSS*, III. I, p. 123, #103].

344. Equality-2

To welcome means that Amida receives us, awaits us. Hearing the inconceivable selected Primal Vow and the holy Name of supreme wisdom without a single doubt is called true and real shinjin; it is also called the diamond-like mind. When sentient beings realize this shinjin, they attain the equal of perfect enlightenment and will ultimately attain the supreme enlightenment, being of the same stage as Maitreya, the future Buddha. That is, they become established in the stage of the truly settled. Hence shinjin is like a diamond, never breaking, or degenerating, or becoming fragmented; thus, we speak of "diamond-like shinjin." This is the meaning of *to welcome* [*Notes on "Essentials of Faith Alone,"* I, pp. 454-455].

345. Equality-3

They then attain birth means that when a person realizes shinjin, he or she is born immediately. "To be born immediately" is to dwell in the stage of non-retrogression. To dwell in the stage of non-retrogression is to become established in the stage of the truly settled. This is also called the attainment of the equal of perfect enlightenment. Such is the meaning of *they then attain birth.*

Then means immediately; "immediately" means without any passage of time and without any passage of days [*Notes on "Essentials of Faith Alone,"* I, p. 455].

346. Equality-4

Immediately (soku) means at once. *Immediately [attain] birth* is to become settled in the stage of the truly settled without any time elapsing, without a day passing. This is expressed, *when they become mindful of the Vow, they are immediately brought to the attainment of birth.*

Soku also means to ascend, which describes the status of one who will necessarily rise to a certain rank. In secular usage, to rise to the throne of the country is "ascension to rank." The person of the rank of crown prince necessarily rises to the rank of king. Likewise, ascending to the stage of the truly settled is similar to holding the rank of crown prince, with ascension to rank—enthronement in the case of the prince—corresponding to the attainment of supreme great nirvana. Amida has vowed that the person of shinjin, having reached the stage of the truly settled, shall necessarily attain nirvana. This is called *the essential purport*, meaning that the realization of the enlightenment of nirvana is taken to be fundamental [*Notes on Once-Calling and Many-Calling*, I, p. 488].

347. Equality-5

Immediately enter the stage of the definitely settled: The moment persons entrust themselves to the Buddha, they enter the stage of the definitely settled. *Enter the stage of the definitely settled*: When a person thinks on Amida truly, without fail he or she becomes established in the stage of the truly settled [*Notes on the Inscriptions on Sacred Scrolls*, I, p. 499].

348. Equality-6

*Contemplating the power of the Buddha's Primal Vow, I see that
no one who encounters it passes by in vain:* Beholding the power
of the Tathāgata's Primal Vow, I see that people who entrust
themselves to it do not meaninglessly remain in samsaric life
here.

*It quickly brings to fullness and perfection the great treasure
ocean of virtues: Able to bring quickly* means that the great
treasure ocean of virtues is effectively brought to perfect fulfillment in the persons who entrust themselves to the power
of the Primal Vow. The boundlessness, expansiveness, and all-
inclusiveness of the Tathāgata's virtues is likened to the unobstructed fullness of the waters of the great ocean [*Notes on the
Inscriptions on Sacred Scrolls*, I, p. 502].

349. Equality-7

Grasped by the karmic power fulfilled through the great Vow,
one is brought to the attainment of birth. This refers to the
person who has already realized shinjin in ordinary times, not
to one who becomes definitely settled in shinjin and who is
blessed with Amida's compassionate grasp for the first time
at the point of death. Since persons who have realized the
diamond-like mind have been grasped and protected by the
light of Amida's heart from ordinary times, they dwell in the
stage of the truly settled. Thus the moment of death is not the
crucial matter; from ordinary times they have been constantly
grasped and protected, never to be abandoned, and so is said *to
be grasped by the power of the Vow and brought to attainment of
birth* [*Notes on the Inscriptions on Sacred Scrolls*, I, pp. 506-507].

350. Equality-8

There may be people lacking true shinjin in ordinary times
who, by the merit of having long engaged in saying the Name,
first encounter the guidance of a true teacher and realize shinjin
at the very end of their lives; at that moment, being grasped by
the power of the Vow, they attain birth. But those who await
Amida's coming at the end of life have yet to realize shinjin

and so are filled with anxiety, anticipating the moment of death
[*Notes on the Inscriptions on Sacred Scrolls*, I, p. 507].

Note: In the context of Shinran's time, people long engaged in saying (reciting) the
nembutsu could mean those persons who had been engaged in self power practice in
another Buddhist sect. As we explained above, quantitative and self power practices
can arouse anxiety concerning the sufficiency of one's practice in attaining salvation.
However, meeting with a Shin teacher, they come to know the Other-Power of the
Vow and receive assurance of their birth into the Pure Land.

351. Equality-9

Since those who have realized shinjin necessarily abide in the
stage of the truly settled, they are in the stage equal to the perfect enlightenment. . . . Although they differ, the terms "truly
settled" and "equal to enlightenment" have the same meaning
and indicate the same stage. Equal to the perfect enlightenment
is the same stage as that of Maitreya, who is in the rank of succession to Buddhahood. Since persons of shinjin will definitely
attain the supreme enlightenment, they are said to be the same
as Maitreya. . . .
. . . Know that persons of true shinjin can be called the equal
of Tathāgatas because, even though they themselves are always
impure and creating karmic evil, their hearts and minds are
already equal to Tathāgatas. . . .
. . . In the *Hymns [on the Samadhi] of All Buddhas' Presence*
Shan-tao, the Master of Kuang-ming [Shan-tao] temple, explains
that the heart of the person of shinjin already and always resides
in the Pure Land. "Resides" means that the heart of the person
of shinjin constantly dwells there. This is to say that such a
person is the same as Maitreya . . . the person of shinjin is equal
to the Tathāgatas [*Lamp for the Latter Ages*, Letter 3, p. 528].

b. Rejection of Deathbed Rites

Note: One of Shinran's boldest teachings is the rejection of the deathbed rites of
traditional Buddhism. The focus on the last thought before death has a long tradition going all the way back to ancient India and the *Upanishads*. It accompanied the
idea of transmigration. There was widespread belief that the form of one's new birth
was concentrated potentially in the last thought in life. It was important therefore to
keep the mind pure, because that moment is unknown. It was and still is an anxious
moment, since the wrong thought can doom a person to an unfortunate birth.

However, Shinran swept this tradition away. He proclaimed that that moment was inconsequential because Amida's embrace never abandons and true entrusting frees the devotee from the fear of adventitious conditions in that moment. He repeatedly comments that to continue in that belief is a mark of attachment to self power practice which places the burden on the person to achieve the constancy and purity which would avoid unfortunate outcomes. This teaching is evidence of Shinran's effort to liberate people from all forms of fear and spiritual intimidation.

352. Last Moment-1

The idea of Amida's coming at the moment of death is for those who seek to gain birth in the Pure Land by doing various practices, for they are practicers of self-power. The moment of death is of central concern to such people, for they have not yet attained true shinjin. We may also speak of Amida's coming at the moment of death in the case of those who, though they have committed the ten transgressions and the five grave offenses throughout their lives, encounter a teacher in the hour of death and are led at the very end to utter the nembutsu.

The practicer of true shinjin, however, abides in the stage of the truly settled, for he or she has already been grasped, never to be abandoned. There is no need to wait in anticipation for the moment of death, no need to rely on Amida's coming. At the time shinjin becomes settled, birth too becomes settled; there is no need for the deathbed rites that prepare one for Amida's coming [*Lamp for the Latter Ages*, Letter 1. I, p. 523].

353. Last Moment-2

It is saddening that so many people, both young and old, men and women, have died this year and last. But the Tathāgata taught the truth of life's impermanence for us fully, so you must not be distressed by it.

I, for my own part, attach no significance to the condition, good or bad, of persons in their final moments. People in whom shinjin is determined do not doubt, and so abide among the truly settled. For this reason their end also—even for those ignorant and foolish and lacking in wisdom—is a happy one [*Lamp for the Latter Ages*, Letter 6. I, p. 531].

354. Last Moment-3

There is nothing I can do about your fellow-practicers, who say that they await the moment of death. Those whose shinjin has become true and real—this being the benefit of the Vow— have been grasped, never to be abandoned; hence they do not depend on Amida's coming at the moment of death. The person whose shinjin has not yet become settled awaits the moment of death in anticipation of Amida's coming [*Lamp for the Latter Ages*, Letter 18, I, p. 549].

4. The Goal of Religion (*Gensō Ekō*)

Note: This teaching is a part of Mahāyāna Buddhist tradition as the culmination of the bodhisattva practice and a stage just prior to attaining Buddhahood. It shows that religion in Buddhism is not a selfish pursuit but has as its primary goal the salvation of all beings together. Salvation in Mahāyāna Buddhism is indivisible and if one is to be saved, all must be saved.

As a Mahāyāna teaching, the ideal was also a part of Pure Land teaching, but it was overshadowed in popular tradition by the desire to gain birth in the Pure Land and be free of the sufferings of this world. However, as an aspect of the total working of Amida Buddha, whose Vows set the pattern for religious endeavor, the salvation of all beings was central. For Shinran it was also a major concern for the devotee of true entrusting, whose mind becomes conformed to the ideal of Amida Buddha. Shinran emphasized this feature, devoting one volume of the *Kyōgyōshinshō* to it. In the Volume on Realization Shinran highlights the Twenty-second Vow (See 59. Vows-1), which depicts the bodhisattva's one birth before attaining Buddhahood.

355. Return-1

This is the Vow (22nd) of the Tathāgata's directing of virtue for our return to this world. Since this is directing of virtue for return to this world that is Other Power, neither self-benefit nor benefiting others arises from the practicer's own aspiration; they are the working of Bodhisattva Dharmākara's Vows. The great master [Hōnen] said: "In Other Power, no working is true working" [*Passages on the Two Aspects of Tathāgata's Directing of Virtue*, I, p. 635].

356. Return-2

[Directing Virtue for Our Return]

Second is Amida's directing of virtue for our return to this world. This is the benefit we receive, the state of benefiting and guiding others. It arises from the Vow of necessary attainment of the rank next to Buddhahood, also known as "the Vow for the attainment of Buddhahood after one lifetime." It may further be called "the Vow of directing virtue for our return to this world" [Twenty second Vow]. The passage declaring the fulfillment of this Vow in the *Larger Sutra* states:

The bodhisattvas of that land all fulfill the attainment of Buddhahood after one lifetime, except those who, for the sake of sentient beings, have established their own original vows and, thus adorning themselves with the virtues of universal vows, seek to bring all to emancipation.

With these sacred words we know clearly that this is the working of the universal Vow of great love and great compassion; it is the vast and inconceivable benefit. Through it one enters the thick forests of blind passion to guide beings, compassionately leading them in accord with the virtue of Samantabhadra [*Passages on the Pure Land Way*, I, pp. 301-302; See also *KGSS*, IV. I, p. 158, #14; IV. I, p. 174, #18].

357. Return-3

Those who reach the Pure Land of happiness
Return to this evil world of the five defilements,
Where, like the Buddha Śākyamuni,
They benefit sentient beings without limit
[*Hymns of the Pure Land*, I, p. 329, #20].

358. Return-4

People, once born in the Pure Land of happiness, later conceive in their hearts the wish to be born in the three realms to teach and guide sentient beings; they then abandon their life in the Pure Land and receive birth in accord with their aspiration. Though they are born into the flames of various births in the three realms, the seed of supreme enlightenment will never rot. Why? Because they are sustained by the good of Amida, the perfectly enlightened [*Treatise on the Pure Land* [Vasubandhu], *KGSS*, IV. I, p. 155, #7].

5. Attainment of *Nirvāna* (Buddhahood)

Note: The spiritual goal of all Buddhists is to attain *Nirvāna*, the freedom from the bondage of finitude, from birth is the stream of births and deaths with its attendant sufferings. While initially the emphasis in early Buddhism was on *Nirvāna*, as Mahāyāna Buddhism emerged, the goal transformed to becoming Buddha and working for the salvation of all beings. The attainment of Buddhahood was more positive and embracing than simply achieving a personal *Nirvāna*.

However, Buddhahood itself is Nirvanic. A Buddha has the same qualities as *Nirvāna*. The Pure Land is itself *Nirvāna*. It is light, bliss, purity, and serene. As Buddha represents ultimate and final freedom, so the Pure Land is a realm of absolute freedom, represented in myth as the instantaneous and spontaneous action of the residents. A Buddha is also empty and indefinable. With such fluid conceptions a Buddha can manifest in myriad forms for the salvation of beings.

According to Shinran, birth in the Pure Land, as popularly understood, even the return of the bodhisattva to work for salvation, is not the ultimate conception. Hence he composed the fifth Volume of the *Kyōgyōshinshō*, the True Buddha Land, to depict the ultimate goal, the realization of Buddha-nature, enlightenment or Buddhahood. Though it is difficult to express ultimate conceptions in ordinary language, beyond the mythic portrayals, we become one with Amida, the Infinite, embracing all reality with compassion and wisdom.

359. *Nirvāna*-1

Since shinjin arises from the Vow,
We attain Buddhahood through the nembutsu by the [Vow's]
    spontaneous working.
The spontaneous working is itself the fulfilled land;
Our realization of supreme nirvana is beyond doubt
[*Hymns of the Pure Land Masters*, Shan-tao, I, p. 382, #82].

360. *Nirvāna*-2

On reaching the land of the Vow,
We immediately realize the supreme nirvana,
And thereupon we awaken great compassion.
All this is called Amida's "directing of virtue"
[*Hymns of the Pure Land Masters*, I, p. 366, #20].

361. *Nirvāna*-3

The realization attained in the Pure Land way is the wondrous fruition attained through Amida's perfect benefiting of others. It arises from the Vow of necessary attainment of nirvana, also known as the "Vow of the realization of great nirvana." It may further be called "the Vow of realization, which is Amida's directing of virtue for our going forth." This realization is purity, reality, and no-birth (nirvana), ultimate and consummate [*Passages on the Pure Land Way*, I, p. 300].

362. *Nirvāna*-4

With these sacred words of the Buddha we know clearly that when foolish beings possessed of all blind passions—the multitudes of beings caught in birth-and-death and defiled by evil karma—realize the mind and practice that Amida directs to them for their going forth, they come to dwell among the truly settled of the Mahayana teaching. Those who dwell among the truly settled necessarily attain nirvana. When one necessarily attains nirvana, [one attains] eternal bliss. Eternal bliss is great nirvana. Great nirvana is the fruit that manifests itself in the field of benefiting and converting others. This body is the uncreated dharma-body. The uncreated dharma-body is the body of ultimate equality. The body of ultimate equality is tranquility. Tranquility is true reality. True reality is dharma-nature. Dharma-nature is suchness. Suchness is oneness [*Passages on the Pure Land Way*, I, p. 301; See also *KGSS*, IV. I, p. 153, #1].

363. *Nirvāna*-5

Thus, when one has boarded the ship of the Vow of great compassion and sailed out on the vast ocean of light, the winds of perfect virtue blow softly and the waves of evil are transformed. The darkness of ignorance is immediately broken through, and quickly reaching the land of immeasurable light, one realizes great nirvana and acts in accord with the virtue of Samantabhadra. Let this be known [*KGSS*, II. I, p. 56, #78].

364. *Nirvāna*-6

Thus we clearly know from the Tathāgata's true teaching and the commentaries of the masters that the Pure Land of peace is the true fulfilled land. Delusional and defiled sentient beings cannot, here, see [Buddha-] nature, for it is covered over by blind passions. The [Nirvana] Sutra states, "I have taught that bodhisattvas of the tenth stage see a little of Buddha-nature." Hence, we know that when we reach the Buddha-land of happiness, we unfailingly disclose Buddha-nature. This is through the directing of virtue by the power of the Primal Vow. Further, the [Nirvana] Sutra states, "Sentient beings will, in the future, possess a body of purity adorned with virtues and be able to see Buddha-nature" [KGSS, V. I, p. 202, #37].

365. *Nirvāna*-7

When foolish beings possessed of blind passions, the multitudes caught in birth-and-death and defiled by evil karma, realize the mind and practice that Amida directs to them for their going forth, they immediately join the truly settled of the Mahayana. Because they dwell among the truly settled, they necessarily attain nirvana. To necessarily attain nirvana is [to attain] eternal bliss. Eternal bliss is ultimate tranquility. Tranquility is supreme nirvana. Supreme nirvana is uncreated dharma-body. Uncreated dharma-body is true reality. True reality is dharma-nature. Dharma-nature is suchness. Suchness is oneness. Amida Tathāgata comes forth from suchness and manifests various bodies—fulfilled, accommodated, and transformed [KGSS, IV. I, p. 153, #1].

366. *Nirvāna*-8

The realm of nirvana refers to the place where one overturns the delusion of ignorance and realizes the supreme enlightenment.

Realm means "place"; know it as the place of attaining enlightenment.

Nirvana has innumerable names. It is impossible to give them in detail; I will list only a few. Nirvana is called extinction of passions, the uncreated, peaceful happiness, eternal bliss, true reality, dharma-body, dharma-nature, suchness, oneness, and Buddha-nature. Buddha-nature is none other than Tathāgata. This Tathāgata pervades the countless worlds; it fills the hearts and minds of the ocean of all beings. Thus, plants, trees, and land all attain Buddhahood [*Notes on "Essentials of Faith Alone,"* pp. 460-461].

367. Nirvāna-9

The city of nirvana is the Pure Land of peace. Through entrusting oneself, one is enabled to enter. These words exhort us to know that the person who has realized true and real shinjin is able to enter the true land fulfilled through Tathāgata's Primal Vow. Know that shinjin is the seed of enlightenment, the seed for realizing the supreme nirvana [*Notes on the Inscriptions on Sacred Scrolls*, I, p. 513].

368. Nirvāna-10

"Right-mindedness," then, is the settling of the shinjin of the universal Primal Vow. Because of the realization of this shinjin, a person necessarily attains the supreme nirvana [*Lamp for the Latter Ages*, Letter I. I, p. 523].

369. Nirvāna-11

When a person has entered completely into the Pure Land of happiness, he or she immediately realizes the supreme nirvana; he realizes the supreme enlightenment. Although the terms differ, they both mean to realize the enlightenment of the Buddha who is dharma-body. As the true cause for this realization, Bodhisattva Dharmākara gave us the Vow of Amida Buddha; this is known as directing virtue for the sake of our going forth in birth. This Vow of directing virtue is the Vow of birth through the nembutsu. To entrust oneself wholeheartedly to the Vow of birth through the nembutsu and be single-hearted is called wholehearted single practice. In terms of the Tathāgata's two forms of giving, true shinjin is to entrust oneself to the Vow of giving and be single-hearted; this shinjin arises from the working of the honored ones, Śākyamuni and Amida [*Lamp for the Latter Ages*, Letter 21. I, p. 555].

GLOSSARY

Ajātaśatru—The evil prince who murdered his father Bimbiśāra and imprisoned his mother Vaidehī in the central Pure Land legend recounted in the *Contemplation Sūtra* and in the *Nirvāṇa Sūtra*, quoted by Shinran in *Collected Works of Shinran*, KGSS, III, pp. 125-143, under the topic "The Person Difficult to Save." The prince is an example of the power of the Buddha to save.

Amida Buddha—The Buddha of Eternal Life and Infinite Light; ruler of the Western Paradise (Sukhāvatī) or Pure Land. According to the Pure Land teaching, the Buddha who established the way to Enlightenment for ordinary people; the center of worship in Pure Land Buddhism through the recitation of the *Namu-amida-butsu. See Nembutsu.*

Amṛta—The nectar of immortality, associated with Amida Buddha.

Anjin—The settled or tranquil mind; a parallel term to *shinjin*, true entrusting.

Avalokiteśvara (Japanese: Kannon)—Sanskrit name of the *Bodhisattva* of Compassion; companion of Amida Buddha, as personification of his virtue of compassion, along with Mahāsthāmaprāpta (Japanese: Seishi), the personification of wisdom.

Avīci—The lowest hell, of endless pain.

Bhikṣu, bhikṣunī—Male and female forms respectively for monk or mendicant.

Bombu—Japanese term for foolish being, common mortal, passion-ridden being; the object of Amida's compassion.

Bosatsu—Japanese for *Bodhisattva*, one destined to become Buddha.

Contemplation Sūtra—Short title of the *Sūtra on the Contemplation of Immeasurable Life.*

Devadatta—An evil accomplice of Ajātaśatru.

Dharmākara—Sanskrit name for the *Bodhisattva* who through five eons of practice perfected his Vows to establish an ideal land where all beings can easily attain Enlightenment. On completion of his Vows he became Amida Buddha and established the Western Pure Land.

Eighty Four Thousand Dharma—Symbolic term for the infinity of Buddha's teachings; signifies that there is a teaching for every condition of being. For Shinran, it meant the provisional teachings of the Sage Path of self-power that lead to true entrusting in Amida's Vow.

Ekō—Japanese term for transfer of merit, which in traditional thought was directed from the devotee to the Buddha so as to apply one's merit toward attaining Enlightenment. In Shin Buddhism, the direction is changed and Dharmākara-Amida's merit is turned toward beings to enable them to achieve Enlightenment.

Genshin (942-1017)—A major figure in the Japanese development of Pure Land teaching; author of the *Essentials of Rebirth [in the Pure Land]* (*Ōjōyōshū*), a manual that popularized the teaching and illustrated the path to salvation. His writing was instrumental in Hōnen's discovery of Shan-tao's teaching of *nembutsu*. In Shinran's lineage he was the sixth great teacher.

Gonja—a manifestation or incarnation of a Buddha or *bodhisattva*.

Hanamatsuri—The festival of flowers in Japan, commemorating the birth of the Buddha. It is held on the lunar calendar, fourth month, eighth day; solar on April 8.

Hijiri—Term for a wise and holy person; a wandering monk.

Hīnayāna—A term of criticism used by the early Mahāyāna sūtra writers to chastise followers of the Buddha who were too narrow in their understanding of the Buddha's teaching. The term means "small, narrow vehicle," compared the "spacious, large vehicle" of the Mahāyāna.

Hisō-hizoku—A term used by Shinran when he was sent into exile; it indicated that he was neither a monk nor a layperson, and that his faith transcended these institutional and social definitions.

Hōben—Japanese for *upāya*.

Hōnen (1133-1212)—Founder of the independent school of Pure Land (*Jōdo*) Buddhism in Japan. He maintained that the traditional monastic practices were not effective in the Last Age (*mappō*) nor universal for all people, as intended by Amida's Vow. He incurred opposition from the establishment Buddhism and went into exile with several disciples, including Shinran. His major treatise, which was a manifesto of his teaching, was *Senchaku hongan nembutsu shū* (Treatise on the Nembutsu of the Select Primal Vow, abbreviated to *Senchakushū*). He is the seventh great teacher in Shinran's lineage and his direct teacher.

Hongan—Primal or Original Vow, particularly the Eighteenth Vow of Amida Buddha.

Honzon—The object of worship in a Buddhist altar; also *gohonzon*, with honorific prefix.

Hōzō—Japanese reading for the name Dharmākara.

Hua-yen Sūtra—A major Mahāyāna sūtra which expresses the philosophy: "the one is all and the all is one"; in Japanese, the *Kegon Sūtra*; in English, the *Garland* or *Wreath Sūtra*.

Icchantika—A person who lacks the seed for Buddhahood and who has no potential or wish to become Buddha.

Jiriki—Self-power in contrast to Other-Power or the working of the Vow.

Jishin kyōnin shin—Shan-tao's motto for the way to repay the Buddha's benevolence. It means "to teach (share) the faith (true entrusting) which one has received oneself."

Jōdo—Japanese term for "Pure Land." Though all Buddhas have their Pure Lands, the Land of Amida Buddha became the most well-known and desired in China and Japan because of its comprehensive nature, its popular propagation, and its ease of entry through recitation of his Name.

Jōdo Shinshū—Literally "The True Teaching (sect) of the Pure Land"; generally accepted as founded by Shinran, who was a disciple of Hōnen. In contrast to Hōnen's other disciples, Shinran stressed the centrality of true entrusting, or faith, as the fundamental basis of birth in the Pure Land and Enlightenment, and not the merit of practices directed to that end.

Jōdo shū—Literally "The Pure Land Teaching (sect)." The tradition maintained by the successors of Hōnen.

Kannon—*See* Avalokiteśvara.

Kaṣāya—*See* below.

Kesa—The stole or scarf worn by clergy, indicating their ordained status.

Kimyō—"I take refuge," equivalent to *namu/namo* as the expression of dedication to the Buddha.

Kōbō Daishi (774-835)—Founder of the Japanese Shingon sect; center on Mount Kōya.

Kotis of *nayutas*—An inconceivable number; an infinity.

Larger Sutra of Eternal Life—The *Sukhāvatī-vyūha Sūtra* which gives an account of Dharmākara *Bodhisattva*'s Vows and his eventual fulfillment of them. The central sūtra for Shinran and part of a threefold complex of sūtras that include the *Sūtra of Contemplation* and the *Smaller Pure Land Sūtra*, which describes the Pure Land in detail. The title of the sūtra appears in various forms: *Sūtra of Adornment of the Realm of Bliss, Sūtra of Immeasurable Life*, or *Sūtra of Limitless Life*.

Lokeśvararāja—The name of the Buddha under whom Dharmākara *Bodhisattva* made his Forty-eight Vows to establish the Pure Land, as recounted in the *Larger Pure Land Sūtra*.

Mahāsthāmaprāpta (Japanese: Seishi)—The counterpart to Avalokiteśvara (Japanese: Kannon), symbolizing wisdom and strength; associated with Amida Buddha.

Maitreya—Popularly known as the future Buddha; symbolizes for Shinran the certainty of Enlightenment for those with true entrusting.

Mantra—A word or phrase with special power when chanted.

Mappō—A theory of the progressive degeneration of Buddhism after the passing of the Buddha. In the Pure Land tradition it was believed that Amida gave his teaching primarily for beings of the last age, who were spiritually decadent.

Mara—An evil being; a deceiver, seducer; symbol of evil.

Maudgalyāyana—A major disciple of Buddha.

Myōgō—The Name of Amida Buddha in Shin Buddhism, i.e., *Namu-amida-butsu.*

Myōkōnin—Wondrously good person; the person exemplifying true entrusting.

Naga—A dragon or serpent; a mythical being.

Namu Amida Butsu—The *nembutsu*: "I take refuge in Amida Buddha."

Namu Fukashigi Kō—Alternative form of *nembutsu* used by Shinran. It means: "I take refuge in the Inconceivable Light."

Namu Mugekō Nyorai—Alternative form of *nembutsu* used by Shinran. It means: "I take refuge in the Unobstructed (unhindered) Light."

Nembutsu—General term for "thinking on the Buddha." It can mean meditation in general Buddhism, but in Pure Land teaching it came to refer chiefly to the recitation of Amida Buddha's Name. For Shinran it also had the meaning of true entrusting to the Buddha.

Nirgrantha—Followers of heathenish teachings; a naked mendicant and opponent of Śākyamuni Buddha.

Nyorai—Japanese for *Tathāgata.*

Nyūdō—A layman who continues to live at home, while taking tonsure as a monk devoted to Buddhism.

Obon—Festival of the dead, traditionally held in Japan on the eighth lunar month, fifteenth day. Presently, by the solar calendar, July 15 or August 15.

Original Vow—*See Hongan.*

Paramitas—The six virtues in Mahāyāna Buddhism: giving, discipline, endurance, endeavor, meditation, wisdom. They make up the discipline for attaining Buddhahood.

Parinirvāṇa—Complete Nirvāṇa, final Nirvāṇa; contrasts with Nirvāṇa with residue, when Buddha decided to remain in the world to share the teaching with others.

Piṇḍala—A painless hell.

Pitaka—A "basket" or division of Buddhist sacred scriptures.

Pratyekabuddha—A Hīnayāna follower who pursues Enlightenment without a teacher, focusing on the principle of interdependence.

Primal Vow—*See Hongan.*

Ranks of the Truly Settled (or Stage of the Truly Settled)—Based on the Eleventh Vow, the assurance that one will definitely attain Enlightenment; the stage of non-retrogression. In traditional Pure Land teaching, it is attained on Birth into the Pure Land. For Shinran it comes at the moment of true entrusting.

Sage Path—The path of meditation and practices to gain Enlightenment based on self-power, or self-effort.

Saha world—This world; the world of birth and death.

Samantabhadra—An important *Bodhisattva* and a symbol of the practice of meditation and discipline; often represented on a white elephant and an attendant of Śākyamuni Buddha.

Saṃvara—A painless hell.

Śāriputra—A leading disciple of Śākyamuni Buddha.

Śāstra—A Treatise.

Seishi—*See* Mahāsthāmaprāpta.

Senju Nembutsu—The sole practice of *nembutsu;* a designation of Hōnen's interpretation of the centrality of the *nembutsu* in the last age and a basis for the independent Pure Land movement.

Shan-tao (613-681)—An important scholar of Chinese Pure Land Buddhism whose teaching greatly affected Hōnen and Shinran through his commentary on the *Sūtra of Contemplation* and by his systematization of Pure Land doctrine. He is credited with stressing the recitation of the *nembutsu* as the central act of Amida's Vow and Pure Land devotion.

Shaku—A scepter; a ceremonial instrument.

Shingyō—Joyous trusting; the term from the Primal Vow denoting the mind of *shinjin.*

Shinjin—The term for "true entrusting," which according to Shinran is the primary cause for Birth in the Pure Land. The Western term "faith," commonly used to translate this term, does not completely express the special meaning given to this Japanese word. In Shinran's view it is the transference or infusion of Amida's true mind of compassion and wisdom into the person, yielding complete reliance on Amida's Vow for one's certainty of Birth in the Pure Land. With this assurance of deliverance, recitation of *nembutsu* or religious practice becomes an expression of gratitude.

Shōjōju—*See* Ranks of the Truly Settled.

Śrāvaka—A follower of the Hīnayāna; a disciple of the Buddha; a hearer.

Śrīmālā—An ancient Indian Queen who expressed her faith in Buddhism in the *Queen Śrīmālā Sūtra,* for which Prince Shōtoku composed a commentary.

Sūtra on the Contemplation of Immeasurable Life—A text of sixteen meditations or visualizations of Amida and the Pure Land.

T'an-luan (476-542)—A major Chinese Pure Land teacher whose thought greatly influenced Shinran. The third in the lineage of seven great teachers.

Tao-ch'o (562-645)—The fourth in Shinran's lineage of great teachers.

Tariki—Other-Power; refers to the power of Amida's Vow working in our life to bring us to Enlightenment; contrast to *jiriki*—self-power.

Tathāgata—A title of the Buddha, meaning: "Thus-come thus-gone one." Buddha emerges from truth and returns to truth.

Tendai—A major sect of Buddhism initiated by Chih-i (538-597) in China on Mt. T'ien-t'ai and introduced to Japan by Saichō (767-822). It is centered on Mount Hiei, from which it exerted great spiritual and social influence in Medieval Japan. Kamakura era (1185-1332) teachers such as Hōnen, Shinran, Dōgen, and Nichiren came from Mount Hiei and had studied Tendai teaching based on the *Lotus Sūtra* and the holistic philosophy grounded in the Kegon teaching.

Tripiṭaka—"Three Baskets," referring to the three sections of the Buddhist scriptures: Sūtras (teaching), Vinaya (discipline), and Abhidharma (commentaries or discussions).

Udumbara—A tree that produced fruit without flowers every 3000 years; a symbol of the rarity of the Buddha's appearance.

Upāya—Compassionate means, tactful device; the method of teaching according to the level or capacity of students and guiding them to higher levels of understanding and insight. A major Mahāyāna principle.

Vaidehī—The wife of King Bimbīsara (cf. the story of Ajātaśatru above); the model of true entrusting in Pure Land tradition and Shin Buddhism.

Vasubandhu—A major Mahāyāna teacher who laid the foundation of the Consciousness-Only school. In Pure Land tradition his commentary to the *Larger Pure Land Sūtra* is a central text. The second great teacher in Shinran's lineage.

Vimalakīrti—A legendary lay disciple of the Buddha, renowned for his wisdom. The center of the *Vimalakīrti Sūtra* for which Prince Shōtoku wrote a commentary.

Yamabushi—Buddhist mountain ascetics who prostrated on mountains and cultivated spiritual power for healings and exorcisms, etc. They worked among the village people.

Zenchishiki—The "good friend" or "good teacher" who assists and guides a person on their path in Buddhism.

For a glossary of all key foreign words used in books published by World Wisdom, including metaphysical terms in English, consult: www.DictionaryofSpiritualTerms.org.
This on-line Dictionary of Spiritual Terms provides extensive definitions, examples and related terms in other languages.

SELECT BIBLIOGRAPHY
FOR FURTHER READING

Amstutz, Galen. *Interpreting Amida: History and Orientalism in the Study of Pure Land Buddhism.* Albany: State University of New York Press, 1997.

Bloom, Alfred. *The Promise of Boundless Compassion: Shin Buddhism for Today.* Honolulu: Buddhist Study Center Press, 2002.
_____. "The Life of Shinran Shonin: The Journey to Self Acceptance." In *Numen,* Vol. XV, 1968. Revised Edition, IBS Monograph Series 1; Berkeley, Institute of Buddhist Studies, 1994. On-line edition, http://www.shin-ibs.edu/pdfs/BloomLS.pdf, 1999 (PDF).
_____. *Shinran's Gospel of Pure Grace.* Ann Arbor, MI: Association for Asian Studies, 1965, 1991.

The Collected Works of Shinran, 2 vols. Translated by Dennis Hirota, Hisao Inagaki, Michio Tokunaga, and Ryushin Uryuzu. Kyoto: Hongwanji International Center, 1997.

Dobbins, James. *Jodo Shinshu: Shin Buddhism in Medieval Japan.* Bloomington, IN: Indiana University Press, 1989.

Foard, James, Michael Solomon, and Richard Payne. *Pure Land Tradition: History and Development.* Berkeley, CA: Regents of the University of California, 1996.

Hirota, Dennis, ed. *Toward a Contemporary Understanding of Pure Land Buddhism: Creating a Shin Buddhist Theology in a Religiously Plural World.* Albany: State University of New York Press, 2000.

Hisao Inagaki. *The Three Pure Land Sutras.* Kyoto: Nagata Bunshodo, 1994.
_____. *A Dictionary of Japanese Buddhist Terms.* Kyoto: Nagata Bunshodo, 1984

Kanamatsu, Kenryo. *Naturalness.* Bloomington IN: World Wisdom Books, 2002.

Kikumura, Norihiko. *Shinran: His Life and Thought.* Los Angeles: Nembutsu Press, 1972.

Machida Soho. *Renegade Monk: Honen and Japanese Pure Land Buddhism.* Berkeley, CA: University of California Press, 1999.

Matsunaga, Daigan and Alicia Matsunaga. *The Foundations of Japanese Buddhism,* 2 vols. Los Angeles: Buddhist Books International, 1974, 1976.

Soothill, William E. and Lewis Hodous. *A Dictionary of Chinese Buddhist Terms.* Taiwan: Buddhist Culture Service, 1934.

Suzuki Daisetz Teitaro. *Collected Writings on Shin Buddhism.* Edited by the Eastern Buddhist Society. Kyoto, Shinshu Otani-ha, 1973.
_____. *Shin Buddhism.* New York: Harper & Row, 1970.

Tamura, Yoshiro. *Japanese Buddhism: A Cultural History.* Tokyo: Kosei Publishing Co., 2000.

Taitetsu Unno. *Tannisho: A Shin Buddhist Classic.* Honolulu: Buddhist Study Center Press, 1996.
_____. *Shin Buddhism: Bits of Rubble Turn into Gold.* New York: Doubleday, 2002.
_____. *River of Fire, River of Water.* New York: Doubleday, 1998.

Takahatake Takamichi. *Young Man Shinran: A Reappraisal of Shinran's Life.* Waterloo (Ontario): Wilfrid Laurier University Press, 1987.

Takeda, Ryusei. "The Pure Land Buddhist Notion of Faith." In *Buddhist-Christian Studies,* 14 (1994), pp. 43-55 (with a response by John B. Cobb, Jr.).

Ueda, Yoshifumi and Dennis Hirota. *Shinran: An Introduction to His Thought.* Kyoto: Hongwanji International Center, 1989.

INDEX OF SELECTIONS

BIOGRAPHICAL NOTES

ALFRED BLOOM was born in Philadelphia. After enlisting in the Army in 1944, he had the opportunity to study Japanese. Greatly influenced by his Christian background, this occasion motivated his decision to become a missionary. However, an encounter with Buddhism stimulated his interest in other religions. After graduating from a seminary, Bloom began his study of Buddhism. Upon receiving a Fulbright grant, he traveled to Japan where he studied the life and thought of Shinran (1173-1262), the founder of Shin Buddhism. In 1963, he completed his doctoral studies at Harvard University. Dr. Bloom has since taught at a number of universities, including the University of Oregon and the University of Hawaii. After retiring from the University of Hawaii, Bloom became the Dean of the Institute of Buddhist Studies in Berkeley, California, a seminary and graduate school sponsored by the Buddhist Churches of America and affiliated with the Christian Graduate Theological Union.

Throughout his 35-year career, Bloom has participated in the research and study of world religions and in the Buddhist-Christian dialogue. He was ordained as a Shin minister and presently lives in Hawaii, where he is a member of the Honpa Hongwanji Mission and is active in ecumenical Buddhist activities.

Dr. Bloom is the author of numerous books and articles, the most important of which is *Shinran's Gospel of Pure Grace*, which has been translated into both Japanese and Korean.

RUBEN L.F. HABITO, Ph.D. Tokyo University, 1978, taught at Sophia University in Tokyo. Since 1989, he has been at Perkins School of Theology, Southern Methodist University, Dallas, Texas, where he is currently Professor of World Religions and Spirituality, and also Associate Dean for Academic Affairs. His works include *Experiencing Buddhism: Ways of Wisdom and Compassion; Living Zen, Loving God; Healing Breath: Zen Spirituality for a Wounded Earth; Shinran to no Deai Kara* (From My Encounters with Shinran) and many others in both Japanese and English. He was President of the Society for Buddhist-Christian Studies from 2003 to 2005, and serves as spiritual director and Teacher (Roshi) at Maria Kannon Zen Center in Dallas, Texas.

Titles in the Spiritual Masters: East & West Series by World Wisdom

The Essential Sri Anandamayi Ma: Illustrated,
by Alexander Lipsky, 2007

The Essential Swami Ramdas: Commemorative Edition,
compiled by Susunaga Weeraperuma, 2005

The Essential Shinran: A Buddhist Path of True Entrusting,
edited by Alfred Bloom, 2006

Frithjof Schuon: Messenger of the Perennial Philosophy,
by Michael Oren Fitzgerald, 2010

The Golden Age of Zen: Zen Masters of the T'ang Dynasty,
by John C.H. Wu, 2003

Honen the Buddhist Saint: Essential Writings and Official Biography,
edited by Joseph A. Fitzgerald, 2006

Introduction to Hindu Dharma: Illustrated,
edited by Michael Oren Fitzgerald, 2007

The Laughing Buddha of Tofukuji:
The Life of Zen Master Keido Fukushima,
by Ishwar C. Harris, 2004

Messenger of the Heart: The Book of Angelus Silesius,
by Frederick Franck, 2005

Paths to Transcendence: According to
Shankara, Ibn Arabi, and Meister Eckhart,
by Reza Shah-Kazemi, 2006

Samdhong Rinpoche, Uncompromising Truth
for a Compromised World,
Tibetan Buddhism and Today's World,
edited by Donovan Roebert, 2006

The Sufi Doctrine of Rumi: Illustrated Edition,
by William C. Chittick, 2005

A Spirit of Tolerance: The Inspiring Life of Tierno Bokar,
by Amadou Hampaté Bâ, 2008

Timeless in Time: Sri Ramana Maharshi,
by A. R. Natarajan, 2006